TOM RUSSELL

THE GODFATHER OF ROCK

A COLLECTION OF MEMORIES
AND PICTURES

Published by Beard Books
A Tom Russell Company

First printing: October 2016
Copyright (c) 2016 by Tom Russell.
All rights reserved.

The right of Tom Russell to be identified as the sole author has been asserted by him accordance with the Copyright, Designs and Patents Act 1988. No part of this book may be used or reproduced in any manner whatsoever without the permission of the author, except in the case of brief quotations embodied in critical articles and reviews. For more information, e-mail all enquires –
tomrussellrocks@gmail.com

Go to tomrussellrocks.com for more pictures and details that will compliment this book

A CIP catalogue for this title is available from the
British Library.
ISBN: 978-1-326-79998-4

This book is also available in Kindle.

FRIENDS OF TOM

Livingaire Air Conditioning	Isabel Reade
Dan and Irina Livingston	Lynn Scott
Robert Mackie	Mike Storrar
Alistair Keith Watson	Ian Storrar (Jan)
Stuart Geddes	Ian Storrar (Stubby)
Kenny Simpson	Mike Sword
Lesley Simpson	Joe Reape
Indra L. Joyce	Ritchie Birnie
Lesley White	Mark Buchanan
Karen Ballantyne	Best Wishes, Gordon Smith
Sam 'Oliver' Bowman	John Henry
Stewart Eadie	John A.J. Ramsay (A.K.A. Ramses)
Lance Morton	Karen Pointon
Joe Cairney	Kenny Pointon
Max Sykes	Wee Jim
Gordon Elrick (DJ - Burns Howff)	Big Mel
Billy Paterson	Hell Evilheart

FRIENDS OF TOM

To Ruth, from Tom

To Darren,
(thanks for being a friend and supporting me all these years)

Debbie Smith

Jennifer MacFadyen

Campbell Stewart

Derek Chapman (DMC Photography)

Dez Burleigh

Graeme (Big G) Lang

Christopher Kidd

Nicola Kidd

Sarah Ferguson Furie

William Campbell

Alan MacDonald

Paul Hugh Murray

Iain McMeechan

Ciaran O'Toole

Gordon Hotchkiss

Owen Ramsay

freefor.co.uk

D.A. MacQuarrie

Jean McCabe

Heather and Richard Royan

Neil Russell

Jenny Cross

Emma Royan

Rebecca Royan

Peter Royan

Jim Crawford

Colin and Esra McCabe

Gordon Hotchkiss

Zach McCabe

Angela Jobb

Jamie and Eleanor McCabe

Chris Glen

James and Sandra Taylor

Jay Crawford

FRIENDS OF TOM

Laura Jane Clements	Paul Murdoch
Paul Logue	Ricky Warwick
Angela Job	Martin Jarvis
Peter McLean	John MacCalman
Stewart and Ruth McCabe	Alan Nimmo
Robert Fields	John Dingwall
Gordon Robertson	Dougie White
Shock City	Joe Elliot
Gordon Wallace	Ian Martin
Allie Barr	Robert Fields
Paul, Dante, Giuliano, Alex and Andy from GUN	Ian (Fergie) Ferguson
Jim Killens	Lisa Wilkinson
Davy Anderson	Babs Matheson
Iain Forbes	Alison Stroak
Audiorayz	Andy Lenihan
Jim Keilt	Laura A. White
Martin Jenkins	John Morrison
Loanhead	

*This book is dedicated to my daughter Heather,
my son Neil
and all my wonderful grandchildren.*

INTRODUCTION

Some words of welcome from just a few of the people I've worked with over the years

Ozzy Osbourne (Black Sabbath)
'Tom Russell – the man who rocks Glasgow.'

Angus Young (AC/DC)
'Tom puts on a great show – but he should be playing just a little bit more AC/DC.'

Slash (Guns N' Roses, Velvet Revolver)
'Of all the people that I know in the world with great beards, Tom Russell is definitely one of them…'

Robert Plant (Led Zeppelin)
'I've no objection to Tom playing the odd Zep track on the radio. On the other hand, you could say, "bollocks".'

Eddie Van Halen (Van Halen)
'The man who loves loud guitars – Tom Russell!'

Jon Bon Jovi (Bon Jovi)
'Tom's the one and only man to have kept the faith for rock.'

Joe Elliott (Def Leppard)
'Tom said to me years ago, 'How on earth, in the song Women, did you think you'd get away with the lyric "What's that smell?" To which I responded, 'Actually Tom, it's "What's that spell?" To which Tom responded, 'Ach, a thousand apologies!' I will never forget that as long as I live!'

Meat Loaf
'Tom Russell: Scotland's very own Bat Out Of Hell.'

David Coverdale (Whitesnake)
'Never mind Made In Japan. Tom was Made In Scotland.'

Lzzy Hale (Halestorm)
'A lot of people talk about how they love rock'n'roll. They play some records and dress the part. But our friend Tom Russell lives, eats, breathes and dies by rock'n'roll. Not only has he been a supporter of our recorded music, but he's never been one to hide in a studio behind a mic – he's been a staple in the live music scene in Scotland for years. He's a huge part of our journey as a band. You can see him in his natural habitat at the biggest and smallest of venues, beard and all! Thank you Tom, for your passion and friendship. With love and rock'n'roll, we'll rule the world!'

Giuliano 'Jools' Gizzi (Gun)
'Tom and i go back many years to when he used to have his record shop in Duke Street. I'd go in every week, bugging him to play our demos on his Friday Night Rock Show on Radio Clyde. To this very day, Tom has shown immense support to myself and Gun – we're forever grateful – supported all the local rock bands by playing their demos on his show, and going to gigs to check out the up-and-coming bands. A true pioneer in rock music and great friend indeed.'

Mick Box (Uriah Heep)
'I've known Tom for a long time, and for as long as I've known him, he's lived and breathed music. He has dedicated his life to the cause, and in doing so, he has enlightened many people's lives along the journey. Long may he continue!'

The Quireboys
'Thanks for all your support over the years, Tom. We've had some funny times together in Glasgow. This man knows his rock'n'roll, folks!'

John Fred Young (Black Stone Cherry)
'Tom is one of the last real rock'n'roll DJs and he's made a huge impression on us! Ever since the first time he interviewed us, we've loved hearing stories of his musical journey and the artists he'd been involved with. We can only hope and pray that younger generations will have a chance to be influenced by a music historian of such class and interfaith.'

Airbourne
'Tom is still standing up for rock'n'roll.'

Harry James (Thunder)
'What a man! Tom played our records when no one else was interested. Did live radio sessions with us when no one else cared. It's all his fault we became successful, so please blame him! Seriously – what he doesn't know about rock music isn't worth knowing. He's quite simply a rock'n'roll legend.'

Steve Rothery (Marillion)
'Tom Russell is a legend to touring musicians; a DJ who asks intelligent questions and has an obvious passion for the best rock music. He's always a great interviewer.'

Ted McKenna (The Sensational Alex Harvey Band, Michael Schenker, Gillan, Rory Gallagher, Band Of Friends)
'I've known Tom longer than I can remember and, as for long as I can remember he's had music, the spirit of rock'n'roll, as a driving force in everything he does.'

Doogie White (Rainbow, La Paz, Yngwie Malmsteen, Michael Schenker)
'Uncle Tom and I have shared a few adventures over the years – be it with snakes, grab-a-granny nights, or indeed in a bath. Uncle Tom gave rock music a voice on the Scottish airwaves a long long time ago. I thought he was an old bugger then… He must be by now, surely.

'No one has done as much for rock music in Scotland, and for Scottish rock music, than Uncle Tom Russell. Under the bearded mantle beats the heart of a real rawker. Proud. True. Loyal. No one does it better.

'Uncle Tom's gentle and knowledgeable interview technique always gets the subject to reveal that something we all wanted to know. A wise master of his craft.'

Ricky Warwick (Thin LIzzy, Black Star Riders, The Almighty, The Fighting Hearts)
'Tom has been a great friend and supporter of my musical journey through the years. He is the voice of rock in Scotland and beyond – the real deal: knowledgeable, honest. And he understands'.

Dan Reed (Dan Reed Network)
'Tom is one those rare breeds who lives, loves and breathes music. He continues to be a beacon of light for fans of rock'n'roll. Even now, he continues to discover new artists for us, making all our lives a much more colourful journey!'

Alan Nimmo (King King)
'Tom's tireless dedication to keeping rock alive in Scotland is the very thing that keeps rock alive in Scotland.'

Scott Holiday (Rival Sons)
'I met Tom on our first-ever tour through Europe. He was one of the first people to play us on the radio and did one of our first on-air interviews too. A good man, helping to keep the rock'n'roll torch burning.'

Jay Crawford (Programme Director, Rock Radio)
'Keep the Faith would be a good anthem to sum up Tom Russell. While music trends come and go in the charts, Tom always knew that the quality of his preferred genre would endure.

'When I was setting up Rock Radio in Scotland, there was one name I had to have on my programme schedule. Without Tom it would not have been credible. Tom lives and breathes rock music – I knew he would breathe life into Rock Radio and help us to live the dream.'

Tony Wilson (Producer of BBC Radio 1's Tommy Vance Rock Show, boss of Total Rock Radio)
'Tom is one of the pioneers of rock broadcasting in the UK, who's brought succour to the rock-starved ears of the gentle folk of Glasgow for almost 40 years. He's a true original, who has earned the respect of musicians, fans and rock broadcasting contemporaries alike for his unfailing commitment to, and love of, the rock genre.'

Paul Anthony (Planet Rock Radio, Rock Radio)
'Tom is an absolute legend in the world of rock radio. He's been there, done it and got all the t-shirts!'

Ciaran O'Toole (Station Manager, Rock Radio)
'I know a lot of good and bad things about Tom – mostly bad. The good thing I know is that he's utterly dedicated to rock and metal music. This legend has been there, seen that, interviewed them all and blagged many t-shirts along the way.'

Billy Rankin (Nazareth, Rock Radio)
'I've known Tom since I was a sixteen-year-old wannabe rock star. From my first band opening his Tom Russell Roadshow in the mid-seventies, he would often lend us new releases from his record bar in Bishopbriggs – so we could play Thin Lizzy's new single live before he could legally play it himself.

'Through his years as Radio Clyde's only rock presenter to showing yours truly the ropes (and whips and chains) with Rock Radio, Tom always shared the same passion for rock music as the musicians he interviewed, and often befriended.

'So much so that I'm inclined to suggest Tom himself is a rock star – with one subtle difference: unlike the rest of us, Tom never did drugs! Which is probably why he can remember enough stuff to write this book.'

Kieron Elliott (Rock Radio breakfast show host, who coined the phrase 'The Beard Of Doom')
'My radio career was mostly a product of being one of the many people to have grown up listening to Tom on a Friday night. Tommy Vance from ten till midnight on the BBC, then Tom from midnight to two on Clyde. Every rock fan in Scotland worth their salt listened to both shows.

'To have the distinct honour, not only get to work with Tom directly on Rock Radio, but to hand over to him every week day morning for a year, was amazing. Tom went from being an idol to being a close, friend which I'll never stop being thankful for.

'Once I got over my mild hero-worshipping, I think I was struck by how quietly and effortlessly he embodied the rock ethos in person – and the beard was very much part of that, in the same way that the lads from

ZZ Top just look 'rock' (apart from Frank Beard, the only person in ZZ Top without a beard!).

'I randomly called Tom 'The Beard of Doom' one morning as I was handing over to him, and it kind of stuck. Tom didn't seem to mind. In fact, he seemed to quite like it, so I just kept it going. It became one of my sayings, like 'random bawbaggery', and it just stuck. I thought it would only be used by us while mucking around but, very quickly, people were coming up to Tom at gigs and saying, 'Hey, it's the Beard of Doom!'

'The fact that it's stuck, Tom likes it, and the rock community still call him it makes me feel very proud. I feel like I've added a really fun element to one of the most incredible personalities in the Scottish rock community.'

Paul Murdoch (Glasgow author, musician and compiler)

It was an absolute pleasure capturing as much as we could of Tom's life in this book. Most of the time he sat in my living room recounting his tales (not necessarily in the right order). We even taped some of our conversations in pubs and restaurants as well as during a few car journeys – one of which was our wee pilgrimage to visit the Bon Scott statue in Kirriemuir. A live pigeon once interrupted proceedings as it fluttered down my chimney, then did a few rounds of my living room. We tried to save it, but I'm afraid it faded away on my front step. I'm sure Tom will go on from here do to much more in the world of rock. His dedication to the genre and the personalities involved is second to none. He told his stories with love and passion. Thanks for spending the time with me, Tom.

Donald MacLeod (Rock Radio, owner of the Garage and the Cathouse clubs)

When Tom asked me to write a few words I was quite honoured, then quite perplexed. What could I possibly say about him? I've known him for nearly forty years. Well, here goes – Tom Russell is......

A monster of Metal
The Rasputin of rock
A raider of riders
The priest of prog
A primer of punk
The defiler of disco

A pilferer of passes
The whipper of headphones
A villain of vinyl
The baron of beer
A crumbler of cakes
The soul who loves solos

A groaner of grunge
The ancient of autocue
An authority of AOR
The gatherer of great music
A filcher of free food
The scratcher of discs

A mixer's misfortune
The computer's calamity
A critic of Coldplay… well, who isn't ?

A lover of ladies
The teller of tales
A lover of live music
The piss-taker of pop
A lover of life
An ambassador of rock

He's all that, and much more. But most importantly of all, Tom is a friend.

1. A BAIRN IS A BAIRN

How I grew up in Kirkintilloch but supported Falkirk ~ my first claim to fame ~ Libyan horror story ~ my night with the Fab Four

There's a good chance, according to my mum, that I spent my first weeks of life lying beside a very famous singer. Although my family were from Kirkintilloch, I was born in Lennoxtown – Lennox Castle, to be precise, in September 1948. Known now as Celtic Football Club's training ground, back then it was the local maternity hospital. It was also, however, the local mental asylum. So, in effect, you had mums and babies in one wing and, well, the 'not so fortunate' in the other. My mum, Grace, bummed for years about being in the next bed to a Mrs Lawrie, who gave birth to a little girl called Marie MacDonald McLaughlin Lawrie. Lulu to you and me.

My dad, James to his own mother but Jimmy to everyone else, was a smashing character. I loved him dearly. He'd been called up at only nineteen in 1940: he got a letter saying, 'Report here.' He had no alternative. He ended up in the RAF as a wireless operator. (Weird to think that our family was into radio even back then.) He spent two years in North Africa and never saw his family in the whole of that time, but he'd met my mum before he was called up, so it must have been hard.

I remember one story about his time in Libya. It concerned one of the 'Brylcreem boys,' which is what they called the pilots. They were all told 'Whatever you do, do not fraternise with the local women – it's one hundred percent out of bounds. It's not done.' But one of them, a smoothie, a real ladies man, went into town almost every night, sniffin' about, seeing what he could get up to. He went out one night and he never came back. About three days later he was found out in the desert, miles from anywhere. He'd been stripped naked and staked out on the sand. His wrists and ankles had been tied, his eyelids had been cut off.

Worse still, his balls had been removed and stuffed into his mouth, which had been sewn up with a needle and thread… and they'd just left him there to die.

I think I was about eleven when my dad told me that story.

My mum and dad hired a room in a wee Kirkintilloch cottage for their first couple of years of marriage. Then, when I was about two or three we got a council house in Hillhead, Kirkintilloch. I was an only child, but I still had a happy time there. I suppose if I was really honest I wish I'd had a brother or a sister. You don't miss it at the time because you don't know any different but, looking back, it's definitely one of my regrets.

Dad came from Falkirk so he used to take me to see Falkirk Football Club – he, I and my grandpa used to all go together. So even though I'd never lived in Falkirk, I became a Falkirk supporter. Years later, I'm proud to say that I carried on the tradition: my own boy, Neil, has continued as a Falkirk fan, a 'bairn.'

By the time I was around ten, Mum was working as a civil servant and Dad was a commercial traveller selling Lindt chocolate. More often than not I was first home, so my job was to clean out the coal fire, set it up again, and have it lit by the time they got in around half-five or so. Another of my jobs was to walk the three hundred yards to the shop with an empty for paraffin. We had a paraffin fire upstairs – there was no such thing as central heating in those days. Dad would often be away with his work, so on many nights Mum and I used to sit in the kitchen listening to Radio Luxembourg. Nice times.

I can hardly think of a cross word that ever occurred between my parents and myself. I loved them both. They brought me up to respect people and to be honest. Even now, when it comes to contracts and stuff, my word is my bond. (Unfortunately there are people out there who aren't quite so decent, who'll rip you off. Yes, it's happened to me, but you just have to shrug it off and think, 'Ah well, you managed to step over someone to get another rung up the ladder – best of luck to you, pal'.)

My primary school was Lairdsland in Kirkintilloch. I still remember sitting the 11-plus then going on to Lenzie Academy. I wasn't that interested in school; If I'm honest, I was a skiver. I would do the minimum to get by, no more. Looking back, I wish I'd found out a bit more about Scottish history, but back then it was boring. The way it was put across didn't float my boat. I had respect for one or two of the teachers, but most of them, just like me, were simply going through the motions.

When I was in second year, at Lenzie, perhaps aged thirteen, one of my classmates told me there was something special going on at lunchtime. So, along with half a dozen other thirteen-year-olds, I headed to 'the moss', a small wood near the school. One of the girls from the class (no idea of her name) was holding court. She got us all to stand back then proceeded to lift her skirt and remove her pants. At least three steps away, she instructed us to 'take a peek'. I don't know about the rest of the guys but my memories of the experience were of complete embarrassment. After two minutes, she pulled her knickers back up and we all trouped back to school for a double period of English. My concentration in class was even worse than usual that afternoon.

So when did I first get hooked on music? I'm often asked that question, but it's hard to say. The story I often tell is of one night, when I was about fifteen, when Dad came home from work and said to Mum: 'Do you fancy a wee night out, Grace? I got two complimentary tickets for a concert from the guy who owns the sweet shop behind the Odeon.'

But Mum had been working all day, and she'd made the tea, so she said, 'I cannae really be bothered, Jimmy. Why don't you take Tom?'

So we went along to this this concert at the Odeon on Renfield Street in Glasgow. A couple of things pop into my head about the gig. One was that I couldn't hear a note – the band had a tiny PA. I think they had two four-by-twelve columns on each side of the stage, and that was it. They were only a couple of hundred watts each, to fill a venue with two or three thousand people inside. Another thing was the constant screaming, mainly women and girls. So it was certainly no introduction to hearing live music.

Then I remember all these girls running down to the front of the stage. The bouncers were really struggling to hold them back. Whether they actually took their knickers off there and then, I can't say, but all these bras and pants were being thrown onto the stage. A blizzard of underwear and pheromones drifted down from the rafters that night, and as a young man jam-packed full of hormones myself, the whole thing seemed wonderful. I thought, 'This is the business for me!'

I'd just seen The Beatles. The date was October 5, 1963. After that they went on to play Kirkcaldy, and after that they become the biggest band of all time. I'd had my introduction to music – but when I went back to school the next day, I'm not sure I even told anyone about it.

2. SETTING OUT

School days ~ first job ~ how I discovered the blues ~the bands that made me want to join the scene

When I left school at sixteen I saw an advert in the local paper for the Star iron foundry in Kirkintilloch. They we looking for a trainee metallurgist. I thought, 'That sounds interesting… what's a metallurgist?' Thinking about it now, I'm still a kind of metallurgist, albeit a heavy metal one. But back then, it meant working in a lab, in a foundry, studying metals.

It would have been nice for my mum and dad to have talked me out of it. You know, 'Stay in school a bit longer, son, get some O levels.' But then again, would they have changed my mind? Probably not.

In the sixties it was pretty common for kids to leave school early and get a job. So I went for the interview and was offered the position on the spot. I'd left school with no qualifications, but I got a day-release to go to college once a week. The job was interesting enough: every morning and afternoon, I'd go down and take a sample of the molten metal coming out of the big cupula.

A few months in, close to Christmas, some of the hard-working rough-and-ready guys in the foundry offered me a whisky. I'd never drunk whisky before but, not wanting to look like a fanny, I took a big swig. Unfortunately, it wasn't whisky, was it? It was pish. A proper 'piss-take' out of the wee boy that worked up in the lab.

There were three of us in the lab, and the chief technician was a fan of blues music. He used to prattle on about the blues and its 'local connection', as he called it. People from Scotland and Ireland who went to America in the seventeenth and eighteenth centuries took the traditional music with them, the ballads and laments. Many Scots who could play the fiddle and sing went to the Carolinas and the West Indies. This technician reckoned that the Scots music influenced the Africans who were taken as slaves. He thought that, as the Africans sat at night and sang their own sad laments – 'Oh God, look what's happened to me. Where am I? What's happened to my family? What was that horrible journey across the sea? Can I ever get home?' – the Scots were singing about missing the mountains and the heather of home. This guy reckoned those threads all merged into what we now know as 'the blues.'

I've since spoken to blues musicians like Joe Bonamassa, Alan Nimmo and Gary Moore, who all reckoned it might have been true.

I remember the technician giving me an LP by Sonny Terry and Brownie McGee. I took it home and plonked it on the record player. My dad was into Sinatra, Matt Munro, the big band stuff; and we had one or two singles lying about, including the first single I ever bought: Apache by The Shadows. When I put this blues album on it certainly made an impression. I suppose you could say that the Sonny Terry album helped me on the road to rock.

I'd begun to collect singles with the little bit of cash I'd pulled together working at the foundry. I soaked up as much of the blues as I could by listening to pirate radio and going to see live acts. It was around this time that a chap called Ian Young opened a rock club in Kirkintilloch. It was called The Graveyard, a wonderful name, and I still have my membership card. Ian had a band on every weekend and one act in particular really blew me away: Beggar's Opera. They were Martin Griffiths (vocals and percussion), Ricky Gardiner (guitar and vocals), Marshall Erskine (bass and flute), Alan Park (keyboards) and Raymond Wilson (drums). They had a song entitled Sarabande which really stuck in my head; and although they never made it big, they did okay in

Europe. Ricky Gardiner went on to become a member David Bowie's touring band.

One of my first-ever gigs was the Spencer Davies Group in Kirkintilloch Town Hall. It was around 1965, and a very young Steve Winwood was on vocals. His voice was so amazing, really unique. The band blew me away – I knew I wanted to be like that... somehow.

Occasionally I would set off for Glasgow city centre and visit a few of the clubs there. There was the Lindella, Sgt Pepper's, the Picasso and the Electric Garden, but it's probably the Maryland that I recall the most. It was in Scott Street, near the Glasgow School of Art. I saw a few good bands in there that stuck out: The Beatstalkers, The Poets, The Stoics, Dean Ford and the Gaylords (who went on to become Marmalade).

The Pathfinders were excellent too, and there were many more, whose names have long faded from my mind. Listening to those bands got me excited about music, and made me even more determined to be part of the scene in some way.

Back in the world of work, I was beginning to get itchy feet. After about a year and a half in the foundry, I saw an advert in a Sunday paper for a Ministry of Defence job. They were looking for student apprentices. Now that I'd managed to get some O levels on day release, I applied. If the truth be told, I only went for the interview because the advert said that they would be taking place in Chorley, a town near Manchester. It all sounded very exotic! And with travel expenses covered, it had the makings of an excellent skive.

So I got the day off and jumped on the train from Glasgow Central station to Chorley for the interview. They told me I would have two months in the blacksmith's shop, two months in the machine shop working on a lathe, two months in the maintenance department with the plumber, then three months at college. After that I'd have three months on the milling machine. Every single bit of it appealed to me – so you can imagine how I felt when, after a month or so, I'd heard absolutely nothing. 'Ah well,' I thought. I'd enjoyed my day off.

A few weeks later, on a Monday, I got a brown envelope in the post addressed to 'Mr T Russell'. That in itself was unusual, but when I opened it I read, 'You've been accepted to work for the MOD. Please report to the Royal Ordnance Factory, Birtley, County Durham, at 8am, on Monday, September 3.'

Yes! I was just about to punch a fist into the sky – but then I took the time to read the letter again.

Point one: the letter had arrived on September 3, the very day I was supposed to report for duty. Point two: I had absolutely no idea where Birtley, County Durham was. I thought it might be in Ireland for a bit as I got mixed up with County Down – but it was in the North East of England. Once I'd figured out that the job was near Newcastle, only about three hours away, and not the other side of the moon, I spoke to my parents.

Part of me was surprised that they were so supportive, but years later Dad told me that Mum had been in tears at the time. That's just the kind of parents they were. They always wanted the best for me, regardless of their own feelings.

So I gave my notice at the foundry and another chapter of my life began.

3. FIVE YEARS IN ENGLAND

Me, Hendrix and an audience of six ~ my first cars ~ my first night of passion ~ the Parachute Regiment ~ starting the band
~ discovering disco

After six months in the North East of England my adventure had already been better than I could ever have imagined. I'd made some friends and there were only around twenty student apprentices. With a bit of luck I was going to become a mechanical engineer.

The bus trips from my first digs to work and back each day were a pain, so I clubbed together with Dave, one of the other apprentices, and we bought a car. It was a Ford Prefect, a late 50s classic. The deal was that we'd take turns using it on holidays – at Easter, I'd use it to come home to Glasgow, then at Christmas it would be my turn to stand in the rain and wait for a bus while Dave went to see his family in London.

My abiding memory of the Prefect is of always getting my feet wet when it rained. One day I looked under the rubber mat on the floor and found a huge hole that went right through to the road beneath. There was no such thing as an MOT in those days. Once I'd realised it was a bloomin' death trap, I coughed up the princely sum of £39 for the first ever car that was a hundred percent my own: a Hillman Minx Convertible.

That sexy soft top served me well for a couple of years. After it gave up the ghost, I got a blue, two-seater MG Midget, an open top sports car. Not particularly fast, but great fun. Then I had a dark green Triumph Spitfire, which was a little bit nippier than the MG. I had some great times in those cars.

I'd made great friends, but sometimes I liked to explore on my own. Quite early on, out in Newcastle one midweek night, I heard this great music coming out of a doorway. The bouncer at the door said. 'Are you alright, son? Do ye wanna go in? It's free tonight – it's a live band rehearsing. Oh, and by the way – are ye eighteen?'

I wandered in. The club was dark and it stank of stale beer and cigarettes. The stage was to the left and the bar was along to the right. A band was playing, but there were only about six people standing watching. The band were loud, and they were excellent. It sounded like blues-rock, but not like I'd ever heard it before. They were a three-piece and the black guitarist was left-handed. I remember him singing a song called Hey Joe.

There were thirty people up at the bar who weren't interested – they were all gathered round this big tall guy, which I thought was strange. He turned out to be one of my heroes: Chas Chandler, the bass player in the Animals.

(I was really into the Animals at the time. In 1965 I'd bought their album Animal Tracks, which was full of great blues-rock songs like For Miss Caulker, Bright Lights Big City and Roadrunner. Eric Burdon's voice was a mixture of gravel and steel. He was one of the first guys to stand proud of the blues as a true rock singer. A few years later Robert Plant and Ian Gillan would come along and raise the bar, but The Animals – Eric Burdon, Hilton Valentine, Chas Chandler, Alan Price and John Steel – set the bar in the first place. Back home in Kirkintilloch, even before I'd moved to Newcastle, I had a poster of them on my wall. They held pride of place on the ceiling, next to a humungous poster of Marianne Faithfull. 'Night, Night, Marianne,' I used to whisper, just before going to sleep.)

Chas was a Newcastle lad, and it turned out he was the manager of the guitarist on stage –who was called Jimi Hendrix. Chas had discovered him in New York and brought him over from the States. I suppose he was keeping an eye on his prodigy that night. I'll always wonder how I managed to see Jimi Hendrix for free, while only six other people watched with me.

After a while, I moved digs to Gateshead, a town that stood on the southern edge of the River Tyne. It was nearer the bright lights of Newcastle, which meant my travel time to work was reduced, and there was less hassle from my landlady about getting in late.

Not long after my move, I lost my virginity. I was the ripe old age of eighteen (well, it was old in the sixties) and one Saturday night I blagged my way into a party with some of my fellow apprentices. We'd been to the pub, got talking to some girls, and finally we were invited along to this girl's house. I remember she was very generous with the booze. I also remember she was also very generous in proportions, especially round the waist and backside.

The night was going well when she invited me to dance. A slow record was on the turntable and I did my best not to stand on her toes. It wasn't my toes, however, that she was interested in. After two slow dances, she grabbed my hand and escorted me upstairs. Well, one thing lead to another – mostly, I may add, encouraged by her – and we… became good friends.

The event, as you can imagine, didn't last very long. To be honest, I hardly knew what was happening, but as I lay there with a smile on my face, my new-found friend, who was not very happy, headed back down the stairs. To my eternal shame, I haven't a clue what her name was; but I do remember that later, I spotted her leading another guy upstairs after a slow dance. Perhaps he fared better.

I had a friend called Jim Cassidy back then, who used to take me out for a pint of Newcastle Brown Ale – a fabulous pint. More importantly, his group of friends made me feel welcome. Okay, they used to call me 'Scotch Jock' and the likes, but that was fine. They were lovely guys. It surprised me that they didn't have much time for the English people south of Watford. They saw a real difference between the people of the North and the people of the South. There was no issue with the Scots, we had the same sense of grievance. We were all fixated on ship-building, the slums and the rights of the working man.

One night, one of these boys, Trevor, told us that he was going to join the Parachute Regiment, The Paras. He was off to sign up that very night, down at the local Territorial Army office. Four Para were based there. 'Listen to this,' he said. 'You get a hundred-pound signing-on fee —' (which was a fortune at the time) — 'and you get five pounds a week.' My ears pricked up, especially when Trevor said the work involved lots of trips to camps all over the place. It really appealed to my sense of adventure.

Jim Cassidy piped up, 'So it's just the TA? And you can bail out whenever you like?'

'Pretty much,' said Trevor.

So five of us, well topped-up with Newcastle Brown Ale, made our way down to the drill hall, and joined up.

Before we were accepted into the regiment, we had to prove that we were fit enough. Pre-Para meant a week down at Aldershot where, every day, they had a whole load of different tortures laid on for us. One day there would be a telegraph pole race, where six of us would wrap a heavy pole in ropes and then race, in full kit, carrying the damn thing through sand dunes. We were always competing with different teams. It was exhausting!

There was an exercise called 'milling' where they put you in a boxing ring with someone roughly the same height, and watched as you knocked the crap out of each other. I couldn't believe how heavy those boxing gloves were. The judges marked you down if you were timid or held back too much.

It was a wonderful feeling when you completed a task. You usually vomited your guts up, of course – but it was great to know that you'd done it.

Two weeks later, after passing Pre-Para we went down to Abingdon in Berkshire, where we underwent our actual parachute training. It was an old RAF station; one thing that stood out was the difference between an army camp and an RAF camp. In an army camp in the early seventies you were lucky if you got a cup of tea and a plate of stew for your dinner. In the RAF camp there was a choice of three starters, four mains and a few puddings. And it was served on real china! Quite a comparison.

We learned how to pack our parachutes, how to check them before jumping out of the plane – and more importantly, how to land without breaking your leg or your back. It was all quite intense. Then the great day arrived... Our first jumps were out of a balloon on a freezing-cold morning. I'd be lying if I said we weren't all shitting ourselves, but you couldn't show it. After our lorry trip to the range, we were taken four at a time, into a rusty old cage at the bottom of a balloon. It was attached to a cable with a reach of six hundred feet, which is pretty high, especially when the wind is howling and the ground is getting further and further away.

We finally got to jumping height and the sergeant dispatcher said, 'Right, number One... three, two, one, go!' Number One jumped out of the cage and we all froze, terrified for the next couple of minutes until he reached the ground. We were given the all-clear, and then it was Number Two. I was Number Three.

I thought, 'Do I really want to do this? In your head you're saying to the sergeant, "Look, I just don't fancy it. I'm off to the pub. Thanks anyway, pal!" Then you realise how embarrassing it would be. You think, 'The chance of this being the one parachute that screws up must be pretty rare. I'll just go for it.'

So out I went, into the abyss. I dropped like a stone for about a hundred feet until the parachute jerked. I looked up. It was a full canopy and I was alive!

Next day we were in a Hercules aircraft, Charlie 1-30. It took off from Abingdon and the DZ (drop zone) was up towards Norwich, in an area where many villages had been evacuated during the Second World War and the Ministry Of Defence had taken the land for training. It was also the place they filmed Dad's Army.

When the big, noisy, propeller aircraft reached eight hundred feet, it was time to go – 'Red On'. You check the guy in front of you, you check the guy behind you and meanwhile the sergeant's giving it laldy: 'You'll be fine, you bunch of bastards – go!'

You fall out the side door of the plane, and as soon as you hit the slipstream, it just feels like you're sliding down a chute. You're travelling at 120 miles an hour and you're dropping fast. Then you have this lovely feeling as there's a jerk on your shoulders. The parachute has opened. It's a full canopy. You begin to relax a little and enjoy the descent. People think that eight hundred feet isn't very high – but remember, if there are people shooting at you from the ground, the less time you're floating about like a sitting duck the better. The whole point is to get a troop of fighters on the ground as quickly as possible.

We did that Hercules jump five times over the next five days. After a total of seven jumps, including the ones from the balloon, we were awarded our wings. We all passed – and I have to say that my parachute wings are one of my proudest processions to this day. My couple of years in the parachute regiment were great fun. The people, the places, the exercises; the whole thing was well worth doing. It certainly hardened me up and gave me a whole new perspective on life.

My twenty-first birthday was in September 1969, and as I was still living in the North East of England, I managed to have two parties – one in Kirkintilloch, mainly for family, and one in Newcastle, for all my Geordie mates. The Newcastle bash ended rather messily. I've no idea what I drank that night, or how much. I only remember being ill the next morning and finding what was left of my shoes. All the leather at the toes was completely worn away. I found out later that the boys had to carry me home across Newcastle's Tyne Bridge. As I was only semi-conscious, my feet scraped along the pavement for about two miles back to my digs in Gateshead.

I had been ticking off as many live concerts as I could during my time in Newcastle. The main venues were The City Hall, The Mayfair and a place called the Club A'Gogo. I went to see an American band called Iron Butterfly at the City Hall one night – but the other band blew them off the stage. They were the progressive rock group called Yes; their musicianship was different class. And Jon Anderson's voice – I'd never heard anything like that before. The emotion that came out of that guy…

Another feature of my life back then was stock-car racing. Newton Aycliffe, a few miles south of Durham, was the venue. I went one Sunday and loved it, especially the destruction derby. At the end of the day's racing, twenty scrap cars were brought onto the track to do battle. You go out there and try to destroy all the other cars until you're the last one moving. Jim Cassidy felt the same as me about it, so with the help of his dad, we bought a scrap Austin A35 and went to work on it.

After fitting special bumpers, cages and seat belts, we removed all the potentially hazardous glass and entered it into one of the races. We drew lots, and as fate would have it, I was to be the driver. I bought myself a helmet, and every Sunday I'd jump into the driving seat until the car was so battered we had to put it into the destruction derby. I remember someone hitting my tail, which made me spin out of control and then roll. Someone in the crowd actually got a picture of that roll.

I also got into water skiing when I lived in Gateshead. There was a club just outside Newcastle, on the River Tyne, and since I'd water skied before, I joined. I eventually got quite good at it. All went well until, there I was, heading up the river on two skis behind the speedboat, when I got too ambitious, tried a stupid move and lost control.

I went into the water head-first. Dazed, I saw… it… coming, but I didn't have the time to avoid it. In those days the Newcastle sewerage system was fairly poor, which is why a big jobby had been floating down the river – straight into my open mouth. It was the most disgusting and horrible experience of my entire life.

I'd also started playing guitar, just self-taught, I concentrated on rhythm guitar. I practiced every night and eventually decided I would join a band. I got myself a Burman amp and cabinet, plus a Hofner Verithin guitar. It was like a Gibson 335, but not quite as cool. All the music shops down there, just like McCormack's in Glasgow, had adverts up on the wall. After a few weeks I spied one that said 'Singer looking for musicians to form a band.' His name was Tom Forman and we hit it off right away. He was a nice guy and he could carry a tune. We had a few more meetings and soon enlisted another member, Les, a fairly decent drummer. Then we found a bass player called Jim.

It was 1968 and all the big rock bands were starting to get it together. The Who and The Stones were out there already, but it was the harder version of rock that drew me in. I'm not a rock snob – If I hear a good pop song, I'm quite happy to say, 'That's great.' But when Led Zeppelin and Deep Purple came onto the scene, it changed everything.

We decided on a name, Strange Brew (after the Cream track) and rehearsed for a while; until Jim, the one of us with the biggest brass neck, went to the local working men's club to ask for a gig. There were only two men and a dug watching us stumble through a few cover versions at that first gig, and we didn't get paid. However, there was a shortage of live bands in the area, so we started getting regular work.

There was one track in particular that I sweated over, because it had a guitar solo and I just wasn't a good enough player to do it justice. I always stressed over that one. We did songs like The Small Faces 'All Or Nothing', Dave Clark's 'Glad All Over' and The Stones 'Little Red Rooster'. After a few weeks we got a guy on keyboards called Allan. Now, he was in a different class, and that pushed us up a few notches. He took over all the solos, which was a relief, leaving me to concentrate on playing rhythm guitar.

Tom was a good singer – but more importantly, he was a babe magnet. He was one of those guys that, for some reason, just mesmerised women. They all fell at his feet. One time we played at RAF Bulmer, about thirty miles north of Newcastle. We went on stage for the first set and this one girl kept looking at Tom. During the second set, in the middle of a big keyboard solo, we spied Tom behind the PA with this girl; her skirt was hitched up and there was no way that he was interested in getting back onto the stage to finish the second verse. Unbelievable! I reckon that was the longest keyboard solo Allan ever played.

Strange Brew actually recorded a single called 'Floating'. Let me see now, it went:

> *Floating along. I'm in a dream.*
> *Reflections of our love. To me it seems*
> *I'm floating, floating in a dream of love.*

Maybe the idea for the lyric came from my water skiing incident on the River Tyne? I should have called it Floater. I've no idea why the song wasn't a hit, although it was played a handful of times on BBC Radio Newscastle. The B-side was another original called Teaser. I've still got a vinyl copy somewhere. It might be worth a fortune on eBay?

Through time, as with most bands, we all fell out. But I managed to stay in touch with our roadie, who, a few weeks after the split, phoned me and said, 'Have you ever heard of a thing called a mobile disco?' This was new – instead of paying fifty quid for a band, a club would pay twenty pounds for someone to come along and play records. 'You've got the PA and the Burman amp,' he reminded me. 'All you need now is a set of record decks. I'll still roadie for you.'

Allan and I were regulars at the Globe Pub in Gateshead so we asked the Manager if we could give it a try. The whole thing just clicked. It was a great success and the start of something that would lead me into another set of adventures.

I know you're thinking that playing records in a pub is doing a live band out of a gig, but progress is progress. I have to admit, I think the advent of discos killed the live acts off a bit. And there in lies my big paradox. I made a living from discos but loved live music. In some ways I probably helped to lessen the very thing got me hooked on music in the first place.

4. DISCO TO DISC SALES

Return from the south ~ setting up home ~ Ark Royal adventures ~ a career wrong-turn ~ my record shops

Fairly soon after I started the discos, my student apprenticeship came to an end. I had my qualification and now it was time to use it. But where? And with whom? I definitely knew it was time to move on – I'd left the Paras and the band had broken up. The mobile disco was still on the go, but that wouldn't keep the wolf from the door by itself. I needed a proper job.

When scanning the papers I noticed an advert by Rockwell Hardness Testing Equipment, who sold and maintained equipment for testing the strength of metal. They were looking for a mechanical engineering graduate to be a sales engineer, covering the whole of Scotland. The salary was good, a car was supplied and it sounded exciting, so I applied for the job, and I got it. Travelling as a sales rep and engineer, testing the hardness of steel, I got to see the whole of Scotland on an expense account – which is thoroughly recommended, if you can pull it off.

The job meant I was financially sound, and it also meant that I was back home. Mum and Dad were delighted. My room was still there, just as I'd left it, with my Animals poster in pride of place and Marianne Faithfull still hovering precariously above my bed. My old friends in Kirkintilloch had moved on to pastures new; jobs had taken them far and wide, so I was on my own again. But in a way it allowed me to throw myself into the new job even more.

As most reps know, getting overnight stays are great fun at first, but eventually it becomes dull and soul-destroying. A Monday night away is fine, Tuesdays are okay, but then Wednesdays and Thursdays are just a pain in the ass. Luckily for me, Aberdeen was booming back then and I got to spend a lot of time there, so things trotted along nicely for a good while.

I began to get into skiing again. This time it was the 'up in the mountains, whistling down the glens' kind of skiing. I joined the local club and went on a coach trip to Aviemore. The bus seemed to stop at every lamp-post on the way up the A9, but I noticed a young lady smiling in my direction the whole time. As I was with my girlfriend, I thought I was probably imagining things, so I purposely ignored the other lass for the last part of the trip.

When we eventually arrived, everyone was well-oiled from the bottles that had been passed around during the journey. Now we had to get to grips with dinner, and even more drink at the local pub, Aviemore's Winking Owl. My girlfriend and I retired to our room at around one in the morning, and she, even drunker than me, passed out before any hanky could be pankied. The girl from the bus had continued to give me the eye all evening. So, being totally oot ma tree, I thought it would be a tremendous idea to leave my sleeping girlfriend and pay the mysterious other a visit. She was, as it happened, in the next room.

I tend to sleep minus pyjamas, so I got up from our bed, staggered out the room, and three or four steps later, I began knocking on her door. There was no reply, so after a couple of minutes, I decided to go back to my own room. It was probably for the best – I wonder what her reaction would have been if she'd answered the door to see me standing there, naked, with a big smile on my face? I'd have probably got the jail!

Then I realised I had no key for our room. I was standing in the corridor, bollock-naked, trying to wake my sleeping girlfriend. She finally opened the door and said, 'What are you doing out there with no clothes on?' I muttered something about mistaking the room door for the toilet door. Pure genius? Naw. Pure madness, and a narrow escape.

After a while I was in a position to look at moving out of my mum and dad's. I was a young single man in my early twenties; and although I enjoyed living at home, getting great meals and my clothes washed, it was time to get a place of my own. I saw an advert in the Kirkintilloch Herald for a flat in Loch Road, an old tenement, for sale at £1250. It had a shared toilet out in the close and needed a bit of work, but I thought it would be great for parties at the weekends, so I bought it. Mum and Dad helped with £100 towards the deposit and I rustled up another £150. The remainder was paid back via a ten-year £1000 mortgage from the council.

I had some wonderful parties there. In fact, I still have the flat to this day, but I hope the parties aren't as wild as they used to be because it's rented out…

During my time as a sales engineer I bumped into an old pal, Dougie Fraser, one of those kids from school who'd faded into the past. He'd started a mobile disco, and once we got talking about our experiences he offered me a bit of work. It was somewhere to go on a Saturday night, but I wasn't playing that much rock at the time. It was the pop of the seventies – Slade, Sweet, Mud and so on. Not rock, but still pretty good. Then, bit by bit, I started getting bookings of my own. I got a Saturday residency at the Reo Stakis Poseidon pub in Bothwell Street, Glasgow – the very spot, as it happens, where I met my wife. She came up and asked for a request, and then one thing led to another. I wonder how many DJs met their wives-to-be like that?

I also played the tunes in the Broadcroft in Kirkintilloch, where I got friendly with an officer on the Ark Royal. His name was Chris Graham, a smashin' bloke. We'd often go for a pint when he came home on leave. (The Ark Royal featured in a TV series at the time, and the theme tune, Rod Stewart's rendition of the Ian Sutherland song Sailing, went to number one in the charts.)

On one of Chris's many visits home, he had some extra time free. The Ark Royal was docked between the Forth Road Bridge and the Forth Rail Bridge for a few days, and he asked if I wanted to go on board and have a look around. My girlfriend and I were delighted. As word spread among Chris's friends, however, we ended up with a party of ten on the day.

A launch came out from the aircraft carrier to Queensferry and we were saluted before boarding the ship. We were taken up onto the flight deck, where I was amazed that there was no fence around the perimeter of the ship; but of course, if there had been a fence, the planes couldn't have landed. It still looked dangerous. After the tour, Chris took us to the officers' mess, where we were served a meal and sampled a few strong drinks including Navy Rum. I think this practice has stopped now, but for many a long year every British sailor on the high seas used to get a tot of rum every day. Chris did warn us, 'Be careful with this stuff because it's dynamite.' After a few shots he took us into a private room where there was a disco. We all danced for a couple of hours before we staggered back onto the launch and were ferried back to shore. What a hangover – but what a great experience.

A year or two later, Chris was back on leave and I was doing my regular Wednesday night disco in the Broadcroft. A wee team of us had a bit too much to drink (as usual), so, as the munchies took hold, we decided to venture into Auchinairn and catch the Indian restaurant before it closed. After the main dishes had been laid out, Chris let out a loud scream. We all stopped chatting, as did the other customers and the staff. Chris pointed at his chicken jalfrezi and shouted, 'That's disgusting!' We all followed his gaze, and saw a rat's tail protruding from the curry sauce. As waiters had gathered round, Chris grabbed the tail and began to lift it – and, it slowly dawned on us that it was a plastic rat. Chris absolutely wet himself, and so did we, but I don't think the staff took it the same way. We made sure we gave them an extra big tip that night.

As time moved on, I began to tire of my stints away in sales – the long drives, the hotel rooms and the pressure to hit target all the time. I was thinking about it as I drove past Jordanhill Teacher Training College in Glasgow one day. It was May, and the sun was shining; the girls were wearing their summer clothes, short skirts etc. So I pulled over for a look.

I'm tempted to say it was divine intervention, but it was more likely the lust-fuelled imaginings of a young man that drew me into the place. I went straight in to college reception and asked if there were any jobs. Someone said that there probably were, if I was prepared to do a one-year course. So I handed in my notice at Rockwell and signed up to start a course at Jordanhill, training to become a technical teacher. Talk about off the cuff!

By September, of course, the sexy summer clothes had morphed into drab winter woollies – and it wasn't long before I started regretting the whole mad notion. Jordanhill reminded me of being back at school. Then when I was sent out on my first practical experience day to Douglas Academy, Milngavie, I realised, for sure, that I'd made a big mistake. When I walked into the staff room they all ignored me, every single one of them. The teachers became preoccupied with their navels or marking homework. Annoyed and yet determined to be as affable as I could under this barrage of unspoken descent, I smiled and said, 'Im from Jordanhill College.' There was still no response, so I sat down with my cup of tea. Then I heard a sharp, communal, intake of breath, before someone said, in a snobby nasal tone, 'That's Mr Smith's chair!' They all shook their heads in warning, as if I was some kind of idiot who was about to sit down on a land-mine.

What the hell had I done? I knew, there and then, that teaching wasn't for me. But looking back, it was probably this one single event that launched my career in music. What could I do now? What was I really interested in? Music was becoming a bigger part of my life – but could I make a living at it?

I'm not sure how it popped into my head, but the notion of owning and running a record shop settled in there. It seemed to make perfect sense. There was already a good record shop in Kirkintilloch called Sound Developments, so Kirky was probably out; and I didn't want to be miles away. I was too nervous to try Glasgow city centre. I didn't fancy competing with the big boys like 23rd Precinct, Listen, HMV and the like. Then I saw an add for a shop lease in Bishopbriggs. The location, about five miles out of Glasgow, seemed perfect.

I'd been with the Royal Bank Of Scotland all my life, so I approached my branch in Kirkintilloch, with a plan, to ask for a loan. I turned up a little ahead of my appointment time, decked out in my best suit, collar and tie. I was shown into a big office where the manager, a man in his mid-fifites, sat behind a large slab of a desk. Seemingly oblivious to my presence, he continued to write as I walked in. He didn't even look up when I stopped in front of him. Unsure what to do, I stood there, until eventually, he lifted his head, scowled, and said, 'Yes?'

I explained I'd had an account at his branch for seven years, and that I wanted to open a record shop. I told him that I'd done a few sums and that I needed £3000 for the lease and about the same again for stock and fittings. I also explained that, although I guessed he would know already, I had £200 in the bank.

He murmured to himself for a moment and then his phone began to ring. Ignoring me, he answered it, then ordered some tea and biscuits. ''Oh,' I thought, 'I could just go a cuppa.' A girl came in with a tray and placed it on his desk. He poured himself a cup, carefully selected a nice chocolate biscuit, and sat back, eyeing me like some scallywag bound for the gallows. He grunted: 'Am I missing something here? You want £6000 – and you only have £200 to put up as a deposit?'

'Well,' I answered, 'My dad will help with another £300.'

He just smirked and said, 'You're wasting my time and yours, sonny. Goodbye.'

So that's it? I blurted out. He ignored me, picked up his pen then pointed to the door without even looking up.

I felt humiliated and angry – but more than anything else, I thought, 'Sod him. I'll show that bastard.' If he'd even given me some tea, or explained, in a reasonable way, that I would need a bigger deposit, I might have gone away and not bothered. But in my opinion, he'd been a complete arse. So as a result of that meeting, I drove straight to Bishopbriggs to take another look at the shop. He'd made me ten times more determined to get that lease, no matter what it took. As I looked at the empty premises again I saw another branch of RBS across the road. Still frothing with rage, I decided to go in and try again.

This time the manager saw me right away. I told him the whole story (although I did hold back about the other manager). He listened politely, then offered me some tea before asking for my projections –profit margins, set up costs and so on. I hadn't properly thought through the running costs and expected income, but he didn't dismiss me like some stupid schoolboy. Instead he told me go away, do some research, and come back and see him in a week.

So I did my homework and even got some more money towards the deposit. My mum and dad chipped in an extra chunk and my grandfather added to the pot, and before long I had £1000. It was 1975, and music was really happening; the second bank manager had done his own research. He'd asked his staff about the demand for music in the area. He'd made a few calls. So, when I came to see him a week later he said, 'If you put down your £1000 we'll add another £4000.'

I was in business!

We got stuck in, did the legal stuff and got the shop opened within a month. Before long it began to make a profit – not a fortune, but enough to give me a wage. Within two years, I opened a second shop in Shettleston; then a third in Mount Florida, and, later, a fourth in Duke Street, near Glasgow city centre. Duke Street was about as close as I wanted to go to the competition. I was still a bit too nervous to go right into the city centre. But I had four shops, all making a wee profit, and life was good.

5. THE REVOLVING WORLD OF RECORDS

The highs and lows of running a wee business ~ meeting Kate Bush and The Bee Gees ~ my dad's card shop ~ experiments in video ~ closing down

When I started the Tom Russell record shops, people were getting rid of their radiograms and buying hi-fis. There were only two media formats: vinyl records and cassettes (eight-tracks hadn't really taken off). When we opened the first shop in Bishopbriggs I got a chap called Steve Jones to do the official opening – he was the breakfast show jock on Radio Clyde, which had started in 1973. He was a great presenter, and for the first few years of the station he was the main man. I had no contacts at the station back then, so I simply phoned them and they passed me onto his agent. He charged about £100, and I remember that he came along in a red suit. I love the picture of him cutting the ribbon with my mum and dad in the background. They were as proud as punch. We got a great crowd, and the launch was a success.

The shop on Shettleston Road was in an old tenement building. One day, a few months after opening, I was paid a visit by a council guy who informed me that he was authorised to inspect the premises; and when he finished, he told me there were two problems.

First, there was a legal requirement for an extractor fan above the front door, to provide fresh air for customers and employees. I couldn't understand because the door opened every ten minutes or so when a customer entered or left. He insisted, and I had to comply. (It was installed… but I don't think the thing was ever switched on.)

Second, and even more ridiculous, was the demand that I build a second toilet in the back shop because I had male and female staff. I told him I'd only recently opened and I had no spare cash; but unsurprisingly, there was no give. His solution was to do the work, sack either the male or female employee – or he'd close me down. Just then I remembered an old, rusty extra key on the shop keyring. On impulse I went into the tenement close, used the key to open a landing cupboard, and discovered the most disgusting, filthy, disease-ridden cludgie. I told the inspector hat the male employee would use the outside toilet and the female would use the one in the back shop. He was raging! But he was stymied and had to admit defeat. When he left with his tail between his legs, I locked the door in the close and it was never opened again.

We had some good times in those shops. Record companies would often do promotional days if one of their acts had a single coming out. They'd take the artist all over the country and line up loads of record shop signings. We once had a band called Dollar come along, who had some hit singles between 1978 and 1982. We had such a big crowd for them at Bishopbriggs that the shop's plate-glass window broke. With the amount of people pushing against it, all trying to get in, it just caved it right in. No one was hurt and the Bishopbriggs Herald gave us some great publicity on the back of it.

We also hosted Guys and Dolls, The Nolan Sisters, and even Spit the Dog from Tiswas. A particularly memorable visit was when Slade came to Bishopbriggs in 1981. They were past the stage of having hit after hit but they were probably still making a good living from Merry Xmas Everybody. They'd just released a single called Lock Up Your Daughters, so Noddy Holder and Dave Hill were there to chat to fans and push the record. They were very polite and great fun.

The Nolan Sisters were big in the early eighties, and their visit to the Shettleston shop was rather eventful. We got a huge turnout, and after ten minutes of signing their singles, one of the sisters asked me if she could use the loo. I escorted her into the back shop and pointed to the toilet. I waited for a couple of minutes to escort her back through to the crowd at the counter – but suddenly, from inside the loo, there was the sound of a flush, followed by a shriek. I'd forgotten that the toilet, being in an old tenement, had a tendency to blow back, soaking any unsuspecting occupier of the cubicle. That's exactly what had happened. Miss Nolan came out in tears, her lovely trouser suit wringing wet. The signing session was sadly cut short and the girls were taken back to their city centre hotel. I suspect that was the first and only time the Nolans visited Shettleston...

A regular customer in the Bishopbriggs shop was a young schoolboy called Billy McLeod, who came into the shop most days and hung around listening to the music. He was a punk, and he didn't have much money, so he rarely bought anything; but that didn't matter. He was a nice lad. When I opened the Shettleston Road shop, I was looking for an assistant, and Billy asked for the job. I told him the money wasn't great and he would have a daily commute, but Billy jumped at the chance.

It was one of my better decisions. Billy was a natural, he grew with the job, he was a real asset; and after a couple of years he left to work with London Records as a rep. A year later, he was promoted to the head office in London, and climbed the ranks to become a senior manager there. Well done, Billy!

There was an inevitable turnover of staff with four shops. Among the memorable employees I had was a chap called John, who answered an ad for a sales assistant in Bishopbriggs. I interviewed him personally and liked him – but there was a problem. I couldn't help noticing he was wearing two ties. After offering him the position, I felt that I had to point it out to him. His reply was, 'Oh yes, I normally wear two ties.' I shrugged my shoulders thinking, 'well... So what?' John started on the Monday and worked for me for a couple of years. Every day, he turned up for work with two ties round his neck; so naturally, we named him Two Ties. Soon regular customers would come into the shop and greet him with, 'Good morning, Two Ties.' John loved it and responded perfectly naturally. He'd even answer the phone with, 'Good Morning, Two Ties here, can I help you?'

Soundtrack was a famous record shop in Mount Florida, near Hampden Park; a very popular place that specialised in imports, a bit like 23rd Precinct. I heard through the grapevine that it was up for sale. So I made some enquiries and ended up making that my third shop, after Shettleston. I employed a girl to run it for me, and all went well for a year.

Then I got a call telling me the shop was on fire. It turned out that the gas heater had gone up. All by herself on a cold winter's afternoon, she'd shut up the place as usual and turned the heater off, but instead of going off, it had exploded. Unhurt but terrified, she quite understandably legged it. So a year after buying it, the shop was gutted. It was in a tenement, so it could have been a real tragedy; thank God the fire brigade had arrived on the scene before it could spread. Insurance paid out eventually, but we had to refurbish the whole place. It took us six months, by which time many of my regular DJ customers had moved on elsewhere.

One of the best things that came out of the Mount Florida experience was the friendship I struck up with one of the diehard customers who stuck by us after the fire. His name was Jim Symon, and he came into the shop every week like clockwork. He was a hairdresser's rep at the time and called on the shop next door, a snazzy little place called Blow Your Top. One day Jim told me about another record shop that was up for sale – one of the Bruce's shops, in Duke Street, Glasgow. That was a big shop at the time, but I decided to go for it, and I got it. Now I had four shops, all turning a small profit. (Bruce Findlay, who owned the shop before me, went on to have a successful career managing Simple Minds.)

Duke Street needed someone to run it, and Jim asked if he could have the job. I told him the wages weren't great, but he still wanted it, so I took him on and he was great. However, he only lasted six months, because he managed to get a job at Radio Clyde. Jim Symon went on to have a very successful career at Clyde for over thirty years, and also did a lot of work with Scottish Television.

Then, as often happens, Sod's Law kicked in and things took a turn for the worse.

It had started, of course, with that fire; the business was never the same again. Then I was informed that the Shettleston shop would have to close for a while. All the Glasgow tenements were getting refurbished and the City Council ordered to move out for six months while the work was done. A shop out of action for another six months meant I'd lose even more customers. Even though I was out of the premises, earning diddly-squat, I still had to pay the rent. Not only that, but I also got a bill for my share of the tenement upgrade… £12,000. The landlord, who lived in Brighton, just sat back and took his rent from me, while I had to pay for his property to be refurbished.

Then, one Saturday, I came home from a party at about one in the morning. (I was married and living in Milton of Campsie by this time.) I was happy; there was a wee sprinkle of snow on the ground; life was good. I was slipping into bed when the phone rang. I had to stagger downstairs to answer it.

'Hello, it's Duke Street Police station here,' said a voice. 'Mr Russell, are you the key holder for the Tom Russell record shop?'

'Yeah.'

'Well, I'm afraid you've had a break-in. You'll need to attend.'

Suddenly feeling like shit, I dressed and got into the car. The Duke Street shop was also in a tenement, and the thieves had chiselled through the bricks in the back of the property. The alarm had gone off and they'd scarpered – but now there was this worrying hole in the back wall. I phoned Hurry Brothers, who specialised in boarding up places after these events. They arrived within half an hour, by which time it was around half past three. The place was secure, but I was now down in the dumps. I got back into the car and drove all the way home. I stripped off, got into bed, eased under the covers — and the bloody phone went again. "It's Duke Street police station again. You've had another break in, sir!'

The thieves had come in through the boarding and, even although the alarm went off again, they'd got into the front shop and nicked a few LPs. I had to attend again. The hole was boarded up a second time, I reset the alarm and got back home about six in the morning.

I was exhausted and in a foul temper. Everything seemed to be going against me. The supermarkets had begun selling records and cassettes. My sales were slowing down. I lay awake thinking about what I should do.

There was this new thing called 'video clubs' – not the big ones like Blockbuster, who hadn't even started yet, but one or two of the local shops were starting to try the video rental thing. I thought, 'This might be a good fit.' So I set up Tom Russell's Video Club, and invested in buying some videos.

I began signing people up. People could borrow out whatever videos they wanted for a couple of nights, in return for an annual membership fee. It did okay for a couple of years, but then it became a continual drain. There was a big demand for new videos all the time. As a business model it was difficult; I either had to go into it in a big way and sign up hundreds of members, or get out. And before I could get organised the big chains all opened.

My plan had failed to stem the sales drifting over to the supermarkets. Woolworths and WH Smith had begun to cut prices and squeeze the wee guys out. And now, every Tom, Dick and Harry had moved in on the scene. As far as my shops were concerned, the words 'nail' and 'coffin' came to mind. It was time to move on, branch out, try something new, before I was sucked down into a black hole...

You used to get problems with records jumping, but nine times out of ten it wasn't a faulty disc, it was a faulty needle. They'd wear out and go blunt, meaning they couldn't sit properly in the groove. A customer would come in and say, 'I bought this last week and it jumps.' You'd put it onto the shop turntable, it wouldn't jump, and you'd say: 'It's probably your needle.' Sometimes the customer would say, 'There's nothing wrong with my needle – change it over!' You'd give them a refund or hand out another copy. Other times the customer would take a new needle, then come in later and say, 'Thanks, that fixed it.'

Tony Rimkus, who managed the Shettleston shop, was another good laugh, and a great record salesman – quite often if someone came in for one LP, they'd leave with two. One day a 'wee worthy' came in clutching an Elvis LP and said to Tony, 'It's this record. it's jumping!'

Tony said, 'Jumping? How do you mean, sir?'

'The record's jumping!'

'You mean the needle's jumping across the record, sir?'

'Aye! That's what I said!'

Tony took the record out of the sleeve and showed it to me. It looked as though the guy had eaten his breakfast off it – what a state it was in. Tony said, 'I'll just go round the back and check it out.' So he went behind the partition and we heard this bang–bang-banging, while the customer looked quite anxious.
After a minute Tony came out and put the LP back in the sleeve, put it back into the sales bag and said, 'That's it sorted, sir. It'll be fine now.'

The customer asked, 'What did you do?'

And with a very straight face, Tony said, 'I put it through the stoatergraph.'

The guy said, 'That's magic – thanks a lot, mate.' And off he went.

'Aye,' said Tony, after the wee guy had gone. 'He was a stoater – so I just cleaned it and put it through the imaginary stoatergraph!'

A week later the guy came in again and Tony said, 'How did you get on with your Elvis LP?'

'Oh,' said the wee guy, 'It's workin' great now.'

The shops were always great fun, but things continued to go against me. One Christmas week morning – which is, of course the busiest week of the year – I was heading in to the Bishopbriggs shop. There was a hold-up, with a policeman directing traffic, and I wondered what was going on. On turning the corner, I saw two fire engines outside the shop, and a black hole where the shop should have been.

Allan, my shop manager, had been filling up his cigarette lighter when the gas canister had fallen on the floor, punctured and started spinning round. Within seconds the gas reached a small electric fire and exploded. Luckily Allan wasn't hurt ,and he'd got out, along with a customer, before the flames spread to the posters that hung from the ceiling. My wee shop was gutted.

Insurance paid out again; but once again, when we re-opened months later, a lot of our regular customers had gone elsewhere. One of the most hurtful things about that episode was the rumours that it had been an insurance job. As if anyone would deliberately set fire to their shop during the busiest week of the year!

I'd got married to my wife, Sandra, by this time; I suppose I could have sold my wee flat to help with the bills, or even to put down a deposit on a decent home. But I hadn't. I'd rented the first flat out to get some income. I worked three nights a week and seven days a week right through the seventies and eighties, and I'd just about got by. But something was going to have to change.

When my dad was made redundant at the age of 59 he decided he wanted to open a card shop. I gave him a corner in my biggest shop, the one in Duke Street. It was a great way for him to test the water – If it did well he could take it further. Things did go well, but after about two years he told me that he and Mum were going to sell their house in Lenzie and buy a place in Anstruther. That surprised the hell out of me. But they explained that, when I was a wee boy, we'd used to holiday round that area: Pittenweem, St Andrews, Crail. There were lots of great memories and they'd always dreamt of retiring there.

About six months after they'd moved, Dad announced that he was opening a shop in Anstruther. Suddenly, together day and night, Mum and him had been snapping at each other. He'd been away as a sales rep all his days, but now he was at home getting under her feet. So I hired a van and took his stock of cards over to Fife. He traded there for five years until he took ill and passed away. Mum kept the shop going for a bit until she couldn't do it any more, then she sold up.

In those days the record companies were making so many millions that every time any artist released an album, or even a single, there was a launch party. It was a good way to get a new musician on everyone's radar quickly – they'd have a launch in every big city and invite all the local radio, press and shop guys, in order to hit as many influential people as they could.

One of the most memorable was the launch party for Kate Bush's second album Lionheart in 1978. It was at the Holiday Inn in Glasgow, in one of the big function rooms upstairs. The deal was, you'd sit for forty minutes listening to the whole album, drinking from the free bar and munching the free food. Then you'd get to meet Kate and chat with her. My abiding memory is of how quiet, gentle and shy she was. My photograph from that night is one of my favourites – what a powerful talent, all wrapped up in such a beautifully delicate package.

In 1979 I was invited to the launch for The Bee Gees' album Spirits Having Flown. The band were massive at the time due to the movie Saturday Night Fever. Again, the do was at the Holiday Inn. We went along, sampled the free drink and had our dinner, while listening to the album. Then we were individually introduced to each Bee Gee. Photos were taken, and I came away with the impression that the Brothers Gibb were a decent bunch of guys. (The one with the beard even told me a dirty joke.)

6. ON AIR

My six-week radio contract ~ early interviews ~ the man who made it all happen ~ karaoke with Robert Palmer ~ Vinegar Joe's knickers ~ Getting Ian Gillan barred ~ They're not male strippers… they're a rock band

I first met Richard Park in the late seventies at those record company piss-ups in Glasgow. He was there as head of music at Radio Clyde, and I was there as a guy who had some record shops. Over a glass or two, we would chat about music. Richard was always interested in what was happening, which singles were selling well – whereas I used to slag off Clyde for not playing enough rock music. Richard would contend that there was no demand for rock on the radio. I would counter, telling him that I sold as many rock records as any other genre. That just wasn't reflected on the radio.

Then, one day, out of the blue, Richard phoned and invited me into his office for a chat. He said that he'd been thinking about what I'd said, and he was prepared to offer me a show on the station, late on a Friday night, once a week. I was delighted – and for the next three nights I went into the Clyde studio, where Richard taught me how to present a show on the radio.

It was a six-week contract at £20 per show. But after the six weeks was up nothing was said. So on week seven, I went in again… Then week eight, nine, ten and so on. I just kept going in, doing a show and submitting my invoice.

If my memory serves me correctly, the very first tune that I played on Radio Clyde was Eruption / You Really Got Me from the first Van Halen album.

I was very nervous before my first interview for Clyde. It was with Ricky Medlocke, the singer-guitarist who ended up in Lynyrd Skynyrd, but at the time, he was frontman for Blackfoot, who were playing the Apollo. I was settled at the station and I'd got friendly with a few of the other DJs: Jim Symon, Dougie Donnelly, Tom Ferrie, Mark Goodier, Bill Smith, Tiger Tim; and of course, Paul Coia. Paul was very popular and he'd landed a gig at STV doing a six o'clock evening show. He interviewed guests there, as well as on Clyde, so he knew his stuff.

So on day of my first interview I asked Paul for some advice. He said, 'Do your homework. You can wing it with a new band, and in some ways it's more spontaneous. But if you interview someone like Jon Bon Jovi and say, "Have you ever been married?" and it's common knowledge, you'll look like a complete tosser.'

I went away and listened to some of Blackfoot's albums – Strikes, Marauder and Highway Song. I did a bit of digging, found out that some of the guys were of Native American extraction, and the interview went really well. That was the first and only time I interviewed Ricky Medlocke. Skynyrd have been here a few times since Ricky joined, but the way the interview rota for the band has gone, I've never met him again.

I once did an interview with Japanese band Vow Wow. Their bass player was Neil Murray of Whitesnake, and they were headlining the Apollo on a Friday night. So I began my show that night by telling the listeners that we'd be joined live in the studio by the band.

About quarter-past twelve the buzzer went, and it was Eric, the security guard, who said, 'I've got some people here for you, Tom.' So he sent them up and about a dozen of them piled into the studio. Neil Murray wasn't with them, but the four other guys in the band, all Japanese, were there with three very attractive young ladies. One of them had a huge camera with her, which she clicked non-stop. It was like something from a Monty Python sketch – she took pictures of the Radio Clyde ceiling, the carpet, my shoes… anything. There was also a guy from Sounds magazine, who'd been doing a review. On top of that there was the band's manager, the tour manager, Uncle Tom Cobley and all.

I got them all to squeeze round the desk in the studio. The track that had been playing was almost finished, and I was getting a bit nervous because I knew I still had to find their single and cue it up. So I changed from 33⅓ to 45RPM, and got ready. The mic was live so I said, 'We've got some special guests in the studio… a band that's just come off the stage at the Apollo tonight. Welcome to Scotland, Vow Wow! Your first time at the legendary venue, The Glasgow Apollo. How did the show go tonight?'

They all looked at each other, and the girl sitting next to them, who had listened carefully to my question, spoke to the band in Japanese. They replied to her in Japanese and she turned to me and said in English, 'It was very good.'

Meanwhile my heart was sinking, as I realised, 'I'm in deep shit.' The band didn't have a word of English amongst them, and this was their official interpreter. The record company never thought to tell me. So the whole interview was a nightmare. I couldn't just say, 'Piss off!' I had to plough on and try to get to the end. Not one of my greatest moments.

I soon started getting to know some of Scotland's home-grown talent pretty well. One of the earliest things Dan McCafferty of Nazareth told me about was dealing with being a rock star. In recent times, Nazareth were no longer a huge band here in the UK – but they still do pretty well in Canada, South America and the Far East, although Dan retired a couple of years back.

He told me that there's one thing that always brings him back down to earth: 'You're touring, getting treated like rock stars, fancy hotels, limousines to the airport and all the rest of it. Just like it was back in the seventies. It's great, and you make a few bob.'

'Then you fly back home. You do the the big long-haul to Heathrow and then whizz up to Edinburgh, still buzzing, and there's my wife, waiting for me. It's so good to see her, but it's frightening how quickly the limos and the posh treatment fades away. It's straight into the Big List: "The lawn needs cut, the dining-room ceiling needs painting. The garden's a mess and there's shelves to get put up … The life of a rock star, eh? I'm just the same as anyone else." I asked him if it made him want to turn around and go straight back on tour. 'Not really,' he said. 'It's good to be brought down to earth now and again.'

Dan went on to tell me about writing songs: 'You get up one morning. the postman's been. You pick up an envelope and it's from the Performing Rights Society. You open it, and it's an itemised cheque for quite a bit of money. Air play royalties for Broken Down Angel or Bad Bad Boy, from all over the world, for the previous three months.'

He explained that Bad Bad Boy had taken him and bass player Pete Agnew about ten minutes to write one night in a pub. They rattled it out over a packet of nuts and a few pints. Forty years later, it still gets them a wee cheque now and again. Everyone wants to be the star in a band, the frontman – But it's the songwriter that makes the money. They're the smart ones.

Dan and Pete are just like Morecambe and Wise when they get together, a great double act. They once told me that, back in the sixties in Dunfermline, they were playing in a covers band called the Shadettes. They had special stage get-ups – everybody did back then. They wore bright yellow suits with big red, polka-dot ties. They all still had daytime jobs; one was a painter, another a plumber and so on, but two or three nights a week they'd go out and play. (This was before the days of those nasty mobile discos, I might add.) It was a Thursday in August, and they had a booking in Kirkcaldy. Now, the distance from Kirkcaldy to Dunfermline isn't that far, but there were no motorways back then, just a few winding roads, some of them still single track.

Dan told me: 'We finished the gig about midnight and packed the gear into the back of the van. We're all knackered as we're driving home. It's a wee narrow road and we come to a roadblock. The police are standing there – we all moan and think, 'What the heck is this all about?' So we pull in, roll down the window, and this big sergeant asks where we've been. "We're in a band. We're the Shadettes."

'Then he asks us for all our addresses and points to the gear in the back. I explain that it's our equipment, but he's not satisfied. He wants us to pull it all out onto the road. I complain that it's nearly two o'clock, and that we've got our work in the morning. But he insists and we have to humph everything out onto the road and watch as the polis check it over with their torches.

'The big Sergeant eventually sighs and tells us to be on our way. So we load the stuff back in and we're just about to move off when Pete winds his window down and asks the big sergeant why he's stopping all the traffic. The big man just says that there's been a robbery, a big robbery, and they're stopping all suspicious vehicles.

'Pete asks where this robbery has taken place. The sergeant just says it was further down south – a train was pulled in and robbed by a gang. Then Pete comes away with: 'Did they say the guys who did it were wearing bright yellow suits with bright red polka-dot ties?'

The Shadettes had played their gig in Kirkcaldy on August 8, 1963 – the night of the great train robbery.

Just when The Cult began to break big, singer Ian Astbury came into Radio Clyde for an interview. He reminded me of Jim Morrison as he swept into the studio, every inch of him a big rock star. Accompanied by a minder, he had a real aura about him.

He was from the north of England and I said something like, 'There's definitely a wee American twang there in your accent.' I wasn't being nasty – it was just a friendly dig.

He replied, 'Yeah, I was born in Cheshire, the band hails from Bradford, but I spent a few of my formative years in Scotland. I lived here from age thirteen to seventeen.'

'Whereabouts in Scotland?' I asked.

'Kirkintilloch,' he replied.

Now I'm thinking, 'Is he winding me up?' I said, 'I'm from there too.'

He said, 'The first time I was ever arrested was in Kirkintilloch.'

'Oh, aye?'

'Yeah – one night I'd been in the Broadcroft and had a couple of pints. I was about seventeen. I was heading up the Cowgate desperate for a pee. So I stood in the door of Woolworths and had my pee. But a police car stopped right behind me, mid-stream, and I ended up in the cells.'

It was all true.

One of the bands I enjoyed most back in the early days was Uriah Heep. They were massive in the seventies. They were going to be one of the shining lights, along with Zeppelin and Black Sabbath – but then their singer, David Byron, passed away. They tried rearranging the lineup but never quite kept the momentum going. They were still making a decent living but I don't believe they got to where they should have been.

Mick Box, the guitarist, is the guy I know best in the band. One of the best stories he told me took place just when the Cold War was beginning to thaw, and suddenly there was an opportunity for Western rock bands to play in Russia. The powers that be put on a huge rock show in Moscow featuring Bon Jovi, Motley Crue, Guns N' Roses and the like. Heep were on the bill and they flew from London to Moscow on Aeroflot, the Soviet state airline. Even before they took off from Heathrow they were getting into the drink because the plane looked on its last legs. By the time they got to Moscow they were five sheets to the wind.

Having a laugh throughout the journey, they convinced themselves that once they got to Moscow, they'd be interrogated by the KGB. They joked that there would be spy cameras everywhere; and possibly fantasised that there would be the odd honey trap here and there. So when they checked into their Moscow hotel, still steamin', the drink-induced paranoia was really building. Mick was sharing with Bernie, the singer, and they decided to check their room for hidden cameras. They searched lamps, pictures and mirrors. Eventually their chief roadie was called in and he started tearing bits of the bathroom apart.

Mick was walking across the bedroom floor when he felt something under his foot. He rolled back the carpet, and in the middle of the floor, there was a great big hexagonal metal thing. 'That's the bug!' he declared. The roadie whipped out his tool box and started to unscrew the big bolt. After ten minutes, a hotel manager rushed into their room screaming in Russian, 'Come with me now!' He took the band downstairs into the ballroom. There, in the middle of the floor, was a chandelier... shattered to bits.

As I did more and more interviews with bands I used to get them at the end of the interview, to record a few words for me that I used as jingles. Some of then were memorable and I used them every week for a number of years ... for example 'Hi Tom Araya from Slayer here with Tom Russell who just loves dead bodies' ... random, but good fun.

In 1984 I interviewed Bryan Adams for the first and only time. He was with A&M Records, and not too well known. I'd played a few of his songs on Radio Clyde, so A&M offered me an interview at the Playhouse in Edinburgh where Bryan was opening for Tina Turner. The interview was to take place in his dressing room at eight-fifteen, after he'd played. I found him to be genuine, honest, and happy to be out on tour. It was a great interview and I was surprised that for the past 30 odd years, I never got to meet him again.

When I left Bryan's room to go back to my seat, I was pounced on by two large American security guys who pinned me against the corridor wall. Another four security guys appeared, making sure that all was cool for the great moment that Tina Turner walked through the corridor and onto the Playhouse stage. Talk about over the top…

On one of my early Radio Clyde assignments to London I had to interview a certain famous singer who, after our chat, asked if I wanted to go for a bite to eat and a pint. We ended up in a pub with a karaoke machine. After a few jars, my companion was persuaded by the compere to do a song. No one but me knew who this guy really was; it was dark and dingy in there. The singer went up, sang Addicted To Love and sat down. The compere said, 'You know – you sounded just like Robert Palmer there.' The guy simply smiled and shrugged. To this day, I'm sure that neither the compere nor anyone else in the place realised that it was actually Robert Palmer himself.

Another story regarding Robert Palmer was relayed to me by Eddie Tobin, one of the senior staff at the Apollo back in the day. Eddie's still around and he's a great bloke. When he was at Glasgow University in the early seventies, he became social convener. He'd only been in the job three months and all his bookings had bombed, when he got a phone call from a whizz-kid agent in London. It was the usual patter: 'I've got this great band! They're gonna be huge! They're gonna be featured in the NME, they'll be on the telly, I'll let you have them cheap. They're called Vinegar Joe.'

So Eddie did the deal, got the posters up and printed the tickets. After a fortnight he'd still only sold four tickets. He was starting to panic ('It's not going well!' he'd always say.)

With four days to go, he went into the beer bar at the men's union, the GUU as it was called, and ordered a pint. He turned to the guy next to him and asked, 'You going to this gig on Saturday?'

The guy looked at the poster on the wall and said, 'Vinegar Joe? Never heard of them. No. I'm not paying ten shillings to see a band I've never heard of.'

Eddie said, 'Did you no hear? They've got a girl singer.'

'Aye, well, even so,' said the guy.

'Aye well, you'll miss out,' replied Eddie, 'because she wears a mini skirt on stage, and —' he paused for effect — 'she doesn't wear any knickers.' After those words he slipped away quietly. That afternoon he sold four tickets. The next day, he'd sold another sixteen. By Thursday the gig was sold out. The rumour mill had kicked in.

On the night, Robert Palmer was on guitar and Elkie Brooks was 'the singer'. Right enough, she was wearing a small leather mini-skirt – but I bet she couldn't understand why all these guys were pushing to get to the front of the stage. It was, of course, a lot of shite. Eddie had made the whole thing up.
I'm not sure if it was linked, but Vinegar Joe's career took off after that.

Much later, Eddie went on to open a great Glasgow venue called The Rockin' Horse. I helped, a wee bit, to get some of the bigger names there – Nazareth, Big George and the Business, Fish, The Quireboys and so on. The Party Boys, made up of ex members of The Sensational Alex Harvey Band, would have a guest singer each time they played. I'd play some rock songs then the band would come on, then my pal Jim would do that last half-hour because I had to dash off to Radio Clyde.

The Party Boys – Zal Cleminson, Chris Glen and Ted McKenna – were managed by a friend of mine, a local guy, Jim Killens. Quite a businessman, he started getting them gigs all over the country. One time, at a venue down south, they pounded into their first number, Faith Healer, only to look up and see a host of blue-rinsed ladies all looking a wee bit disappointed. Jim hadn't bothered to tell the venue that The Party Boys were a rock band... not a male stripper outfit.

It wasn't just the Robert Palmer interview that led to a night on the town with a rock legend. In the early eighties Deep Purple's Ian Gillan came in to record an interview about his solo career as Gillan. He had Janick Gers (now in Iron Maiden) as guitarist in his band, and powerhouse bass player John McCoy.

We'd had a good laugh doing the interview, then Ian said he fancied a pint, so we headed out in Glasgow with my pal Gordon Hotchkiss. It was a weeknight and the pubs shut shop at eleven. You know what it's like – you have five pints in you and you're looking for more.
'Where can we go?' said Ian.

Gordon replied, 'How about the Tuxedo Princess?'

It was a ferry, moored under the Kingston bridge on the River Clyde, that served as a disco as well as a casino. I explained to Ian that it wouldn't exactly be rock music in there; but he just said, 'I don't give a toss. Do they sell drink? Let's go!'

We went up the gangplank and came face to face with a big security guard. Gordon was also on Radio Clyde at the time, doing the folk programme. It was very unusual for me to do this – it just shows how pissed I must have been. But I said, 'Tom Russell and Gordon Hotchkiss from Radio Clyde here, and this is Ian Gillan from Deep Purple! Any chance of getting in for a nightcap?'

He let us aboard and we went down to what must have been the car deck at one time, but was now a disco with lights flashing everywhere. We were the only people in there apart from the staff. We downed a pint, then it was time for a pee – but could we find the toilet? There was probably a big sign somewhere, but in our state of inebriation it was totally invisible. We searched and searched, but because it was so quiet, there was nobody to ask. So we stepped over a couple of ropes and past a 'no entry' sign.

There we were on the bridge of the ship, right on the top deck. There was no toilet there either. So, in unison, the three of us pulled our zips down and let it flow, in triplicate, right into the Clyde. Big sighs of relief and zips up. But as we turned round, the big bouncer was standing right behind us. 'Right, boys. Off! You're barred!'

I think Gordon likes to take a risk when he's out for a swally with me. I remember one night when we were drinking with David Walters, who ran the Paris nightclub in Paisley. One night around one o'clock, slightly the worse for wear, David said, 'Do you fancy a plate of steak and chips and a few more pints?'

We fancied the idea of a few more pints anyway, so David took us to a casino in Glasgow city centre. We staggered up to the big gorilla on the door who said, 'Sorry boys, you can't get in tonight.'

David said, 'I'm a member.'

'Okay, you can get in,' said the bouncer, and pointed at Gordon. 'And this wee fella can get in. But the one with the beard – he's no' getting in.'

'Why not?' David said. 'He's my pal. He's alright.'

'He's not got a tie. End of.'

I said, 'I don't own a tie.' But the bouncer wasn't for budging. Then David disappeared. I found out later that he'd gone back to his car, and in the boot he'd found a dirty old bit of rope. He came back to the casino, out of breath, and said, 'Here, Tom – put this on.'
I tied the thing round my collar and we presented ourselves to the bouncer again. 'Can we get in now?'

The big guy smiled, 'Aye, in you go, ye daft buggers.'

So we were in this posh casino. David was playing poker, Gordon was on the gin and I was sitting like a haddie with this bit of dirty rope round my neck. Ah well. I signalled to the barman. 'Another pint, please.'

I owe a lot to Richard Park. He gave me my break on Radio Clyde, he encouraged me and he taught me the basics. He even suggested that I develop a gravellier voice for the rock audience. However, he did have a reputation for keeping his wallet under lock and key.

He eventually left to join Capital Radio in London. He always said, as a lot of bosses do, 'If you're ever in town, look me up.' Maybe three months after he left, I happened to be in London doing an interview. I had to do it at lunchtime then see the band at night, so, as I had a bit of free time in the afternoon, I phoned Richard and asked if he wanted to catch up. He said, 'Yes, Tom – I'd be delighted to show you round Capital.'

So here's me chatting with the big boss and getting shown round Capital, when Richard tells me about a well-known London DJ he's had to let go. He'd informed the guy that the show he'd just done was his last. 'I'm changing things around a bit,' he told me. The ex DJ, of course, went ballistic, and all sorts of rants echoed along the corridors. The guy went over Richard's head, up to see the managing director – but it was still his last show. It's not always nice being a boss.

When Richard asked me what I was doing that night, I told him I was going to the Marquee. (He was never one for live music, especially rock. He's more into pop, soul, R&B, motown – that kind of stuff.) He asked if I'd eaten. I hadn't. 'There's a lovely Italian across the road from the studio. Would you like to join me for a bite?'

A bottle of red and a plate of spaghetti bolognese later, we're full-up and ready to leave, and the bill comes to about £50 – not cheap. It's at this point Richard said something like, 'Oh, Tom, you're not going to believe this…' He's doing the Scottish 'pat the pockets' thing. 'I've left my wallet in the office,' he said. 'Look, next time it's on me, okay?'

So I paid. I just laughed. To be honest, Richard's head must have been full of so much stuff that he probably genuinely forgot. He's a great guy. (Richard is currently the boss at Global Radio, which is massive.) I certainly owed him a nice Italian meal – at the very least – for all the things he'd done for me over the years.

Radio Clyde's Anderston base in Glasgow city centre was a good location; but after a few years we moved to a purpose-built, modern studio complex in Clydebank, which also had a swimming pool, canteen, bar and gym. It was fantastic – but in a way, not as good. It was that few miles out of the city centre which made it a bit more difficult to soak up the city feel and get to gigs.

I didn't have anything to complain about… my six-week contract for the Friday Night Rock Show was going to end up running for over twenty years, and I loved every minute of it.

7. FESTIVAL SEASON

Monsters Of Rock ~ Reading ~ T In The Park ~ East Kilbride ~ further afield ~ Tricks for blagging interviews

I thought it would be really useful to attend the Monsters of Rock festival at Castle Donington, so I went to the boss of Radio Clyde, Alex Dickson (an old-school ex-newspaper man – I got on well with him) and asked, 'Any chance of a tank of petrol and some expenses to go?' Alex agreed, and all I had to do was work out the logistics. I still had the shops along with my Friday Night Rock Show. So I was in the shop all day on the Friday before the festival, then I went into the radio station and did my show, which finished around 2am. I had a coffee, got into the car, and drove all the way to Donington. I stopped for a toilet break at Scotch Corner and slept in the car for an hour once I was there.

I managed to blag my way backstage, and as it happened, I met loads of great people – many of whom are still great friends. People like Brian Pithers from Radio 210 in Reading (sadly no longer around), Chris Tetley from Piccadilly Radio in Manchester, Kevin McDempster from Liverpool, Paul Anthony from Stoke-on-Trent, Andy Fox, Neil Jones and many others.

I got stuck in, doing interviews with all these big bands that didn't get that many interviews with radio here in the UK. The American artists couldn't believe it – every little town in their country had its own rock radio station; and, to Americans, the UK was the home of rock. The Who, Led Zeppelin, Black Sabbath – they couldn't understand why there was so little radio airplay for rock in the UK.

The festival finished at eleven on the Saturday night; It was just a one-day event back then. So I'd sleep in the car for three hours, wake up around two and start driving home. I usually made it back to Glasgow in time for a hearty Sunday breakfast.

Going to the festivals each summer was a great way to build up the record company contacts, who'd then phone me up to arrange interviews or invite me to showcases. I was flexible because I had my own business, so I mostly said 'yes'. They'd fly me down to London and put me up in the same hotel – a rock'n'roll place called the Columbia, at Lancaster Gate. I'd do interviews in the afternoon, with a select handful of other rock presenters, then we'd head to the Borderline, the Marquee or the Hammersmith Odeon to see whatever band it was play live. We'd invariably get merry on the record company money, then it would be back to the hotel and a flight back to Glasgow the next morning.

When I went to the Reading festival in 1983, it was the only time I ever met Phil Lynott. The Thin Lizzy frontman was laid back, gentle, very approachable and friendly; and there was a twinkle in his eye. You just knew he was an intelligent guy. It was one of my unofficial interviews: he was just standing on his own, smoking a fag, so I said, 'Hi, Phil, I'm Tom Russell from Radio Clyde in Glasgow.'

'Oh, Glasgow – great place,' he said.

'I've not seen you since last time at the Apollo.'

'The Apollo is great! We have a lot of fans there. I love playing Glasgow.'

'Any chance of a wee five-minute interview?'

'Sure!'

So I whipped out the portable and did it there and then.

Reading was great – they had two stages side by side. You'd watch a band on one stage, and when they finished their set, turn and watch the band on the other stage. There was a man-made tunnel underneath that led from the VIP section at the front, all the way to the backstage area. Most of the official interviews took place in the backstage area.

The first time I went to Reading I felt a bit out of my depth. I had no idea who anyone was and I just had to brass-neck it. Backstage, I'd see a girl with a clipboard and I'd say, 'Hi, I'm Tom Russell. I do the Radio Clyde Rock Show in Glasgow.' I'd just leave that hanging. She'd either say, 'Okay, nice, bye.' Or she'd say, 'Nice to meet you, Tom. I'm such-and-such from record company X. I'm looking after band Y and band Z. Would you like to interview them?' It was as simple as that. As years progressed these girls would have all the interviews pre-scheduled, but the first couple of times, I just had to wing it.

I tend to like most of the different strands of rock, everything from hard rock to soft rock, prog rock to metal and classic rock to some indie rock. My favourite, however, is probably still blues rock. One year at Reading, I had the pleasure of watching a full set from Stevie Ray Vaughan. He was superb. Cool as anything with his battered old Strat and that cowboy hat. I didn't get an interview though, which was sad, as he died not long after in a helicopter accident.

I remember an event that I compered at Calderglen Country Park, East Kilbride, in August 1984. It was going to be an annual thing and the council put a lot of money into it. There was Nazareth, Frankie Miller, The Dead Loss Band, Chasar, The Bluebells, Scheme, Waysted, H2O, Glasgow and Pallas.

At the time the big number-one band was Frankie Goes to Hollywood and their record company were giving out shirts that said, 'Frankie Who?' That's all it said. At this festival the merch stands were selling T-shirts that said, 'Frankie Who?' on the front, but on the back they said, 'Frankie Fucking Miller, That's Who!' Brilliant.

It was a great day, but the midges were hellish. During the festival there were a few inevitable gaps between bands and, as compere, I had to entertain the troops. It was blistering hot, and during a particularly long gap, someone suggested a wet T-shirt competition. So I asked the crowd if they were up for it. A girl at the front shouted 'What's the prize?' Making it up as I went along, I said, 'You can have half an hour in private, with any member of any band you've seen today.'

We got about a dozen entries on the spot and once they were on the stage, one of the security guards sourced a big bucket of cold water and we kicked off. Everybody entered into the spirit of things, with the audience deciding the winner by the loudest round of applause. It eventually got down to the last three, who were neck and neck. So I'm afraid we picked the first girl who took the game to next level – a quick flash of her boobs to the crowd secured the prize.

Out of all the big artists she could have picked, she chose Mick Boyle, the singer in the band Glasgow. Off she went backstage to meet her hero, and they had a very innocent but fun get-together. Mick was the perfect gentleman.

After bit of pressure from some of the girls standing down the front, we decided, with a view to equality, to have a wet Y-front competition. It was not as successful as the ladies' event!

(Mick did okay after Glasgow – he got a job as a driver with one of the tour companies that handled the big rock bands. In the nineties I regularly met him at Heathrow. One time he was on his way to Moscow to pick up a truck that had been with the Tina Turner tour. His job was to drive it to Rome for the next concert.)

Back when T In The Park was in Hamilton, a Canadian singer called Alanis Morissette was playing. Her album Jagged Little Pill had gone through the roof, selling more than thirty-three million copies. I asked her record company for an interview, thinking, 'No chance', but I got the thumbs up. Alanis was really professional, and she mesmerised me. There's no way a beautiful twenty—five-year-old was going to fancy an old rocker like me, but she made me feel as if I was Brad Pitt. It was lovely, swimming in my own delusion. I asked her about one of her songs, Isn't it Ironic – I said, 'That title… it's a bit like sod's law, isn't it?'

'No, Tom,' she replied, gazing seductively into my eyes, 'It's a bit like Murphy's law.'

I guess it was lost in the translation.

While Clyde was still at Anderston I'd started to become confident enough to phone up the record companies and ask about a band. Most of any company's time was invariably spent with the main pop acts, so it wasn't unusual for me to request an interview, only to be asked: 'Who? Are you sure they're on our label?'

'Well, yes. I'm holding their record in my hand and it's got your logo on it.'

'Oh! Oh, yes, them, of course they're with us.'

It was as bad as that. Rock acts weren't the focus of attention.

One of the advantages of having the record shops at the same time as being on radio was that there were two reasons to ask me to band parties, and for company reps to give me white label copies of new releases. After I'd had a listen, the rep would ask how many copies the shop would like. One time I'd been given a white label of an album by

Manowar, called Battle Hymns. As soon as I heard the first track I thought, 'Whoa!' So I said to the rep, 'Any chance I can hold onto this? I'll play it on the radio.' I was delighted to play it for the first time on Clyde that Friday night. Now, that wouldn't make much difference to Manowar's career, but it was something I loved to do. Discovering something new and getting it out there. I think the folk who were listening felt the same way – letters started coming in from all over the place, asking for songs and saying thanks for playing Thin Lizzy, UFO, Deep Purple, AC/DC, Sabbath and so on.

I've done things like that over my entire career on the radio. Sometimes a band would send me a cassette in the old days. There's one band I'm thinking of in particular, and I've actually still got the cassette. This Scottish band came from nowhere; they sent their recording to me with a note saying, 'Hi, Tom, we've only been going a few months but we've managed to get a record deal and we're doing a gig at Night Moves.'

I was impressed with the tape and I played it on my demo slot. (I always took the view that, in a two-hour show, three minutes devoted to an unknown act wasn't going to do any harm.) The band was The Almighty, featuring Ricky Warwick. I'm sure he appreciates the fact that his music was first played on Radio Clyde. Ricky now lives in Los Angeles with a lovely wife and daughter, and sings with Thin Lizzy and The Black Star Riders.

Once I was established on the interview circuit, the record companies would think nothing of flying me all over the place. I remember interviewing Judas Priest twice, once in Marbella and once in Philadelphia. I got the Marbella interview while I was working down in London with the Metal Hammer magazine. That was a good time for interviews – I could give a band coverage in Metal Hammer as well as on radio. We interviewed the band on the beach, in front of Sean Connery's house, all of us sitting in shorts and Hawaiian shirts. Most of the band were golf fanatics and they had houses over there. KK Downing, one of the band's guitarists, invested his money in land in Shropshire and actually built a golf course. He turned this old run-down stately home with a hundred acres, into a country club with the full works: golf course, spa, hotel. Amazing! He retired from the band a few years ago but he still owns the golf course.

Video came back into my life as well. I'd met Harry Doherty, the Irish editor of Sounds magazine, at a couple of parties, then again when he came up to Glasgow for an interview because Sounds was having a relaunch. We'd got on well and he'd appreciated the airtime. A couple of years later he called me with an idea: he'd started a company called Hard'n'Heavy Video Magazine with big American money behind it. He wanted to video bands and he needed somebody to do the interviews. He offered me a retainer and brought me in as needed.

We launched Hard'n'Heavy and produced a few editions, which were available through record shops and newsagents. It was £7.99 and it was doing okay. Think about it – people didn't get to see their rock heroes that much on the telly. A rock star with a new album struggled to get TV coverage. A pop star, no problem, but a rock star? Twenty-five years ago, before YouTube, you'd never see interviews on TV with these rock guys. Maybe on The Old Grey Whistle Test, but that was it. Even someone like Ozzy, until he did his reality TV show, wasn't that well known to anyone other than rock fans.

The video magazine lasted for about a year and a half, then there seemed to be some management disagreements. On top of that, MTV kicked off. They launched their Headbangers Ball, so there was no need for people to buy a monthly video magazine any more.

8. ROUGH WITH THE SMOOTH

'Baldy! Baldy!' ~ nights out with Robert Plant and Jimmy Page (nearly) ~ flight upgrade ~ a brush with the law

While working on Clyde was a joy most of the time, I'd end up in some fixes as a 'well-known' rock DJ –and I'd sometimes get a bit of a slagging too. You had to take the rough with the smooth.

In the eighties I was very self-conscious about my hair loss. Most of it had gone on top by the time I was twenty-five. I refused to hide it by wearing a hat or a wig; but still, it was a pain. The pain got worse the day I was compering my first Radio Clyde Kelvingrove Festival (in Kelvingrove Park, Glasgow). A chant began to rumble through the crowd, growing louder and louder: 'Baldy! Baldy!'

It was just drunk Glasgow guys. But when you're nervous anyway, you're self-conscious about your hair loss, and you're trying to keep it together to introduce the next band, it's the last thing you need. I wanted to shout, 'Fuck off, the lot of you!' but then, your brain is telling you. 'Don't be silly… that will just make it worse.' I just had to hang on to the microphone and keep going. I found that, by speaking loudly, I could hear my voice through the monitors louder than I could hear the chants. It didn't drown them out completely, but I was able to concentrate enough to keep going.

When I was asked to go back for the second year, I wasn't looking forward to that aspect of it. However, a plan formed in my mind – I bought this really cheap and nasty woman's wig and put it in my bag, and I also brought along a fishing rod. When I went on stage there was a wee bit of the 'Baldy! Baldy!' chant.

I was trying hard not to let them see it was upsetting me, but it reminded me of school. I thought about all the nasty things I might have said in my life. Karma can be a bastard.

I went on to introduce the second band with the wig on. I saw a few of the drunks going, 'What the...?'
I started my spiel while one or two were still shouting at me. Then, as I'm speaking, the wig – which was attached to the fishing line – started to lift off my head. John MacCalman was behind the speakers with the rod, reeling in the line. The whole place erupted into laughter. It didn't stop all the 'baldy' comments, but it made me feel a bit better.

Perhaps twenty years later, when I'd become a wee bit better-known with the rock crowd, I'd be at the Academy or the SECC, and guys would come up and say, 'Look, I owe you a bit of an apology. I used to shout "baldy" at you, and as you can see...' They were having the same problem as me in the hair department – it was just happening to them a little later in life.

It doesn't bother me now. But back then, I was overly effected by it.

Of course, there were a lot more positives than negatives as I became better-known. One of the biggest positives was the amount of time I got to spend in the Glasgow Apollo – a brilliant venue, remembered just as much by the bands that played there as the fans themselves. I often did my interviews in the backstage area of the Apollo, and sometimes I actually took rock stars along to see other acts.

I've interviewed Robert Plant four times over the years. The first couple of times were at the beginning of his solo career – I'd never have got within a hundred yards of him when Led Zeppelin were at their peak. My first Clyde interview with Robert went on for about an hour, mainly because he was enjoying himself. He'd been kept in a bit of a cocoon with Zep, but now there was no time pressure, so we talked about the blues and his early influences. He was quite keen on Scottish traditional music, and he told me he'd regularly visited Scotland during his Zep days. He and his wife would come up for a week, drive about then stop at a bed and breakfast somewhere for the night.

I once asked him about Knebworth, Zeppelin's concert in August 1979. He had a tear in his eye while he discussed it as if it was yesterday – the sun going down on the stage and the sense of expectation surrounding the event. He told me that they hadn't been totally ready to play because it was their first gig after a long lay-off. They'd played some songs too fast, others too slow. Almost 400,000 people soaked the thing up over two nights and he had nice memories of the event.

Robert's Pictures at Eleven album was released in 1982 and it did fairly well here and in America. I asked him if he'd be slipping in the odd Led Zeppelin song on tour. There was a categorical 'no' to that.

I said, 'Not even an odd wee track? We all appreciate you moving on, but you have to remember where you come from.'

He replied, 'No way. Definitely not.'

The first night he played the Apollo there was electricity in the air. He came on in this outfit, looking like Tony Hadley from Spandau Ballet – I remember him wearing a pair of white slippers. There was a huge cheer when he walked to the front of the stage. Playing with a great band, he did songs from the new album for about an hour or so. But you could sense people were starting to lose interest. When he went off stage, everyone thought he'd do a Zeppelin song for his encore, but he didn't. He simply came back on and played another couple of his new songs. I was disappointed. But that's just the way it was for a while. Robert came back in 1983 with his second album, The Principle Of Moments, and this time the Apollo wasn't quite as full. It was only during his third tour that he eventually began to slip in a few Zeppelin tracks. Whether he'd just exorcised his demons, or whether it was management advice, who knows?

Then in the mid-nineties there were the Page and Plant tours, along with two brand-new albums, No Quarter and Walking Into Clarksdale. They were very strong, with live performances to match. The drummer was Michael Lee who'd been in Little Angels – a superb musician who tragically died in 2008.

I've met Jimmy Page a couple of times but never had the pleasure of an official interview. I did see him playing the Marquee in London with Aerosmith, during a warm-up gig for the Monsters Of Rock festival. He joined in on Train Kept A Rollin'. A few days later, I was backstage at the festival and I bumped into Page. I said, 'Hi Jimmy – I'm Tom Russell. I do a rock show up in Glasgow.'

He was very polite: 'Oh, hi! Nice to meet you.'

'I saw you playing on Thursday at the Marquee when you came on with Aerosmith. I was blown away.'

'Yeah, well, we're doing it again tonight,' he replied.

'Can't wait. I'll make sure I'm out front to watch that.' Just a nice wee conversation.

The second time I met Jimmy Page was at the Classic Rock Awards in London. I worked the red carpet up until about nine o'clock, and I noticed that everyone else was well-on, so I decided to catch up, which I'd done by nine forty-five. It was then that I spotted Jimmy, putting his coat on, just about to head for the door. And to my eternal shame, I shouted out, in full-on Glaswegian: 'Hey… Jimmy!' He turned his head, gave me a withering glance, and moved on. Not my proudest moment. You wake up the next morning and think, 'Aw naw… I didn't, did I?' (It's amazing who you can end up sitting beside at the Classic Rock Awards. One year I ended up at a table eating dinner. On one side was Myles Kennedy and on the other was Joe Bonamassa. I kept my inner 'bawdy Glaswegian' in check that time.)

Another time I interviewed Robert Plant, he had a bit of time to kill. The chat went well, and afterwards he asked if there were any bands playing in town. I said ZZ Top were playing the Apollo. Their album Eliminator had just come out, so they were starting to get huge. I got hold of the PR guy and got an extra ticket for Robert. We watched from the press balcony and, because Robert knew the boys in the band, we went round to meet them after the gig. Then the boys in ZZ Top asked if there was anywhere they could go, now the gig was over.

Like many of their contemporaries in those days, they were staying at the Albany Hotel. I said, 'There's a sixties night at a club called Henry Afrikas. I can probably get us in.'

Robert and ZZ Top drummer Frank Beard went back to the hotel, but Billy Gibbons, Dusty Hill and I jumped into a car and went down to the club. At the door the big bouncer's face was a picture. He dashed in, got a camera and dragged the manager out onto the pavement to take a photograph. The photo was eventually put in the glass case at the front door, where it remained for years. There was a Budweiser promotion on, so we couldn't have picked a better night. The guys got into some of the sixties songs and we had a wee sample of the promotional Buds. A memorable evening!

There's another time that becoming a bit well-known turned out to be a positive thing. I'd been down in London, doing some work for Metal Hammer, and I had an open ticket for my flight back to Glasgow. The last flight out of Heathrow was around nine o'clock on the Friday evening – but when I tried to check in, it was full. Breaking out in a cold sweat, I tried to tell them that I was due on Radio Clyde at midnight for the rock show. As you can imagine, no one was interested.

Just as I was contemplating my P45, one of the pilots walked past. He came up, introduced himself and told me that he was a fan. I told him about my predicament and he said, 'Hang on... I'll see what I can do.' Five minutes later escorted me onto the British Airways flight; but instead of turning right into the cabin, I followed him left, straight into the cockpit. I sat on the bucket seat all the way to Glasgow. What an experience – the views were incredible. We landed at ten-fifteen and I got to Clyde at eleven, just in time to get organised for the show. Talk about adrenalin! (I took a note of my saviour's address and the next day, I posted him a nice package of albums and a thank-you note. Lucky white heather.)

I was having a great time on the Friday Night Rock Show. Not just on the show itself, but with all the other stuff that seemed to orbit my life at the time. There were live concerts to attend, festivals to go to, DJ work in clubs, interview trips and all those backstage parties to contend with. However, all was not totally completely rosy in my rock garden. I've made a few mistakes in my life. I'm not perfect by a long shot – and here's a story about a post-concert piss-up that really turned sour...

Iron Maiden were the headline act at the 1992 Monsters of Rock festival in Donington. As usual, they were very generous when it came to after-show parties, and I decided to indulge a bit. Maiden's manager, Rod Smallwood, knew how to put on a great spread, which that year included a tipple called Eddie's Evil Brew. As the band put on a big fireworks display, and with all my interviews done, I had about three pints of it.

Stupidly, at one o'clock in the morning, I got into the car and drove to my digs in Nottingham, where I had my digs. I know what you're thinking, and there's no excuses. I'd told the guest house that I was at the festival and I'd be back late, so they'd left access open for me. The thing was, I knew the road the guest house was on, but not the exact spot. I was driving along, slowing down to look for the address, when I saw the blue lights. Thinking, 'Oh, shit!' I pulled over and wound down my window.

The policeman said, 'Hello, sir. Is there a problem?'

'No, Officer. I'm looking for number 72, a guest house.'

'Oh, that's up there on the right,' he told me. 'By the way sir, have you been drinking?'

'Well,' I said, 'I had a pint earlier on.'

'If that's the case sir, I'm going to have to breathalyse you.' So he did his bit, and I was over the limit.
He said, 'I'm going to have to arrest you and take you back to the station.'

Stomach churning, I went with him, gave a urine sample, and the results were positive; so I was charged. It was already three in the morning, but I had to wait until four, so that I was below the limit and I could drive home. It was a horrible journey. I felt rotten about it. I felt I'd let myself down.

Maybe a month later, I got a summons to attend Nottingham crown court. There was a note saying not to drive in case I was banned. I got the train down by myself – it was the first time I'd been in a court. Full of remorse, I was asked, 'Anything you'd like to say?'

'I'd like to apologise to the court,' I said. 'I thought I was okay to drive, but obviously I made a mistake. And I need the car for my job.' As I looked up, however, I saw the magistrate wasn't even listening.

'Oh, are you finished?' he said. 'Clerk, read out the police statement.'

I was stunned – It was full of absolute shite. 'We found the occupant slumped over the steering wheel. The car was swerving across the road. The driver was not coherent.' All untrue.

'Banned for a year and a three-hundred-pound fine!' the magistrate announced.

I asked, 'Can I say something?'

'Well, it's highly irregular.'

'It's fine,' I said. 'I'll take my punishment. I was in the wrong. But I wasn't slumped over any steering wheel nor was I swerving about. It's a disgrace that one of your officers feels it necessary to lie, just to boost his case.'

But again, the magistrate wasn't even listening.

So I had a hell of a year. Anyone who's lost their licence will know what I mean. Drinking and driving was prevalent back in the day, but still very wrong. I deserved what I got. I hope it will make others think. I've certainly learned my lesson.

Tom 18 months meets Santa   Tom, aged 4, with Mum and Dad

Tom on the day of his first parachute jump

Tom's stock car, No. 50, rolling over…

Tom in the band – Strange Brew

Tom in his 20's doing a mobile disco.

First shop opening with proud mum and dad

Dave Hill and Noddy Holder of Slade at Bishopbriggs shop

The first shop – Bishopbriggs

An early Radio Clyde picture   Compering at Kelvingrove

Wurzel and Lemmy from Motorhead, outside Radio Clyde

Interviewing Status Quo at the SECC

Carrying on with Brian and Angus of AC/DC at the Holiday Inn

Watching Baseball a day after getting 'attacked by a snake' in Atlanta

An early Bon Jovi interview

Bruce Dickinson wins a Go-Kart race. Tom came second

In NewYork, interviewing Europe

9. MEN OF ACTION

Chris Rea falls off stage ~ Lemmy goes to the Dial Inn ~ Bon Jovi push a van ~ Tiger Tim touches his toes

Commercial radio was great, but there wasn't a lot of money to be made just doing one show a week. So it was good when that and the record shops fed into each other. One time a label rep called Matt called in at one of my shops. He sold me his new batch of albums then asked if I was doing anything that night, because he had a band on at the Apollo and a couple of complimentary tickets. He hung about until I closed the shop and then we headed into town, ending up in the Burns Howff (another classic Glasgow venue).

Soon this guy appeared, a Geordie, who was the label act's support at the Apollo. It was about half-five and we offered him a drink. Round after round ensued and we began complimenting the pints with shorts because time was getting tight. Although the guy was due on at seven-fifteen, he never panicked. He was enjoying himself, telling stories, having a laugh. It turned into a great wee session, but at seven the guy said, 'I need to get up the road. I'm on stage in fifteen minutes.' We helped him up the road and got him into the Apollo, but he literally staggered up to the dressing room as we positioned ourselves in the stalls.

There were only about two hundred people there at the time. (In those days it wasn't that fashionable to watch a support band. Everybody was across the road in Lauder's Bar.) The guy came on and he did a great set. He got a good reception all the way through.
But after the last song, the applause inspired a touch of theatricals, and he jumped off the stage. Now, the Apollo stage was a good height, so it wasn't pretty.

Years later I was scheduled to interview him for Clyde – the station often got me to do a lot of interviews, even pop ones, because the other DJs didn't like doing them and also because I was self-employed and I had more free time than others. I went to London for the interview, and it was the first time I'd seen him since that night. He was a big star by this time.

I started the interview with: 'The last time we met, we had a wee drink together before you played the Apollo…'

His eyes widened. 'You, ye bastard!' he said. 'You're the one that got me all those drinks and then I jumped off that bloody stage. I twisted my ankle real bad – and from that day till this, every winter, that ankle still throbs like hell!'

The headline band at the Apollo all those years before had been Lindisfarne. I really loved them after coming across them during my time in Newcastle. The support act, now a big star, was the man I set on The Road to Hell – Chris Rea. Sorry, Chris…

Bands would often come into the studio at Clyde after they'd played the Glasgow Apollo. Other times they would come in beforehand to do a pre-record. One guy who did both on separate occasions was Lemmy Kilmister. Around 1983, Motorhead's record company phoned to say the band had a new album called Another Perfect Day, and asked if I'd like the guys to come along live after playing the Apollo. Brian Robertson was in the band at the time, having joined up in May 1982, so I said, 'Sure.'

That night I started my show at midnight as usual; and, fifteen minutes later, Eric at reception buzzed me to say that my guests had arrived. In came Lemmy and Brian, and I could tell that they already had a good bevy in them. I said, 'How was it tonight, boys?'

Lemmy could be tricky – he loved putting you down with a one-word answer if he thought you'd asked a stupid question. He didn't suffer fools gladly. This time it was worse than that. Two minutes into the live interview, he produced a tin and began spooning out white powder. I was terrified, but I just got on with it and it went okay. Now, it could have been a big wind-up by Lemmy and Brian, but how was I to know?

Lemmy was cool, each of the ten times I interviewed him. He never made out that he remembered you, and maybe he didn't. He once came into the studio to pre-record an interview on a Tuesday night. We'd finished for about eight o'clock and he said, 'Where is there to go in Glasgow on a Tuesday? I'm at the Albany Hotel.'

I said, 'They've usually got a live band on at the Dial Inn, next to the Odeon.'

So Lemmy and I went down to the Dial Inn. I wasn't that well-known then, but Lemmy was. You could see one or two people looking over and thinking: 'That's no' Lemmy from Motorhead, is it?' You could see them mouthing the words and then shaking their heads: 'Nah… It cannae be.' No one came over. We had two or three pints, watched a band (no idea who it was) totally uninterrupted, and then we went back to the Albany.

Recently, I was talking to a guy at a gig and he said, 'Years ago, did you and Lemmy come into the Dial Inn for a pint?' When I replied in the affirmative, he punched the air. 'I knew it!' He'd been there that night, but no one had believed him when he said that it was Lemmy.

I obtained a brilliant Motorhead souvenir when was I was working in London on the video magazine. After Lemmy and the band played the Hammersmith Odeon, a couple of the Hard'n'Heavy crew and I blagged our way backstage and went to the band's dressing room. We were made welcome and told to help ourselves to a drink, which we did.

Lemmy was nowhere to be seen; but, just as I was pouring myself a large Jack Daniel's, he entered the dressing room and said something like, 'Leave my Jack alone, you Scottish git!' He then removed his Motorhead 1916 T-shirt, which was sodden with sweat, and threw it at me. Quick as a flash, I wrung it out and stuck it in my bag. I still have that shirt to this day.

Most people didn't see the softer side of Lemmy. But around 2010 I was due to interview him and I happened to mention it on air. Later I received an email from two listeners who were getting married the following week, and were big Motorhead fans. They asked if I could get them a message from Lemmy.

So after my interview, I asked the man himself, and he was delighted to record a personal message for the couple. He wished them all the best in his own inimitable style. I transferred the message to cassette (remember those things?) and posted it to them. A week later, I got a lovely letter from the bride to say thanks. They'd played the cassette after the best man's speech and got the biggest cheer of the night from the assorted wedding guests.

When Radio Clyde moved to Clydebank in 1983, we went from one studio to three – two main studios with a news studio in the middle. When presenter Peter Mallan, who did the show preceding mine, finished at midnight, he'd hand over to the newsroom for three minutes. In that time he had to stand up, unplug his headphones, pick up his records and get out of the studio. Then I'd move in and cue up my first record. If it happened to be track seven it wasn't so easy, and of course, you're panicking… Then the newscaster would finish, you'd hit the jingle and you'd be off: 'Hi, Tom Russell here, welcome to The Friday Night Rock Show…'

The DJ on the slot before Peter was Tiger Tim Stevens, the loveliest, nicest guy, but full of mischief. Now, because I only did one show a week, I would get very nervous beforehand – especially if it was track seven that I had to cue up. That three-minute section of news goes by really quickly. On this particular night, Tim was still about while I was getting ready as usual; trying to remember the speed of the track (thirty-three or forty-five?) and testing my mic. Then the newscaster finished: 'We'll be back in an hour with an update.' I hit the jingle, opened the microphone and lifted my head.

Tim had timed it to perfection: he stood up on a chair that he'd put in front of me, loosened his belt and turned his back on me, all while I was concentrating on track seven. Just as I opened the mic to say, 'Hi, Tom Russell here,' Tim's trousers and pants dropped to his ankles. And if that wasn't bad enough, for that extra-special effect he leaned forward... and touched his toes.

You can imagine the sight. You can imagine my reaction. I dissolved into a stuttering wreck.

Sometimes a band would come into Radio Clyde before their Apollo gig, and they'd cut it a bit fine for their soundcheck. That's what happened to an American band who came to the UK for the first time in 1984, supporting Kiss. They'd released a single called Runaway and I'd got the album on import. I'd played the track a few times on the radio; and again, because there were so few avenues for rock back then, I got access to these guys no problem. Glasgow was to be one of the bands first British gigs, and I would record one of their first-ever radio interviews in the UK.

It was early winter, around October. The band arrived around two o'clock in a wee minibus, and they did a smashing interview. I showed them round the building afterwards – the American bands were always blown away at a radio station with a swimming pool!

We chatted over a coffee as snow began to fall. After another twenty minutes the band's tour manager said they had to leave for their soundcheck. But they couldn't get the minibus out of the Radio Clyde car park. The wheels were spinning in the snow. So my colleague John MacCalman and I helped Jon Bon Jovi, Richie Sambora and Dave Bryan push their bus in the snow. I'm glad to say that we eventually got them moving and they made their soundcheck. I have a lot of good photographs, but I always regretted not getting a photo of that one. I've interviewed Bon Jovi a good six or so times since, and I always bring it up. They always say they remember it. (Whether they do or not, who knows?)

I always loved discovering and helping new bands. Tom's talent radar was on, looking for opportunities for the next up-and-coming acts. When the band Glasgow sent me a demo, it was their name that attracted me first. After I played their tape on the Friday Night Rock Show, they sent me a letter, thanking me and inviting me to Linwood to see them play. So I drove over to the gig and introduced myself to Mick the singer, Archie the guitarist, Joe the drummer and Neil the bass player. As we sat and blethered, I thought, 'You guys have got potential.' They put a on a show in that wee Linwood pub as if they were headlining the Apollo.

Over the next few months, I became friends with the band; until one day they said, 'Tom, we've got a gig at Whitley Bay near Newcastle. Do you fancy coming?' We drove down in their split bus (gear in the back, seats in the front) with beer flowing all the way and the driver, whose name I can't remember, smoking dope just like a packet of fags. They played two one-hour sets and finished up around midnight. Everyone had a good drink in them by the we set off on the drive home.

On the A69 between Newcastle and Carlisle, there was a sudden bang. We screeched to a stop and the driver said, 'It came from nowhere! Did you not see it?' We got out of the bus and found a deer lying on the road, still alive but wounded. Everyone was coming up with suggestions until some silly bugger with a beard suggested we go to the nearby town of Hexham to find a vet. We lifted the deer onto the bus and continued the journey. Neil stroking the deer's head, all the way to Hexham. While we were wondering how to find a vet at three in the morning, the poor deer expired. Again, there were more drunken suggestions: 'Take it home and eat it.'

'Naw – we cannae do that – it might be diseased.'

Someone else suggested, through the drink, that if we were to get caught driving home with a dead deer, we'd all get the jail. Better leave it in the vet's garden. But we couldn't find a big neon sign that said 'Vet open all night.' This same stupid bugger with all the daft suggestions – who worked on the radio – pointed and said, 'There's the very place for it!' We took the deer from Neil, who was still stroking its head, and propped it up in one of those old-fashioned red phone boxes in the centre of Hexham. We had to use the wire from the phone receiver, wrapped round its antlers, to keep it upright. Then we drove home.
What must it have been like for the first customer wanting to use that phone on the Sunday morning? ... Oh dear!

One day I got a call from United Artists, a subsidiary of EMI, asking for help. One of their touring bands had dumped their support – 'They were absolute shite,' was the comment – and the label asked: 'Is there anyone you could recommend, Tom?'

I said, 'Can I phone you back in half an hour?'

'Can you make it ten minutes?'

'Okay,' I replied. I was already looking up Glasgow singer Mick's number. I got a reply quickly: they were all up for it, except Joe the drummer, who had a daytime job. The rest of the band however, quickly managed to persuade him. There was only twenty quid a night in it, but at least there was no buy-on – in those days you normally had to get your record company to buy you onto a tour, at a very high cost.

I gave the boys a phone number, and the location of the next show on the tour, which was in the north of England. They managed to get on their bus with roadie Bob McBean and got underway.

Mick phoned me the next day. They were supporting Uriah Heep, who were very good to them. Although. as you can imagine, twenty quid a night barely covered their fuel costs, never mind a bite to eat.

There were a few other opportunities after that for Glasgow, but they still never quite made it that last step. On the other hand, Heavy Pettin' did about three shows and got signed to Polydor – and then they were out supporting Ozzy.

Another band I liked was Chou Pahrot, who I thought would be great in the middle of the day for Kelvingrove. I took Clyde's production manager John MacCalman to see them; his attitude was, 'They'll either sink or swim.'

There were about four thousand people at Kelvingrove on the day and it had a great atmosphere. Chou Pahrot came on – a couple of the guys were wearing dresses and one had a violin, playing music that reminded me of Frank Zappa. What a pelting they took! Oranges, cans of beer, the lot. Poor guys… they were just a bit too bizarre. Three songs in, they had to get off. (I met one of the guys a few years ago, when Glasgow City Council had put in a good bit of money into refurbishing Kelvingrove Bandstand, which had been about to fall down. We spent the evening reminiscing.)

Bon Jovi, who'd toured the UK for the first time as support to Kiss, came back as headliners about six months later, then again a year after that. They were doing the Edinburgh Playhouse and the date happened to coincide with the Kelvingrove festival. So I phoned the record company and asked if there was any chance the boys could come through to Glasgow in the afternoon, not to play, but just to make a wee appearance. Bon Jovi said 'yes.'

On the day, around three o'clock, five thousand people were enjoying the sun and the bands at Kelvingrove, when I got the nod that our guests had arrived. The boys came onto the stage and said a few words – what a lovely surprise for the fans in Glasgow. Jon Bon took the mic and told them, 'Thanks for inviting us through!' He talked about their new album and then they spent an hour signing autographs and chatting to fans. Some people don't believe that actually happened – but it did. Ask anyone who was there.

In the mid-eighties I was approached by a guy called Davy Anderson, who I'm still friendly with, to compere the Easterhouse Festival. He'd come into my Shettleston shop to tell me about it. It was round about the time gangs were causing some trouble in the Easterhouse area. I went along to the festival and saw Dicky Bow and the Collars and Scheme. A band called Blind Allez, who soon changed their name to Phobia, were really promising, so I met up with the boys after they'd played. They gave me a cassette to listen to, and I went to see them a couple more times. A few months later, I was thinking about the lineup for the next Kelvingrove Festival and I asked them to perform. They did well that day.

A few weeks later, a guy called Rab Andrew gave me a call. Rab had a recording studio on the south side of Glasgow and had signed the band Texas to a management deal. Their first single was a huge hit and he was on the hunt for another band. He said, 'I think rock has a big future but I don't know enough about it. Is there anyone I should be aware of?'

I rhymed off a dozen names, then told him that three of them were playing Kirkintilloch Town Hall the following Friday. So Rab and I went along and saw Phobia, Abel Ganz and Chasar. I was convinced that Rab would go for Chasar, who were superb musically, but he didn't say much until the end. I hadn't told anyone I was bringing this guy, but I introduced him to all the bands.

A week later, Rab phoned me and said, 'Thanks for the night at Kirkintilloch. I've actually signed one of the bands.'

'Which one?' I asked.

'Phobia.'

'Oh,' I said, 'Why them?'

'I just saw potential,' he said. 'So now I've got them rehearsing.'

A few months later he told me, 'I've got them in practicing five nights a week practicing. They're pissed off with it, but the two brothers are working hard.'

Another few months later he told me he'd got them a record deal. They'd changed their name to GUN and signed to A&M Records. They ended up doing very well – they supported the Rolling Stones, amongst others, but nothing happened for them in America. Sometimes that's how it goes. (I can think of a few other bands like Terrorvision, Little Angels and Thunder, who got so far in the UK. There wasn't enough money to be made here, so unless they broke America it got tricky.)

Eventually Mark, the singer with GUN, got a good job with the Mercury Records promotions department and Giuliano, the guitarist, went back to working in the family restaurant. The good news is that , these days, things are back on the up for GUN.

Polydor Records put a lot of money into another Glasgow band, Heavy Pettin' – their tour with Ozzy helped start a great buzz. They had good songs and good musicianship, and they even had an album produced by Brian May of Queen. Hamie was an excellent frontman. Everything was going well, even in America – then someone at Polydor said: 'We need to recoup some of the money we've invested. We want you to enter the Eurovision Song Contest.'

The band's opinion was that it would destroy their credibility – and it kind of did. Hamie recently told me: 'Yes, they wanted their money back, but there was more to it. Polydor had paid for three albums, world tours and videos for MTV, but they didn't know what to do with us. So we wanted out. We were in the bar of a recording studio in Chelsea when our manager came in with the director of Polydor, who told us that they only way they'd let us go was if we did Euro.

'We thought it was a joke. We knew it would destroy us. But it was either stay, be put on a shelf and held to our contract – or write a song for Eurovision, play on the show, then we'd be allowed to leave with a clean slate and go to one of the American labels that wanted to sign us.

'It was a bad and crazy time. We went out of our way to lose that show and we were Terry Wogan's worst nightmare. I was constantly drunk on Jack Daniel's. Terry would come into our dressing room and tell us: "Now come on boys, let's be professional." We just stared at him, started laughing and kept on drinking.

'I remember being drunk and having sex with one of the other contestants in our dressing room when he walked in. As he was leaving I kept shouting, 'Terry, can I get your autograph for my mother?'

10. GETTING OUT THERE

Clyde's mobile studio ~ the lost tapes ~ opening The Venue ~ travels with Iron Maiden, Guns N' Roses, Scorpions, Pearl Jam and more

Around the time of the Kelvingrove festivals, radio stations were making big profits, so Radio Clyde reinvested some money in a top-of-the-range mobile recording studio. It cost an arm and a leg – but it was only being used a few times a year, once to record the festival and once to record Christmas carols. So some of us suggested to Alex Dickson that perhaps we could use it to record some of the bands playing in Glasgow at the time, with a view to broadcasting them. Some people dismissed the idea, saying we'd never get permission to broadcast.

So I said, 'Our gear is as good as The Rolling Stones' mobile or any other mobile in the world. Why don't we record concerts, do a great production on the tapes, send them to the bands and say, 'This doesn't get broadcast anywhere until you say so"?'

I don't think any of the bands we recorded over the next few years said 'no'. The late Pete Shipton was the main engineer. He had a great ear and an excellent team, who mastered recordings of Nazareth, Magnum, Simple Minds, Runrig, Rory Gallagher, Thin Lizzy, Ian Gillan, Whitesnake, Dio, Wings, GUN, Roxy Music and more – so many fantastic recordings of bands at their peak, playing the Glasgow Apollo or the Barrowland.

They were originally recorded onto a huge two-inch master tape. Once it had all been mixed, it went onto a half-inch reel to reel. The usual deal was that we were allowed to play it on air twice. Sometimes the band would take a track and put it on the B-side of a single.

So what happened to the tapes? They were kept in a big cupboard, until, down the line, Radio Clyde was sold. The new owners came up for a look around and said, 'What's all this rubbish?' John MacCalman, head of production said they were old live recordings. 'Just skip them,' he was told. John tried his best to fight the decision but, to tell you the rest of the story, I have to go off-piste a little…

Jimmy Devlin was quite a character, who started off as bass player in an Edinburgh band, Bilbo Baggins. They had a minor hit single called Saturday Night. Later, he got a job as a record sales rep and he used to come into my shop. Then he was promoted to head office in London, and within five years he'd become managing director of Polydor. They had a lot of rock acts: Magnum, Van Morrison, The Almighty, Rainbow, and more.

I was often down at Polydor doing interviews. I didn't see Jimmy that much – he was the big boss – but one day I was down interviewing someone when Jimmy came into the room. He gave me a big cuddle and we had a blether, then he took me up to his office. Big leather chairs, huge table, the works; and behind him, facing me, on the wall, was a big painting of the band Bilbo Baggins, including Jimmy in his white tartan trousers.

Jimmy told me, 'I get these characters coming in here with the fancy titles like head of A&R, head of promotion and so on. I have them in for a bollocking at times. I get them to stand on that carpet. No seat. And I say, "Tell me… that album by so-and-so was a great album. How come it only sold a thousand copies when it should have sold a hundred thousand?"

'They make up all these excuses. Then I say. "There's only one way you're going to keep your job, ya bastard. I'll stand aside, and then you'll apologise to Bilbo Baggins."

'They usually protest a bit, but I tell them I'm not kidding. Then they look at the painting and say something like, "Sorry, Mr Bilbo Baggins." Then I tell them to fuck off out of my office and they can keep their job for another month – but any more fuck ups and they'll be out!' Presumably the poor buggers marched off, head hung in shame, suitably chastised.

Jimmy ended up back in Edinburgh and he set up a company called River Records. One day they approached Radio Clyde and said, 'Any chance we can buy some of these live tapes and release them on CD?' They were probably thinking that they wouldn't sell millions, but there'd be enough business to make a profit.

So suddenly, the company that owned Clyde were interested in those old tapes. John MacCalman said, 'You told me to skip them.'

'Oh no – that wasn't us.'

'Aye it was.'

'So they're gone?'

'Well,' said John, 'I put some of them up in the loft.'

So they found a few – Magnum, Whitesnake, Marillion, Thin Lizzy, Simple Minds, Status Quo. Brilliant material that was eventually released on River Records.

In 2013 I got an email from David Coverdale's personal assistant: 'We're doing a retrospective "Best of Whitesnake". David remembers doing a recording in Glasgow when you were involved. Can we use it?' I phoned John, but the tape was long gone, possibly to River Records. David's PA said. 'Could you maybe ask around and see if anyone has a copy? David's memory of it is good.'

So I put it on my Facebook page, and one guy told me, 'I recorded it when it was broadcast. the quality is good. I can send you a copy.' I sent it to Phoenix, Arizona, where Coverdale lives, and they selected one track which, I think, ended up on the album.

In the early eighties it was normal for pubs to shut at eleven o'clock, and after that the only place that you could get a drink was a night club or a disco. There were quite a few of these places in Glasgow – but none of them played rock music. I thought that was unfair. A substantial part of the population happened to like rock music, but if they went out on a Saturday night, they were stuffed after eleven. Most of them didn't want to go to discos and listen to the latest pop drivel.

So I spoke to Richard Park at Clyde, and he put me in touch with Ross Bowie, George Bowie's dad. Ross had been a mover and shaker in the area over three decades already; he owned a few clubs and discos at the time, including the Mayfair (now the Garage). It had a downstairs room, not as big as the Mayfair itself, but it still looked as if you could hold a decent night there. I chatted with Ross, who agreed to put on a rock night.

Being full-on with my shops and the Friday Night Rock Show, I was a bit too busy to book bands and hire a PA, so Ross brought in a guy called Allan Mawn. A partnership was set up between Clyde, Allan, Ross and I and we started doing a Friday night there. We had to think of a name, and after a lot of consideration and head-scratching, we called it the Venue.

Some of the best bands around played that place. Every Friday the doors would open about eight o'clock, with me playing the music. I had to carry in a big pile of vinyl singles and LPs – there were none of your USB drives back then. Thankfully, Ross's sixteen-year-old son George, (who went on to have some success himself on Radio Clyde) used to meet me in the car park and help me carry in my records. I'd play the rock tunes and introduce the live band before scooting back to Clyde in time to to get ready for my Friday Night Rock Show.

After a few months, it had become very successful – and the best thing was that the rock fans of Glasgow had a place to go to on a Friday night, and enjoy themselves until about two o'clock. Touring bands enjoyed the option too.

Ross and Allan eventually took the whole thing over, and that was fine. Soon, a few other businessmen started running a Saturday night rock club in Glasgow. Donald McLeod was one of the main guys – he opened a club in Brown Street and called it the Cathouse. At the beginning, the rock club was on level one, and down in the basement, there was a grab-a-granny night (a sixties night for older singles). Mature divorcees downstairs and hard rock fans upstairs… I'm not sure if one lot mixed with the other, or even became the other, but it was all good fun. It became very successful, with Robert Fields booking the bands. After a few years the Venue faded a bit and the Cathouse took over. Donald's company became so successful that it ended up buying the Garage and a few other clubs in Glasgow.

In 1987 Geffen Records invited to me to London for an overnighter. They'd signed a Los Angeles band called Guns N' Roses, who were playing a couple of gigs at the Marquee. I had an interview in the band's hotel in the afternoon. When I was shown in, the guys were lounging about, drinking, smoking and listening to some music, which I recognised as Nazareth. As I was setting up my tape recorder, Axl Rose heard my accent and asked me, 'Are You Scottish?'

When I replied, 'Yes, I'm from Glasgow,' the whole band got excited – they offered me beer and asked me if there was any possibility that I knew Nazareth? When I said 'yes,' Axl asked if there was any chance that, if Guns N' Roses ever came to Scotland, I could fix up a meeting with Nazareth. They were one of Axl's favourite bands, and as a teenager, he used to follow them round the USA when they toured.

Incidentally, the gig at the Marquee that night was breathtaking; one of the best I've ever seen.

I got on particularly well with Duff McKagan, the bass player. He's another one that who's always like, 'Tom! How you doing? How's the scene in Glasgow?' A good guy. He's also a money whizz-kid – when he left Guns N' Roses, he went to university and took a degree in financial studies.

(Duff and Slash enjoyed another lease of life with Velvet Revolver in the 2000s. After they split, he formed a band called Loaded. One time when I interviewed them, Duff was wearing a t-shirt that had an arrow pointing to his left and the words: 'This guy likes to suck cock.' So anyone standing on his left was in trouble.)

Country rock singer Steve Earle is probably best known for his song Copperhead Road, which I loved playing on air. I interviewed him once, in Glasgow on a Monday night around 1988. We pre-recorded the chat, then Steve suggested we go out for some Mexican food. I was happy to go along, and we both ended up steamin' on the tequila. I remember him telling me that he'd been married five or six times – the first time when he was only eighteen. He was sitting on his front porch one afternoon when an angry guy pulled up in his truck, marched up to Steve with a loaded shotgun, forced him into the truck and drove him to the local church, where he was escorted up the aisle at gunpoint. The guy stood there, shotgun in hand, until the pastor conducted the marriage ceremony between Steve and the guy's pregnant daughter. A genuine shotgun wedding! … The marriage didn't last.

I've interviewed most of the members of Deep Purple, but I've only met Ritchie Blackmore once. The band were playing the Edinburgh Playhouse in the late eighties, and I went through to interview bass player Roger Glover. He's a lovely, professional guy and he asked me to go back for a drink after the gig. The show was superb – a great mix of old and new Purple songs, and there was magic in the air. After the main set, the band left the stage, and there were the inevitable shouts for more; but after a couple of minutes, the house lights went up. The shouts for more quickly turned to boos as the fans were refused an encore.

Half an hour later I was in the backstage area, waiting for my after-show drink; and as I went in to the dressing room, I passed Ritchie. Perfectly pleasant, he said hello, so I introduced myself and asked why there was no encore. He replied that there had been – but that the band had simply not gone off stage then gone back on again. I politely pointed out that the crowd didn't know that, hence the boos ... Ritchie didn't seem that bothered.

I knew I was very lucky to be working on a radio rock show when media outlets for rock were limited. That's the reason, for example, I was invited to the launch of a Scorpions album in Munich, Germany. It was 1990 and the album was called Crazy World. After hearing the record and piling into a mountain of drink, I got back to my hotel about three in the morning. A rock journalist pal of mine, Jerry Ewing, fancied a swim. The hotel, however, had prevented the lift from stopping at the pool on the fourteenth floor after midnight. It was specifically to stop numpties like us going for a drunken swim. But Jerry said, 'I know what we can do – we can go to the fifteenth floor and then go down the fire escape to the fourteenth.'

'Great idea,' said I. Being a courteous guy, I let Jerry go first; and soon realised it was a wise move. He got himself locked out on the exterior fire escape, in freezing temperatures, with no way down to the fourteenth floor or back onto the fifteenth. To my eternal shame, at this stage of the proceedings, I became tired, returned to my room and went to bed.

Eventually Jerry made his way all the way down to the first floor where, still locked out, he had to break a pane of glass to get into the hotel. That resulted in a badly-cut leg. Blood pished out over the plush hall carpet, and there was quite a hefty bill for the record company the next morning. Poor Jerry didn't get invited to anything by that record company for ages.

In 1991, with the Friday Night Rock Show doing well, I was invited to New York to interview a band called Masters Of Reality at their studio in Syracuse. I rated them highly, but they never made it to the heights I felt they deserved. I got one well with bandleader Chris Goss that day. I never saw him again until 2014, when I bumped into him backstage at the Download festival. He'd done well as a producer, working with Kyuss and Queens of the Stone Age, and we spent a pleasant hour in the sunshine, reminiscing.

During that New York trip I was invited to see some record company people at the famous CBS building on Sixth Street. Over a coffee, I was given an advance promotional cassette of a band that they'd just signed. They were from Seattle, but the first album had been recorded in England and it was about to be released. I'd heard of the band in the underground press, but I hadn't heard any of the material. I was made to swear on my life that their cassette would be 'for my ears only.' When I got back to my hotel room, I played it while lying on a massive king-size bed; I clearly remember being absolutely blown away by this album called Ten by Pearl Jam.

A few months later, Pearl Jam toured the UK for the first time. The Glasgow show was at the original Cathouse, in Brown Street, and it was phenomenal. I interviewed singer Eddie Vedder on the afternoon of the show, taking my six-year-old son, Neil, with me. Eddie made Neil welcome and we had a great interview. Sadly, even though they've had a very successful career over the past 25 years, they've rarely come back to play in Scotland.

I've had some amazing trips to album launches over the years. One of the best was the Status Quo 25th anniversary party in 1990. The band's record company decided to take all the press to Butlin's holiday camp in Minehead, where the band had started out. (I think Francis Rossi and Rick Parfitt may have even met there with their parents.) In London we all boarded The Quo Express, a train hired exclusively to take us to Minehead. We stayed in the chalets and Quo played a gig on the Saturday night. One of the best live acts you'll ever find, in my opinion.

It was a similar to an Iron Maiden special in 1993, put on at Pinewood Studios to honour Bruce Dickinson's 'last gig' with them. He'd brought out a solo album. There were frustrations in the band and eventually Bruce left, but in a fairly amicable way. They decided to stage one final performance together and film it for a video. Their label, EMI, were very good with these things then, and they approached rock DJs including myself, asking us to run ticket competitions, so that real fans could be at the show. Radio Clyde hired a coach and set up a contest to fill the seats.

Twenty winners each received a pair of tickets and the big day came. As we set off, the driver announced, 'There's no drinking on the bus!'

Aye, right!

To be fair, he was decent enough. He kept his eyes on the road and off the piles of beer that were emerging from bags and rucksacks everywhere. We even had additional pit stops at Carlisle and Knutsford for extra supplies before arriving at Pinewood Studios where – you've guessed it – there was more free drink laid on for all invited guests.

With about five hundred people there from all over Europe, it was a magical experience for the Glasgow fans. There was no hotel or anything, so after a great show, it was back to the bus. It was a freezing cold night in the middle of winter as we realised the bus wasn't going to start. Pinewood, (which is where they film the James Bond films) was closing down for the night. All the lights were being switched off and we didn't know what to do. The driver phoned for a tow truck, but I felt responsible for the Glasgow prizewinners, who were all supposed to be getting picked up from Glasgow's George Square later that morning.

I was wandering about trying to find someone who could help when I bumped into Steve Harris, Iron Maiden's bass player. 'How are you doing, Tom?' he asked. I told him what had happened and he said in his strong Cockney accent. 'Fackin'ell! I don't know what I can do. Eh… tell you what, come with me.' I followed him back to the Maiden dressing room, where he handed over two crates of beer from the band's rider. 'Maybe that will help a bit,' he said. It did. Then a replacement bus arrived around three o'clock and we got under way. What an adventure.

That reminds me of another Maiden story, relayed to me by their drummer, Nicko McBrain… Rod Smallwood has been the band's manager since day one, and he did well for them and himself. He's also a big rugby and golf fan. So, maybe twenty years ago, after the band had just completed a world tour and grossed a few bob, Rod decided to do something a bit special for the guys. As a member of Wentworth Golf Club, he arranged to take the band for a golf day. They all met at nine in the morning and had a wee 'livener' to loosen up the joints.

Rod had warned them all to behave themselves. But Nicko remembered that, by the time they'd got to the thirteenth hole, his stomach felt really funny and he was dying for a fart. He'd let a few go already, usually just at the point when Rod was about to hit his putt, so by this time the manager was getting well pissed off. 'You're putting me off, Nicko!'

Then the inevitable happened. Rod was just about to putt for the thirteenth hole when Nicko lifted his leg to let one go. But to his surprise, he produced rather more than a ripping fart – and to a chortle of laughter from the band, he followed through. Iron Maiden erupted into hysterics as Nicko turned to Rod and said, 'Come on boss, what can I do?'

Rod, uptight about any of the club members seeing Nicko in his state, said, 'There's a bush over there. Take this towel and clean yourself up!' Nicko went behind the bushes, dropped the tartan trousers that he'd bought especially for the event, and removed his pants. Then he rolled them up into a ball and tucked them under a bush.
Rod won the round of golf, even with his handicap, and they all retired to the bar. After a while, the door opened and this posh gentleman, Colonel Wipshot-Bagnot, barged in, ranting and raving. 'I'm absolutely disgusted. I'll never come back to this golf course again!' he said. 'I was playing the thirteenth and I'd just pitched a beautiful shot next to the green. I couldn't see where it had landed at first, but then I found it, perched on top of a disgusting pair of pants!'

One of the band piped up: 'Were you allowed a lift and drop?'

Maiden guitarist Dave Murray is a lovely guy. I've interviewed him a couple of times, but one stint on Radio Clyde's Friday Night Rock Show was memorable for a specific reason. Dave was my live guest on the show, but he wasn't particularly comfortable – he could stand on stage in front of thousands of people and play guitar no problem, but speaking live on the radio made him a bit nervous.

Throughout the interview, Dave kept saying 'you know' over and over again, sometimes two or three times in each sentence. It went on for the twenty minutes that he was live on air. So my mischievous self took over. After he left, I offered a prize for the listener who could tell me how many times Dave had said 'you know' during the interview. In those days, entries came in by post and the winner was announced the following Friday. That gave me time to listen back to the recording of the show and count the number. To my astonishment, one guy got the answer spot on: 180 times. He must have recorded the show and counted them up, just as I had.

A couple of years later, at a Maiden album launch party in London I got Dave a drink from the (free) bar and confessed my 'crime'. True to form, Dave and his lady just laughed… you know.

11. ADVENTURES IN BED

A few tales of sex, drugs and rock'n'roll ~ an impostor ~ mistaken identity ~ selling the shops

Rock music will always be associated with sex, drugs and rock'n'roll. But I must admit that, over the years, I haven't come across all that much of it. A bit of sex, yes. A bit of rock, yes. A few pints, yes. Drugs? Never in my case. But the image is there.

I did have various adventures in the bedroom department as a single lad – and one of the most memorable took place when I met a lady in her thirties, a good ten years older than I was, who was recently divorced with two young children. She invited me back to her place for coffee and I was happy to accept. The babysitter headed up the road and the kids were fast asleep in their beds, so we settled down together on the couch to 'enjoy our coffee'.

Nature took over and one thing led to another. Around three in the morning, it had progressed to a full-blown session – in the lounge, on the couch… However, while in the missionary position, I was shocked to be kicked on the back of my calf by my partners heel. It happened a second time and a third. It was sore, but I thought it was some bizarre sex-game type thing and I tried to ignore it.

The kicks continued and I was just about to suspend operations when, glancing down the couch, I spotted the cause. A small dog, belonging to my new friend, had her knickers firmly clamped in its mouth. The knickers were still wrapped around one of her ankles, and the mutt was playing with them. My partner for the evening was simply trying to shoo away the offending puppy without upsetting my concentrated efforts – and that's why she ended up kicking me.

I remember when Marillion were on their second UK tour in the 1980s, and they played a midweek show at the Ayr Pavilion. I got on the guest list and thoroughly enjoyed the show. About fifteen minutes after the band had finished, I thought I'd pop backstage and say hello – just courtesy.

I'd never been backstage at that venue, and I wasn't totally sure where I was. I spied a toilet and thought I might as well use it. On the left-hand side was a row of urinals. On the right-hand side was a row of sinks. The sink nearest the door wasn't being used for washing hands at the time... A very polite young lady was sitting on it. I can still picture her, with her bright red knickers wrapped around one ankle and her legs wrapped round the bare backside of one of the guys with the band. The girl was first to look up – she just said, 'Flipping heck!' or words to that effect. Then the guy turned round and said, 'Oh, Tam! I didn't know you were in the audience. I'll be out in a minute.'

I closed the door, went along to see the rest of the guys and chatted for about five minutes, until the man in question came into the dressing room. He chatted away, quite the thing, as if the episode in the bog had never happened.

I've been fairly friendly with Fish over the years, even after he left Marillion, and I was delighted when I got an invite to his wedding. He seemed to have been a wee bit unlucky in love in the past, so I was pleased for him. He lived in Haddington, near Edinburgh at the time, and he'd built a residential recording studio there. I went through by myself and got there in good time for the kick-off. Willie Docherty, another rock jock was there too – Willie actually came from Haddington.

Fish was holding court, but he looked a wee bit sheepish. The wedding had been called off the day before. I never quite got the whole story, but the bride was nowhere to be seen and that was that. However, the wedding party wasn't cancelled. They still had the band, they still had the hog roast, and there was a ton of drink. So we just had a big party. Besides, Fish's new album was coming out the following month, so we celebrated that instead. Willie and I joked that the big man probably put the expenses against his studio costs.

(A few years later, at the Tartan Clef Awards, I was presenting one to Fish. I did my usual spiel then a preamble about his career, rambling on about Marillion and the success of his solo work. A lot of the audience weren't particularly aware of him, or Marillion, for that matter. A few had maybe heard their single Kayleigh, but that was it. There was just a ripple of applause for him. Fish got up, with a few jars in him by that time, and started this ten-minute rant against the music business. Most people lost interest and resumed their table conversations. Okay, it was a bit awkward – but it was also so rock'n'roll.)

Towards the end of my Radio Clyde days, I was doing a weekly show on Clyde 2 on a Saturday Night. The music wasn't great, but I more or less had freedom to do what I wanted. So, one night, in a mischievous mood, I decided to open the phone lines for listeners to call in with their confessions on a feature I called 'The Risky Romp Hotline.'

The first couple of callers were okay, but line number three was memorable. She said she'd been on holiday with her parents in Spain, she'd met a guy, and they'd hit it off. They'd had a romantic meal followed by a midnight stroll along a moonlit beach. After a smoochy kiss, they decided to find somewhere to cement their relationship. (Remember, this was all going out on live radio).

They came across a newbuild hotel, still under construction, and the front door was open. It was dark, but they found a pile of cellophane-wrapped mattresses on the ground floor, made themselves comfortable and proceeded to have rather noisy sex.

Everything was fine until the 'lie back' – while they were catching their breath, a loud cough was heard from the direction of the reception area. The night security guard was sitting with a smile on his face. His desk was just a few metres away…

Luckily, none of the Clyde bosses heard that particular show.

I was told a great story once by one of the guys at the Dreadnought rock club in Bathgate. Years previously, when he'd worked as a roadie for a well-known rock band who were touring Germany, another of the roadies got lucky. He became 'very friendly' with a local girl and they retired to a hotel room for the evening. The guys from the band, on hearing the news, sneaked into the roadie's room and found the couple naked and locked together. The band pounced, and, using gaffa tape – every roadie's favourite accessory – they bound the couple tightly together. The hilarity finished with the band carrying the giggling, naked, tightly-bound couple into the hotel lift. They pressed the button to take the lift to reception, and went off to their own rooms for a good night's sleep. No one knows what happened next… I can only imagine the reaction when the lift reached the ground floor and the door opened.

A few years ago on a midweek night, a good pal (who will remain nameless) and myself ended up near Glasgow's St Enoch car park in this club, the Warehouse. My pal, recently separated from his wife, was out for a blether and a pint. He wasn't out looking for girls; he's not that type. But he was asked to dance, and, not wanting to offend, he got up and did the best he could. You know, the dad-dance stuff, like we all do. Still, I could tell that he and this girl were getting on really well together.

At the end of the night I headed home; and when I woke up the next morning with a stinking hangover, I decided to phone my pal to see how he'd got on. He told me they'd left the club together and ended up in his car. He couldn't remember what happened after that. Next thing he knew, it was daylight, his head was pounding and he could hardly breathe. Then there was this thumping noise: Bang–bang–bang. When he opened his eyes fully he realised his head was resting between the girl's naked legs, and her dress was up around her waist, she was still fast asleep. A car park attendant was knocking on the roof of the car., shouting: 'Haw – you'll need to buy a ticket!'

The car park was free overnight, but it was now six-thirty in the morning.

Jim Crawford, a great character, would often help me out in the record shops. One day he came in very excited. He'd met this very nice lady, a divorcee who he fancied quite a bit. She was well-spoken, very respectable and good company. There was a wee peck on the cheek at the end of each date; nothing more. He was just taking his time.

Then she said, 'I need to go to Carlisle next week, and I don't like traveling alone. Would you come with me? We might have to stay over.'

Jim, of course, said, 'No problem.' What a buying signal!

They got to Carlisle and checked into their hotel. She went off to do some business and Jim was left to have a pint of Guinness at the bar. She came back around six and they had a meal. Then, after a few romantic drinks together, they retired to their double room and quietly consummated their friendship.

However, around six in the morning Jim woke up, put his hand out, but there was no one there. He thought, 'She must be in the bathroom.' Now, Guinness has a bit of an effect on our James, an effect of the gaseous variety. Judging that the coast was clear, he decided to let one go. It was a ripper, it reeked. It was absolutely Abraham Lincoln. Jim lifted up the duvet to clear the air, and took a deep, slightly self-indulgent whiff of his own fart.

Just then he heard a wee cough. Startled, he looked around in horror – and there she was. His lady friend was not in the bathroom, she'd been standing at the window the whole time.

Probably wisely, she decided not to come back into the bed. The breakfast was rather frosty, as was the drive back up to Glasgow. Needless to say, he never saw her again.

One winter night, I ended up at Glasgow's Central Hotel, where Jim was the DJ at a widows, divorcees and separated disco. I was just in for a pint, but Jim announced, 'We have a special guest tonight... Tom Russell from Radio Clyde!'

The following weekend, Jim was working at the Central again, when a woman came up to him and said, 'Hey you! See that guy you hud on last week, that wisnae Tom Russell, so it wisnae!'

'Is that right?' replied Jim.

'Aye,' she said firmly. 'The guy who's been pumpin' me for four weeks – he's Tom Russell!'

'Oh dear,' said Jim. 'I think the real Tom will be very disappointed. You've been had, missus!'

That's one of the stranger parts of being a wee bit well-known. Other times it goes a different way – you think you're being recognised... but you're not.

I was at the Sonisphere Festival at Knebworth three or four times, and I normally stayed in the same hotel. One Sunday morning I got up for an early breakfast. I was in the lift with six women in their forties, and I could sense there was a bit of a confab going on. Eventually one of them said, 'It is him.'

As I got out of the lift, one of them said, 'Do you mind if we get an autograph?' I'm thinking, 'They must be from Glasgow.' Then they asked for photographs, and I obliged before they wandered off. Just as they turned the corner, however, I saw one of them looking at the autograph and saying, 'Who the hell's Tom Russell?'

Seasick Steve had been playing nearby the night before. You guessed it... They thought I was him.

Festivals, of course, are massive business today. In my early radio days, bands didn't make a fortune out of touring and playing festivals. The money was in their record sales, with big companies making a fortune. How things have changed – nowadays, it seems that touring is the only way to make money in music. The record companies don't have the same financial power that they used to, now we're in the age of downloads.

For example, when I saw Walter Trout recently, he was selling T-shirts, as bands have always done; but he was also selling his CDs and DVDs. During the gig he announced that he'd be at the merchandising area, in person, at the end of the show, to sign anything anybody wanted. There must have been two hundred people queuing up at the end of the gig. In the old days, people would have bought the CDs at a record shop, but those shops are almost extinct now. It's a different business model.

The winds of change had blown over my record shops too. On top of the fires, the renovations and the robberies, cassettes and vinyl had given way to the compact disc format. CDs were easier for supermarkets to sell – the clue is in the name: they were more compact. The space they took up more than paid for the return they generated. It wasn't that CDs were much cheaper in the big chains; it was simply the convenience factor. It was easy to pop one into the shopping trolley. It didn't occur to people that it would do the wee record shop on the corner out of a sale.

So I eventually pulled the plug on the shops and sold up. That led to a period of time when I was just scrambling about trying to make a living, trying to pay the mortgage. It was then that a guy called Tony Wilson phoned me. Tony used to be Tommy Vance's producer on BBC Radio 1, and he was actually the true rock fan in the team. Tommy liked rock, but it was actually Tony who scouted about and found new bands. A few years after Radio 1 cancelled the Friday Night Rock Show around 1993, Tony set up his own radio station, which was eventually called Total Rock. It was on the internet, but in the very early days of internet radio.

You have to remember that there weren't that many experienced radio DJs who happened to be into rock. Most of the people he hired were actually journalists who were really into their rock and metal, but didn't know that much about the technicalities of radio. It's not something you can learn in five minutes. The basics can be taught, but you need to get a good bit of practical experience too.

I'd met Tony on numerous occasions over the years, at gigs, or at interviews in London when Tommy Vance was in at the same time and I was next in line. So Tony called and said, 'Would you be interested in coming down to London for a month to do some shows for us?'

I said, 'Yes – but what's the deal with accommodation, transport and so on?'

He said, 'We'll pay something towards the transport and then we'll sort something out. for accommodation.'

So I went down one Sunday. Even though I was doing the Radio Clyde show on a Friday night, I reckoned I could still cover Tony's show, from ten in the morning till one in the afternoon, Monday to Friday, for a month. The station was operating out of an old run-down pub, which was still trading as a pub. There was a wee side room that housed the studio. Not hi-tech or salubrious, but it did the job.

Tony was about to head home just after I arrived. I asked, 'Do you have any accommodation for me?'

'Oh, yeah. I think we sorted something out,' he told me. Tony's a great guy, but he's a wee bit harum-scarum. It was pretty obvious that he'd forgotten all about it. 'It's not the best, but there's a room above the pub.' It was just a bare room covered in dust – absolutely mingin'. 'Will this be alright?' he said. There was no bed, nothing. Just a room. 'Did you bring a sleeping bag or a pillow?' he asked.

'I just flew down this morning, It wasn't exactly the kind of stuff I was thinking about,' I told him.

He nipped out and came back with a blanket and a pillow. 'Will that do you for the first night? we'll sort something out tomorrow.'

I didn't have much choice, so I tried to make myself comfortable, and eventually got to sleep. I woke up the next morning scratching all over. I was covered in ants. When I went down to the studio, Tony said, 'How did you get on?'

'Well…'

'Oh,' he said, seeing my disgruntled expression. 'Here's twenty quid. Go and get yourself a proper sleeping bag.'

'Is this me for four weeks, Tony?' It was. No carpet, just floorboards. But I roughed it out. At the end of the month's contract we parted as friends. It was actually good fun in the main.

12. BUSINESS CLASS

Visiting Rick Rubin and Slayer ~ the ghost of John Belushi ~ violent welcome to New York ~ The glamourous milkman ~ Metallica, Machine Head and Korn

Rick Rubin has produced top acts like AC/DC, Def Leppard, Johnny Cash, the Beastie Boys, and he's enjoyed a massive amount of success. But he's terrified of flying – any time he goes anywhere it's by train or ship. That's why, when Polygram signed a deal with Rick's own label American Recordings, they asked me to fly to Los Angeles to interview him and Slayer, one of his first signings.

It would have been too expensive to fly all the UK's rock jocks out to America, so they decided to pick one. The chat would be recorded, edited and distributed to the other jocks. It was the first time they'd use the model, and if it worked, they proposed to give someone else the free trip next time.

My flight was from Glasgow to Heathrow, then direct to LA. It's the only time in my life I've ever flown business class. Twelve hours in a big comfy seat, passing right over Greenland, and landing in warm, bright LA. I thought, 'This is no' a bad life…' A young guy with long hair held up a card with 'Tom Russell' written on it, and led me towards a pink 1957 Chevrolet with the top down. As we drive through the city I'm thinking, 'This is the dream!'

The guy asked what I was over for, and I said, 'I'm over to do an interview with Rick Rubin and Slayer.' Then I asked, 'What about yourself?'

He said, 'I sing in a band and we're actually auditioning for Mr Rubin in the studio. He was looking for someone to come and pick you up from the airport, so I volunteered, and he gave me the keys to his car.' Then he said, 'I just love your accent.'

I said, 'Aye, yours is no' bad either.' It was southern, kind of Lynyrd Skynyrd-ish.

'So you're from Glasgow, Scotland?'

'Yip,' I replied.

'Isn't where AC/DC were born?'

'Yes, in a way.'

'They're my favourite band of all time,' said my driver. 'Most people think that they were born in Australia but I know better. The two brothers came from Glasgow and the singer came from Scotland as well.'

A year or so later, I was excited to get hold of the Black Crowes' debut album Shake Your Money Maker – the one with the big single Hard To Handle. I looked at the sleeve and recognised the singer, Chris Robinson, the guy who'd picked me up in Rick Rubin's Chevrolet.

We got to the hotel and Chris said, 'You've really hit it off, staying at this hotel, man. This is some place!' I'd never heard of the Chateau Marmont. It looked a bit old-fashioned, but hey…

'All the big movie stars used to stay here,' Chris told me. 'Errol Flynn, Marilyn Monroe, John Wayne – but these days it's the big rock stars that hang out here.'

I wasn't to be picked up until the next morning, so I had the evening to myself. It was four in the afternoon, and even after twenty-two hours' travelling, it didn't seem like time to go to bed. The hotel looked a bit run-down, and I was thinking it could have done with a lick of paint, when the receptionist said, 'Mr Russell, the good news is that you're in room 6A.'

'Oh, right,' I replied, none the wiser.

'You must have heard of John Belushi?'

'Yes, the guy in Animal House and The Blues Brothers,' I replied.

Then the receptionist said, 'Don't you remember what happened to him?'

'Sadly, I think he committed suicide.'

'Yeah – he was found dead in room 6A back in 1982,' she whispered.

I though, 'I hope it's been redecorated.'

We sauntered along the corridor until we reached a door. She turned the key and we went into a suite… with its own swimming pool. Every room on the ground floor had its own plunge pool. Some of the tiles were chipped – and possibly still full of shotgun pellets – but that was fine.

I went for a walk along Sunset Boulevard, a busy road where every second car was a Lamborghini, a Ferrari or a Rolls-Royce. It was just a different league. The hotel restaurant was dead so I didn't have to make a reservation. It was just me and these two other guys, both at different tables. Being a friendly Scot, I started chatting and ended up having a nightcap together. They were both in the film business. One was a sound man, the other a cameraman and. After the night cap, one of them said, 'Which room are you in?'

I said, '6A. What about you?'

'I'm in 8B,' he said, rather smugly.

'Is there something special about 8B?' I asked.
'It's the room John Belushi killed himself in!'

The other guy chips in: 'I'm in 7C. The girl at reception told me he died in my room!'
The receptionist was obviously on to a good thing with the John Belushi story. She'd probably get a good tip for putting 'special guests' in there. (And just in case any of you guys or gals get the same receptionist – John Belushi sadly ended his own life in Bungalow 3 on the March 5, 1982. So don't tip the receptionist unless you're in Bungalow 3!)

The next morning, I was taken to Rubin's house – a modern mansion up in the Hollywood hills. Rick had long hair and a big black beard, quite an imposing bloke, but very cool and extremely generous.

He showed me round his house and we talked about what we were going to do in the interview. After that, we went for lunch with the guys from Slayer in a swanky Hollywood restaurant. I'm sitting there, stuffing my face and again thinking, 'Tom Russell, you lucky sod!'

In the afternoon we recorded the interview, then, I slotted in an interview with Phil Lewis, who'd been in a band called Girl. He was a Londoner who'd come to LA after the demise of Girl to form a band called LA Guns, who'd become part of the whole Motley Crue and Guns N' Roses scene. Phil turned out to be a decent guy, and he took me on another tour of Hollywood in his own car. My second open-top in twenty-four hours! That night they all took me to the famous Rainbow Bar and Grill.

Next day, after interviewing Slayer, I had to fly to New York for another record company interview. I ended up, just like the night before, in a deserted hotel restaurant. And just like that night, I met a few guys who were up for a night cap. I expected to be in bed reading a book by nine o'clock, but the evening morphed into one of those unexpected nights where everyone got on and one thing lead to another. About ten, one of guys said, 'Let's go to a night club.'

We waved down a yellow cab and ended up at the entrance of the Manhattan branch of Stringfellows. The bouncer thought we were a bit early, but he let us in. We paid the five-dollar entrance fee but soon found out we were the only people in the place. My new-found friends had nipped off for a pee and I decided to get a round in. I went over to this huge circular bar and said, 'Three beers please!' The bartender was on the phone. She turned slightly, gave me a dirty look and then resumed her conversation. I stood for a few minutes, getting more and more pissed off as she talked away. I asked again and got another dirty look. Then I was really angry: 'Excuse me, hen – I'm here!'

This time she picked up a second phone and muttered something down the wire. Seconds later, I was lifted off my feet. A great big guy had my arms up my back, and I was huckled, my feet barely touching the ground, across the dance floor. He opened the emergency door with my head and threw me down ten steps onto the street. I landed hard on the pavement below as the door was shut tight behind me. Of course, the stupid part of me said, 'I'm going straight round to that front door again to demand my money back!' Luckily, the little bit of sense I had left prevailed.

Welcome to New York, Tom.

One of my weirdest interview trips was a flight to America to interview Europe... but it turned out to be one of my best. I was working for Harry Docherty, who'd launched the Hard'n'Heavy video magazine, and he was now running the Metal Hammer Video Magazine. Usually I worked with cameraman Denis O'Regan, a very well-known photographer with the NME, Sounds and Melody Maker. Being a Londoner, Denis knew the place well – he'd point things out all the time, like, 'See that oak tree? That's the one that killed Marc Bolan.'

Denis had worked with Europe before. After the interview and a photoshoot in Greenwich village, New York, we went back to the hotel with the band and had a pool tournament. When we got back to the UK, Harry said, 'Could you write an article about the trip to go with the video?' So I did, and the headline was something like: 'Europe 0, Britain 3'.

Long-haul flights tend to be fairly uneventful, but one trip back from New York on Continental Airways was a bit more interesting. I ended up sitting next to an American lady from the deep South in her forties. I told her I'd been doing some interviews for a radio station, and she told me she was going to Scotland to meet her fiancee. She'd met him online (this was still in the early days of internet dating) and after a few weeks, he'd proposed and she'd accepted. She was flying over to meet him for the first time. I thought, 'Isn't that wonderful?' She'd been married before but had no kids, and she'd been alone for a long time; so was really upbeat and excited at the prospect of meeting her man.
I asked, 'Is he meeting you at the airport?'

'Yes,' she said. 'He lives in a place called Bridgetown, in the Scottish countryside.'

I thought, 'It must be some wee place up near Oban.' I asked, 'What does he do?'

'He's in dairy products,' she said. 'He's an executive in the dairy industry.'

When we landed in Glasgow I wished her all the best. I went through passport control but I didn't see her in the baggage area. As I went towards my car, there she was coming out of the terminal, arm in arm with this guy. The two of them were walking towards an electric milk float. It said on the side,'James Bloggs – We'll Meet All Your Dairy Needs – Bridgeton, Glasgow.' Her man was a milkman from Brigton. She still looked happy, and that's the main thing. Besides, maybe the milkman knew Frankie Miller, a fellow Brigton man.

Another American who was delighted to be in Scotland was Jonathan Davis, singer with Korn, who broke through in the nineties. He told me his grandfather had emigrated from Scotland to the US, that he always spoke with a strong Scottish accent, and that they'd been very close. His grandfather used to take him to the Highland games in California, and when he was nine or ten he learned the bagpipes. All this came out in our first interview; part of me thought, 'This is a wind-up.' But no – at the Barrowland that night he came on during one of Korn's songs, wearing the kilt, blasting out a tune on the pipes.

A few years later, when I spoke to him at the Download festival, he remembered nothing about being in Glasgow or our first interview. It was a bit sad and a bit awkward. Later, maybe in 2013, Korn brought another album out and we talked then too. He was back to that nice open guy again. Actually, it's not uncommon.

Interviews sometimes take unusual turns… I remember talking to Soundgarden, a huge Seattle band who'd come through with Nirvana, Alice In Chains and Pearl Jam. I'd interviewed them during their first visit to Glasgow, but the second time they were really big and I flew down to London to meet them. Singer Chris Cornell and two other members were there, and the chat just clicked – they were in a good mood, I'd done my homework and it sparked. The record company tend to keep out of the way during interviews but this time the girl said,

'That was a great interview. Well done, Tom.' It's lovely when someone says that to you.

A couple of days later, she phoned and said, 'See that interview you did? Would you mind if we put that on the B-side of the next single?'

'Would I mind?' I said.

'We'll pay you a hundred pounds for it!' she added.

I wasn't really bothered about the money. I was chuffed to bits. It's on the B-side of Burden In My Hand, which came out in 1996.

A similar unexpected turn came when I was flown down to interview Lars Ulrich, James Hetfield and Kirk Hammett of Metallica. Right up until the Black Album in 1991 they were a down-to-earth band; but after that they became stars and it became harder to get access. There had been a bit of a wait until Load came out in 1996.

The interview turned out well and at the end of the piece I said, 'It's been a few years between the last album and this one. How long will the fans have to wait until we get the next one?' The answer was, 'Probably not as long, because we actually recorded more than half of the next album already.'

I said, 'Have you thought of a name for the next one?'

Kirk said, 'Let's just concentrate on this one. We haven't even started thinking about it yet.'
So I said, 'Why don't you call it Reload?'

'That's not a bad idea,' they said.

A year later – guess what – Reload came out. Now, that may just have been a coincidence. They might have gone upstairs in the hotel and totally forgotten all about the suggestion. Who knows. But maybe…?

A week later, I got a call from their record company. They told me that the boys really enjoyed the interview and asked if I'd have any objections if they used it for a promo CD to be played on any radio station in the world. 'Eh… that would be fine,' I said. This time, no offer of dosh – but hey-ho. It's a nice wee memento.

Metallica had first played Glasgow with Anthrax in 1986. There was a buzz in California around the 'thrash metal scene' and that buzz was growing. I interviewed both bands at the Barrowland and found them all to be very down-to-earth, as in 'smelly socks and cursing like troopers'. Metallica's bass player, Cliff Burton, wasn't part of the interview, although I remember meeting him at the time. He was killed in September 1986, just a few months later. Band and crew were out on tour in Sweden, all in their beds on the tour bus, when they hit black ice and the vehicle rolled.

When I interviewed Metallica for the second time, a year after the terrible accident, they were still very traumatised by the whole thing. They said it was horrible – you wake up and everything is rolling, then everything comes to a standstill, and you're like. What the hell was that?' Some of them were upside down or hanging out of bed or on the floor.

I remember them telling me how they'd all scrambled out of the broken windows, still in shock, with the bus on its side. They thought it might burst into flames. It was dark and they were all shouting, 'Are you okay? Is the driver okay?' Then someone said, 'Has anyone seen Cliff?' There was no sign of him. It was only later that he was found under the bus – he'd been thrown out of his bunk and through the window just before it landed. He didn't stand a chance.

I did another interview with Metallica in London, after they'd become really big, they played the Hammersmith Odeon and threw a party afterwards. Lars Ulrich told me that he'd been training to be a professional tennis player when he was about fifteen. It was going well, but he also played drums. His mum and dad decided he could make it big as a tennis player so they moved to California to give him the best training environment. But the drumming never stopped. Then he saw an advert for a band looking for a drummer, auditioned and got the gig. Soon, the tennis was dropped.

Back then there was no MTV or internet, so the only way for a band like Metallica to raise awareness in the UK was to play loads of gigs and form a relationship with fans, journalists and the half-dozen or so radio DJs who'd play their music.

However, at the Metallica party there was Brian Pithers, Paul Anthony, myself and a few journalists. We'd all completed our interviews, seen the gig and were now standing at the bar with Lars. He said, 'We owe so much to you guys. We made it big in Britain first because of your support – all that airplay and journalism. We will never forget that. We will always be what you see now: down to earth and a fan's band.'

Metallica are now festival headliners, and as a wee radio station we don't get near them. The last time I met them, about eight years ago, they played the SECC in Glasgow. The record company said, 'No interviews.'

Machine Head were the support on that tour and I had to do their interview backstage at the SECC before they played. I recorded the conversation with my son Neil, who was so chuffed to meet them. We finished the interview and they asked if we were here to watch the show. We said, 'Of course!' I wasn't one to just do an interview and piss off without seeing the band play. They said, 'Great, come back for a beer afterwards,' and we were issued with our passes.

We had a couple of hours so we jumped in a taxi to Rockus bar for a few pints, since 'work' had finished and I could now relax. After a couple of drinks we had to dash back in time to see Machine Head. Neil, Kieron Elliot (Rock Radio breakfast presenter at the time) and I piled out of this taxi, and, as we were in a rush, I managed to scrape my head on the taxi door. Suddenly there was blood running down my face… But when you've had a few, you don't worry about stuff like that – you just grab a hankie and stick it on there!

We watched Machine Head, then Metallica came on, and they were fantastic, as expected. They played 'in the round, which was the fashion at the time: the circular stage meant that each band member was facing the crowd. The we went back to the Machine Head dressing room for our drinks. We were getting stuck in, and Neil was just happy to be there with Machine Head, when the door opened and in walked Lars – he'd popped in to ask if they had any booze left. He went round the room until he came to me. 'I know you!' he said.
I said, 'Yeah, I interviewed you a couple of times back in the day.'

He asked, 'God, what have you done to your head?' There was still a wee trickle of blood running down my forehead. 'I've got just the cure for that,' he said. He picked up a bottle of vodka, took the top off, grabbed me by the shoulders and poured the vodka all over my head saying, 'That will do as an antiseptic.' Neil took a photograph as it was happening, but it didn't turn out, it's just a blur.

13. MEET YOUR HEROES

My moments with Dio, Saxon, Nirvana, Frank Zappa, Motley Crue ~ and the ones that got away

One of my greatest privileges was to interview Ronnie James Dio. The first time was backstage at the Apollo, and it was a great chat. He was so co-operative – no airs and graces, just a good guy. He had a wonderful knack of putting people at ease. As soon as you met him, he'd say: 'Hi Tom, lovely to see you again. How's Glasgow?' I'll never know whether he was just being totally professional, or he had a little book, did his homework, took notes and stuff. I'm going to plump for him being a genius with an amazing memory for names. Either way, he put you at ease immediately.

Not a lot of people know this, but Ronnie was a curry fanatic. He told me that his favourite place for a good curry was Glasgow. I can't believe he said the same thing in every town he visited – then again, some artists stand up on stage and say. 'Hi Glasgow, it's great to be back in my favourite city,' then say the same thing about Edinburgh the next night. Anyway, I believed Ronnie. He said it every time I met him. Backstage after each of his shows, the rider would be plate upon plate of every curry imaginable. One time he asked me, 'What is this stuff?' It was pakora. According to Ronnie, they didn't have it in many places he visited at that time. He reckoned that it was a Scottish invention.

(I met his wife Wendy at Download in 2011, the year after he died. They'd named one of the stages after Ronnie and she'd flown over for the opening.)

I must have interviewed Biff Byford of Saxon over twenty times. They were a big, new wave of British heavy metal band who had great success right through the seventies, eighties and nineties, and then there was a gradual fade. As far as Glasgow was concerned they went right down to half-filling King Tuts. It was quite sad. Biff was slightly bitter at times and he had a love-hate relationship with some of the Kerrang journalists. The band eventually got slagged to bits in the rock press no matter what they did. Then Harvey Goldsmith did a TV show highlighting Saxon's 'downfall', and the 'downfall' of metal in general. I found the whole show very frustrating – strangely, however, it led to the rebirth of the band. All the fans rallied behind them. They were annoyed at the tone of the show. I'm guessing they thought, 'I might not have bought any of their albums for years. But no one is going to slag off one of the first bands to get the rock rollercoaster moving again.' So when Saxon toured straight after the TV show, they began pulling good audiences again.

Around the same time, I wondered if Saxon would do the Rock Radio birthday bash. So I phoned their manager, a German with perfect English, and I put the proposal to him. He said, 'You want us to come to Glasgow, to play for nothing? For some charity I've never heard of? Why should we do it?'

I said, 'Why not? The Garage is going to be packed full of rock fans who will really appreciate you doing this. Next time, when the band comes back for a proper tour, they'll buy the tickets in droves… and it's for a good charity.'

They came to Glasgow and blew the roof off that Rock Radio birthday bash. Six months later they sold out the ABC, and they've toured every couple of years since. Biff is a fantastic frontman and it's so good to see the resurgence of a band like Saxon.

I got to interview Kurt Cobain twice. The first time was in Glasgow, when Nirvana's first album, Bleach, was out. They weren't huge, but there was a little underground buzz. I remember Kurt being a quiet, gentle lad. Quite cerebral – but totally engaged. Maybe two years later, when I was working in London, Nevermind had just come out and the buzz was incredible. They were now selling out sizeable venues. When I interviewed Kurt that time he was like a different person. I don't know whether it was a mental condition, or the drugs; but he just seemed disengaged. His eyes wandered off me. He was somewhere else. Towards the end of the interview I said something like, 'Last time I interviewed you, you were playing to a few hundred people. Now you're playing to thousands. Which do you prefer?'

The question seemed to awaken something inside him. He looked me straight in the eye and said, 'No question about it: I'd rather be playing to a few hundred. Somewhere I can see their reaction, feel their tension, their excitement. When you play to thousands, it's not the same.'

A few years later he took his own life.

Speaking of Seattle bands, around 1993 I recorded an interview with Shannon Hoon, singer with Blind Melon, in London; and two years later I did the same thing again. By this time Shannon had a reputation as being a bit of a junkie. I asked him about it, and he replied that he had experimented with various drugs, but his first child had been born a few weeks earlier. Shannon became quite serious and told me that on the day of his daughter's birth, he'd looked into her eyes and vowed never to take drugs again. He wanted to see her growing up.

Sadly, less than three months after that, Shannon was found dead in the back of a tour bus in New Orleans. The coroner said he'd died of a cocaine-induced heart attack.

I interviewed Frank Zappa once. He was a strange character but quite likeable. I don't remember much about the actual interview, but I remember, as was the practice in these days, giving him one of our red Radio Clyde 261 t-shirts. He told me that he already had one, given to him a couple of years previously by my colleague Dougie Donnelly;

however, he asked if he could keep the new one, as the first one had been pinched by his son Dweezil. A couple of years later, a popular photo and poster of Zappa did the rounds in which he was on stage, playing guitar, wearing his red Radio Clyde 261 shirt. Frank sadly died of prostate cancer in December 1993 – leaving four unusually named children: Moon, Dweezil, Ahmet and Diva.

I've interviewed Motley Crue a few times over the years – I've spoken to Nikki Sixx twice and Tommy Lee once. Nikki told me about the song Kickstart My Heart. He said it was a true story: the band were into overindulging back in the day, when, one night, Nikki just went totally over the top. He was carted off to hospital and his heart stopped beating for a few minutes. The medical people almost gave up, noted the time of death and so on. But they gave it one last go, and eventually got a pulse.

The Crue announced a full UK tour after the Glasgow Apollo had closed down, and many touring bands had switched to the Edinburgh Playhouse. It was similar to the Apollo, but it wasn't as dirty; a bit too plush, in my opinion, which is why they didn't have as many rock bands. Motley booked it up for a night in the middle of winter – but then cancelled a few days before the show. The record company said it was 'due to the amount of snow on the roof of the venue.' Of course, everyone in Scotland was going. 'Whit? There's about half an inch of snow, at most!' I wonder if the boys had simply overindulged again?

Twenty years ago I interviewed Otis Rush when he was about 70, and had his lady friend with him, a blonde lady in her 30s. It was a wonderful chance to ask one of the early icons about the theory I'd heard about when I was an apprentice at the Star iron foundry in Kirkintilloch – the one the lab technician had about Scotland's 'local connection' with the blues.

Otis had hardly even heard of Scotland before our interview, so he floundered a bit before saying, 'Well, there was this English group that did quite well back in the seventies. There was a song on their first album which was one of my songs. But on the album it said that they wrote it. But, when I listened, it sounded very like my song that I'd recorded years before.'

On checking this, I found out that Led Zeppelin had recorded 'I can't Quit You Baby' on Zeppelin 1. It was actually written in '56 by Willie Dixon for Otis Rush, who had a hit with it at that time.

Anyway, Otis continued and he told me that his manager back then had pursued this claim and had got ten thousand dollars in compensation. So, he took his half and he let his manager take half. You could see in his eyes that he was delighted to get so much at the time. Who knows if this really happened or not – but Led Zeppelin have sold nearly two hundred million albums so, if it did, they could probably have afforded it.

At the end of the interview, we took a picture and I asked him to sign his new album. He hesitated a bit, but then took a pen from his pocket and marked a cross on the album sleeve. Probably born in the early part of the century into a poor family, he'd played guitar, sang and wrote songs without much of a problem, but when he wrote a song – it was totally in his head. He'd never learned to write.

In 1989 I did a charity event at the Motherwell Civic Centre. I was asked to come along for an hour or so to introduce a couple of the bands. (I've always done a little bit for charity. You can't do it every week because you have a living to make, but this was one of the times that I said I'd go along.)

The headline act wasn't so much a rock band as a pop-rock band, Goodbye Mr McKenzie. I noticed that the singer, who also played keyboards, was an attractive girl with a powerful personality. The guitarist was an ex-punk band guy. I was impressed – they were good at what they did.

They ended up getting a record deal with Parlophone and had a couple of minor Scottish hits around about the time when a lot of Scottish bands were getting attention: Simple Minds, Horse, Deacon Blue, Travis, Hue and Cry and so on.

Then, perhaps five years later, it was announced that there was a new American band called Garbage. The PR was highlighting the fact that the band had a Scottish singer. One of the members of the band was a guy called Butch Vig, whose main claim to fame was that he'd produced Nirvana's Nevermind album. It turned out that the singer was Shirley Manson from Goodbye Mr MacKenzie. I interviewed Garbage at the time when they were having some success with songs like Stupid Girl and I'm Only Happy When It Rains. As it happened, it was Butch and bass player Duke Erikson who came into the Clyde studios for the chat. It was a good interview and Butch was a nice guy; but I was disappointed not to catch up with Shirley.

One of my few regrets over the years is that I never got a chance to interview Eric Clapton. I've never even met him. I always liked his music – not so much his recent stuff, but the Cream material was just fantastic. I have seen him a few times live, including once in the mid-seventies at the Glasgow Apollo, when he was struggling with all sorts of demons. I was up in the gods, and there he was, this guitar god, one of my heroes, playing the Apollo. And this young guy in the background was taking some of the solos. Eric was playing rhythm most of the time.

The last time I saw him was in 2015 at the Hydro. It was fifty quid a head with eleven thousand people there – a nice wee earner, as they say. Eric doesn't always play what the crowd wants to hear; that's well known. But he did great versions of Layla and Tears in Heaven in the first fifty minutes. The band had a great sound, but around then a buzzing sound started coming out of one side of the PA. Eric got really angry and demanded it was fixed. After another few moments he took off his guitar and stomped off the stage. The rest of the band, including Andy Fairweather Low and Paul Carrack, finished the song. Then Andy said, 'There's a technical fault.'

The band left the stage and the lights came on. The crowd was going, 'Okay, shit happens.' After fifteen minutes it was sorted out and the band came back on again, and played Gin House with Andy singing. Then Clapton himself returned, played a song, then mumbled, 'Good night, Glasgow,' and went off again. Everyone cheered, thinking there was bound to be an encore. But no – the house lights came up and the backing music started playing. Despite eleven thousand people booing, nothing happened.

I remember walking through the foyer and there were almost fights between the merch' sellers and the punters who felt they'd been ripped off. People were going, 'If he's only going to give us an hour, I don't want this bloody shirt – I want my money back.' Not the nicest of memories.

A far nicer memory involves Doogie White, who's been a friend of mine for many years. He first came to prominence in a band called La Paz – they were the business and included guitarist Chic McSherry and drummer Paul McManus, who's now with Gun. In fact, before that Paul was a member of Glasgow. La Paz were another of those west of Scotland bands who were good enough, but never got that lucky break. They never made it and eventually split up.

One night I had Robert Plant in for a live interview on the Friday Night Rock Show. He's a very eloquent, a very intelligent man, so I said, 'Do you fancy opening the phone lines? Let's get the punters to ask some questions for a change.'

Robert said, 'Why not?'

The third person to come on the line said, 'Hello, it's Doogie White here – you know, from La Paz?'

'Hi Doogie,' I said. 'You're through to Robert. What's your question?' Doogie asked how to keep his voice in shape while on tour. He still reminds me of the great opportunity he got to talk to one of the greats.

A few years later Doogie moved down to London, did some session work, tried out for a few bands and eventually landed a job with Yngwie Malmsteen – who's a great guitarist, but a little serious at times. (In fact, he calls himself Yngwie J Malmsteen. I once asked him what the 'J' stood for. He replied, 'That's just to distinguish me from all the other Yngwie Malmsteens...' Aye, right enough – there's about four that I know of in Coatbridge alone.)

Doogie toured the world with Yngwie. It was his first real big break. He also sang with a band called Tank. It was round about this time that Bruce Dickinson left Iron Maiden; and since Doogie was good at making friends, a good networker, he got the call. I think he got down to the last few, before Blaze Bayley got the gig. (Blaze, the singer in Wolfsbane, had a similar voice to Bruce and actually looked a wee bit like him in a way.)
After the Maiden auditions, Doogie surprised everybody by getting the gig with Rainbow. He sang on their last album, Stranger in Us All, then toured the world with Ritchie Blackmore and the rest of the band, before Ritchie rediscovered the lute.

One thing about Doogie is that he'll rarely say a bad word about anyone. If you ask, 'Was Yngwie a bit of an arse?' he might have a twinkle in his eye, but he'll say, 'He was okay to me…' Fair play.

La Paz hooked up again after a Rock Radio Birthday Bash and did an album, which got good reviews but didn't really sell as hoped. But they're now on their third album and the music is getting better and better.

Doogie and I have had various adventures together over the years. One concerned a ten-pound note, which he swore he lent me once upon a time. He'd always ask for it to be returned – but honestly, I can't remember the transaction. Maybe it was just his way of scrounging a tenner off an old mate.

I do remember another of our adventures a bit more clearly. It was after one of the Donington festivals; Iron Maiden had headlined and we'd both managed to blag our way into the aftershow party. Maiden, as usual, were extremely generous with the food and drink, and we overindulged until the party broke up around two in the morning. Neither of us could remember which hotel we were staying in, and were contemplating kipping in a portacabin, when one of the girls from Maiden's management, the lovely AnnRae, came to our rescue. She ordered a taxi, took us back to her hotel and sneaked us into her room. Much to our disappointment, she sourced a spare blanket, ushered us into the bathroom and pointed to our bed for the night – the bath! (The good news, as far as I was concerned, was that Doogie ended up with his back against the taps and not me.)

14. READY FOR MY CLOSE-UP

My acting career ~ that Still Game scene ~ Tony Iommi ~ Geezer Butler ~ Neil Peart ~ Elton John ~ a sad end with Radio Clyde

I don't want to sound cynical – but many bands on their way up are delighted to give you interviews – AC/DC, Iron Maiden, Bon Jovi, Metallica, Guns N' Roses – but when they get to a certain stage in their development you can't get near them. You can't get past the PR person or the management. It's only natural, I suppose; at the top, they only want to do breakfast television or Graham Norton. A wee rock show in Glasgow is no longer important.

Sometimes you get to meet acts on the way back down. They reach a peak for a few years, then they start to lose their way. That's when, out of the blue, you get a call from the record company: 'Would you like to do an interview with band X?' With a wry smile you say, 'Aye, of course I will.' It's all part of the game. You just have to roll with it.

There are exceptions to this 'big wall'... Tony Iommi from Black Sabbath is a man I've had the pleasure of meeting on a number of occasions. He must go down as one of the greatest guitarists of all time; Some of the riffs he's come up with are classics. And he's a nice guy – although he doesn't give the impression that he enjoys the whole interview thing.

The first time I interviewed him in the eighties, I thought he was winding me up. We were chatting about the early days, how Sabbath band got together, how he came up with the guitar sound and so on. He said: 'After I left school I got a job as a sheet metal worker. I used to lift metal, put it under a press. I'd hit the button and the press would shape it.' One afternoon his hand got caught in the press and he was rushed off to hospital, and lost the tips of two fingers.

Tony told me that he thought his guitar-playing days were over. Once his wounds healed, he wondered what he could do to keep going. His mother did a lot of sewing, so he pinched a couple of her metal thimbles that she used for darning. He slipped them onto the end of his fingers and found he could press the strings down onto the frets.

I guess his thimbles are custom-made now – but he's managed to produce some of the best guitar sounds ever. He just had a dogged determination to keep going, no matter what.

Geezer Butler is another integral part of Sabbath, not just as their bass player but their as lyricist. One time, when Sabbath had split and he was doing his solo thing, he did a couple of solo albums with his band called GZR. Up he came to Glasgow and we had a chat. When the interview was over I said: 'What are you doing after this?'

His radio plugger cut in and said, 'Nothing until seven o'clock, with the BBC.'

That was five hours away, so I said, 'Do you fancy a couple of pints?'

'Why not?' Geezer said.

Then about six o'clock I asked, 'Do you fancy a curry?' As we all headed to the curry shop, I'm looking round thinking, 'This is surreal. I'm here in an Indian restaurant on Sauchiehall Street with Geezer Butler... and nobody has a clue who the guy is.'
Geezer told some really funny stories – all, of course, long forgotten. He has a wonderfully dry Black Country wit.

It's fairly normal for a big rock band to be well organised when it comes to interviews. They split the duties. Rush once had a way of working it, with all three of giving interviews, so it depended on your luck. When they played Ingliston in May 1983, I didn't know who I was going to get. On that occasion it was drummer Neil Peart – a really nice guy, and a deep thinker with a sense of humour. Rush fans often comment on that interview. There was a Rush convention at Bathgate a couple of years ago and a guy came up to me and said, 'Tom! I've got that interview you did with Neil Peart in 1983 on cassette, and I still listen to it occasionally.' Even though it was recorded over thirty-three years ago!

I suppose I was in the right place at the right time. Even a band as big as Rush still had very little media exposure in the eighties. Sounds, NME and Radio 1 wouldn't be that interested. So when I wanted to chat to them when they played Glasgow's SECC in April 1988, the record company said, 'No problem – before or after the show?' I was on Radio Clyde live that night so I asked if the band would consider coming in to the station after their gig. So guitarist Alex Lifeson did it. Bands are usually pretty knackered after a live show, so it was really good of him.

My third Rush interview was also with Alex – and on that occasion, I did ask a stupid question. As soon as it came out of my mouth, I was like, 'Fuck... naw!' I said something like, 'You're a great player, but in a three-piece band a lot falls on your shoulders. As a guitarist, do you never envy some of the other great guitarists that are able to go off and do wonderful solos?'

As I said it, I realised what it sounded like; Alex, of course, does some of the best solos on the planet. What a numpty! He was a gentleman, and answered politely... but he was probably thinking, 'What is this guy on?'

That's the thing about a live interview: you can be led down the wrong path for just one second and it can end in disaster. It can be nerve-racking.

My next Rush interview was with Alex again. At that gig the amps at the front of the stage were in the shape of ovens, all with roasting chickens inside. After the usual questions I asked him about the effect. Alex told me, 'Well, we do a pretty long set. It was just in case we got hungry.' Lovely answer! 'In fact,' he continued, 'Did you not notice that I'd take a chicken off now and again and hand it up to the lighting guys? They get real hungry during our live show.' He said it all with a totally straight face.

The last interview I did with Rush gave me the chance, for the first time in thirty years, to talk to bass player and vocalist Geddy Lee. He's hilarious – he has a cheeky sense of humour and certainly isn't as serious as he looks.

The first time I met the boys who became Thunder was in 1985 when they'd just released an album on Epic Records called Black and White. At that time, the band was called Terraplane. It was okay; eighties poprock. They played Night Moves in Glasgow, I recorded an interview and we got on well. Their second album wasn't even marketed or promoted and they were dropped.

A year later EMI announced that they'd signed a band called Thunder. One of their first appearances was at Monsters of Rock. I looked at the names and three out of four of the band were from Terraplane. They were first on that day at Donington – and if there had been a roof, they would have lifted it off.

I've interviewed Thunder more than any other band; probably about twenty-five times. They're always great fun to interview (and I bet they even have a few good stories about me). They've split up a couple of times in the past, but they've got back together again, sounding better than ever and obviously enjoying themselves. In 2015 they released Wonder Days, one of the best albums of their career. They're known for their great live performances, when they're never afraid to blast into a few covers at encore time. Danny, the singer, is a superb frontman; Harry James a brilliant drummer; and Luke Morley, the guitarist who composes all the songs, is, in my opinion, one of the greatest British rock songwriters of all time.

I just love seeing young bands break through. I've argued so often that you can't live in the past – it's dead easy to sit in your local pub and listen to Stairway to Heaven, Freebird and Whole Lotta Rosie over and over again, reminiscing about how wonderful the rock scene was. You have to move on or the rock scene will die. The only way to move on is by embracing new bands.

Over my forty years or so playing rock on the radio, I've done my little bit. It's good to give a new band some airplay. There's nothing I like better than people who come up to me and say: 'I heard band X on your show for the first time. I bought everything they recorded and went to see them on tour. I've become a lifelong fan. Thanks, Tom!'

Yes, celebrate the past, but embrace the new. Listen to the new Alter Bridge song, or the new single from new British band Inglorious. As far as Scottish bands are concerned, there are lots that I've championed. Some have gone onto success, some have disappeared… and, of course, some never made it at all.

Much as I loved the band Glasgow in the 1980s, I more recently loved a band called The Detours. I thought they'd do really well, but they ended up splitting just a few years ago.
There's another new band called The Toi – good songwriters – and a young outfit called Mason Hill: I have high hopes for them. The King Lot also write excellent songs. Attica Rage, who operate at the heavier end of the rock spectrum, are also very good; they've done well, released a few albums and played not only throughout the UK but in Europe.

Alan Nimmo from King King is a fantastic example of never giving up – he's played the Scottish blues rock circuit for more years than even he probably cares to remember. He had some success in previous bands, but it was only when he formed King King that he went on to have well-deserved major success. Dave Arcari is another Scottish player who's enjoying a bit of success – he plays very traditional blues and is well worth checking out.

(There are so many young Scottish bands I could mention, so sorry if I've missed you out. I must however give a plug to Audiorayz and Loanhead, who played at the launch party for this book at the Hard Rock Cafe in Glasgow. Thanks guys!)

With the record shops closed down and just the Friday stint on Radio Clyde I found myself in a bit of debt, which I was determined to pay back. It was hard work and it took a couple of years, but I did it. I'd asked the station about other slots, but as nothing was forthcoming, I decided to sign up to one of the film extras agencies in Glasgow.

Soon I began to get quite a lot of small parts in films. I did one called Unleashed with Morgan Freeman, Bob Hoskins and Jackie Chan that was partly filmed at the Botanic Gardens in Glasgow.

Morgan Freeman was playing a blind man with a stick. You don't pester the actors when you're an extra – but if they speak to you that's different. We were having lunch on the first day, and as I was coming out of a Portakabin toilet, I saw Morgan Freeman at the bottom of the stairs. I thought I'd better be polite, so I said, 'Come up!'

'No, you come down,' he said. I did, and said something like, 'Nice day!' He returned the pleasantry, but he had his eyes shut and he was using the white stick. He went up the stairs into the toilet with closed eyes using this stick, still in character, even though he was taking his lunch hour. I was fascinated!

I did a film in St Andrews called Stroke Of Genius, with Jim Caviezel playing legendary golfer Bobby Jones. We had to report at seven in the morning, and we didn't finish until nine at night, for five long days. It was hours and hours in costume, standing on the golf course, applauding imaginary golf shots.

I've appeared in River City a few times. I was on the Only An Excuse Christmas special. And I even went on to appear on Still Game three times. The last time on Still Game, the director called me over. There had been six of us sitting in a corner and he'd scanned our faces; then he asked if I wanted to earn an extra twenty quid by saying a few words. You made around a hundred pounds a day as an extra for a ten-hour day, and your agent took twenty-five percent. I was expecting to earn seventy-five quid towards the mortgage, so for an extra twenty I said, 'No problem – I do stuff on the radio so I'm happy to do a talking part.'

He replied, 'Aye – but wait till you see what it is first!' He showed me the script, and then a magazine that I had to purchase. It was quite a surprise. 'I'm a married man!' I said.

'You're going to ruin my image for the rest of my days!'

He said, 'Well, you don't need to do it. I can get someone else.'

I replied, 'No way… I'll do it for a laugh.'

It was the episode where the character Navid is away, and Jack and Victor are looking after his shop. I'm at the back, browsing through the magazines and then I bring up my selection. I buy a pack of cigarettes, a loaf, a tin of beans… and 'that magazine' It was called Big Cocks. Jack and Victor react with disgust, calling me a 'dirty bastard' – then they throw me out the shop. It was years ago; but I still get people coming up to me to ask about it.

I used to use a garage in Cumbernauld owned by a guy called Jim Dickson and his son, Big Jim. Two or three weeks after the episode had aired for the first time, I went in for a tyre repair. When I got there Jim said, 'Go inside. Big Jim has got something for you behind the counter. It's a magazine…'

I said, 'Aye. I know what you're on about. It's a wind-up!'

He replied, 'No, seriously, we've got this magazine, and we knew you'd be over here one of these days.'

I was still a bit suspicious when Big Jim whipped out the publication and presented it to me. It was The Farmers Weekly. On the front page there was a lovely picture of a huge cockerel.

As well as film extra work, I started to do discos again – weddings, twenty-first parties – I wasn't enjoying it, but it fed the family. Throughout my radio career I've linked up with clubs and promoters to do my rock DJ gigs, as warm-up for a band, as compere or as a straight-through rock DJ night. I wanted to do a bit more of that work rather than mainstream discos, and my friend Eddie Tobin, who was with Scottish & Newcastle Breweries at the time, asked me to look at a place in Cumbernauld. It was a dance venue six nights a week but didn't open on Sundays. It had a small stage and looked quite promising. We named it the Sax Rock Club, and we took the place over every Sunday. A local guy, Jock Barnson, actually booked the bands and sorted the contracts, and we ran for about two years before it started to fade a bit.

On one occasion the manager of a new band phoned Jock and told him that they were doing a twenty-date UK tour. Jock had never heard of them, and neither had I, but they were only looking for one hundred pounds, so Jock took a risk and signed the contract. Suddenly, two months before the Sax show, the band's album came out and got great reviews, and their single got them on Top Of The Pops. The manager told Jock that the hundred-pound deal no longer covered their costs – but Jock was hard enough to say, 'A contract's a contract.' The band was Ocean Colour Scene. They were very good live and the place was absolutely heaving. Six months later they were selling out the Barrowland.

Another memorable gig at Sax came about after an old contact called me and said, 'Listen, Tom, I've got this American artist coming over to do some promotion on his solo album. He's lead guitarist in a big Seattle band. Would you do an interview? You could come down to London, or I could bring him up to Glasgow.' I said I'd do whatever suited them, and she came back to say, 'He actually quite fancies coming up to Scotland.'

It happened to be on a Sunday, so I chanced my arm: 'I don't suppose he'd fancy doing a wee live appearance?'

That's how Jerry Cantrell from Alice in Chains wound up playing a set at Sax. The rock fans in Cumbernauld couldn't believe their luck.

I always loved a band called Big George and the Business. Big George was a Glasgow blues legend who played an old beaten up Fender Strat. His voice just oozed blues and soul. Unfortunately, he was a bit fond of the bevvy, and he died in his fifites in 2013. But I loved him… One of the few bits of journalistic writing I'm proud of is when I said in Metal Hammer: 'Big George is a Scottish institution. Some people think he should be in one.' He stood me a glass of single malt after he read it.

I was working at Sax in Cumbernauld one night when Big George was playing. He never called me 'Tom', always 'Tam'. Before they played he'd had a few drinks, as usual, but that night he played this amazing blues guitar solo. I saw him turn round to Shifty, his bass player, and nod. Shifty nodded back and with the drummer, carried on the beat while George went to the bar, downed a whisky in a oner, then picked up the solo where he'd left off without missing a beat. Brilliant. But it killed him in the end.

I picked up all sorts of jobs on top. One, around the year 2000, was with the pollsters Gallup. You could pick up thirty quid for a day's work. Sometimes it was simply knocking doors and asking things like: 'Have you heard of Tunnocks?' Other times it was a lot worse... It's East Kilbride shopping centre on a Monday morning, and there I am with my clipboard, raincoat and bunnet. The shopping centre wouldn't let us do surveys inside the complex, so I had to stand outside in the rain.

The questions that day were aimed at 'women of a certain age' and they were about sanitary products. I'd keep asking, 'I'm doing a survey... would you mind if I asked you some questions?' You could totally understand why people didn't want to stop in the rain; then when they did stop the questions weren't the best. It was completely soul-destroying. When I got home I was soaked through and pissed off.

I was also working at planting Christmas trees on the Campsie Hills. I was in my fifties, so I wasn't as fit as I used to be. I was paid thirty quid for every one hundred saplings I planted. It wasn't much money, but it paid a few more bills. It got to the point where I realised that I couldn't physically do it any more. I quit around three o'clock one day and went home.

About ten minutes later the phone went, and it was Radio Clyde. 'Tom, can you help us out? I know it's mostly rock stuff that you do, but we've got an interview offer and no one else can do it.'

I was needed in London the next day. I said 'yes,' picked up the password for the plane tickets, and got some albums out to do some prep for the interview. The trip was exactly what I needed. The next day I was met in London by a really lovely guy called David, driving a big Mercedes. I was taken to a beautiful, old-school, 19th century hotel in

Holland Park to interview Elton John. The first thing he told me was, 'This is ridiculous, us doing this here. My house is just round the corner – but record companies like to show off.'

With bigger stars like Elton, you've got to be careful – they'll have been asked the exact same questions thousands of times. You obviously start out with standards until things get settled: 'We're here to talk about your new album. How was the recording process? Are you happy with it?' They're happy enough to answer those because they want to plug the new release. Once everyone is relaxed, you can ask more interesting questions.

A couple of moments about my conversation with Elton stick in my mind. The first was when I said, 'My favourite album of yours is Goodbye Yellow Brick Road.' It's superb. What are your memories of that?'

He looked me in the eye with a serious expression, and said, 'You know, Tom, that's a great question – but I can't answer it. I remember absolutely nothing about writing, recording, or promoting that album. I was on at least a bottle of brandy a day, plus every pill I could get my hands on. But… thanks for saying you like it!'

I also told him about the time he played the Glasgow Apollo, and it sold out so quickly that I couldn't even wangle a ticket through my record shop contacts. Then it was announced that Elton would do a second show on the same night. He replied, 'God, I forgot about that! Yes, I stayed in the Albany Hotel that time.' Most of the stars did back then. He continued, 'We soundchecked in the afternoon, I did a bit of press and then, with no support act, we went up to the Apollo and did the show. It was fantastic. In those days I played about two hours, plus encores.

'I remember coming off the stage, exhausted. I turned to my manager and said, "Whose idea was it to do two shows, you greedy bastard?" he said, "Well, I did ask you if you wanted another X thousand pounds for one night's work, and you said yes!"

'So I came off stage, got into the minibus and headed back to the Albany. It was around ten o'clock. I got into a hot bath for ten minutes, had a bite to eat, lay on the bed for ten minutes, then jumped back in the minibus and went back to the Apollo.'

I'd bought a ticket for the second show; I think it was as late as eleven-thirty when he came on. He played until one-thirty. What a performer! And what a lucky bastard I was to meet the man himself. I've got a great signed picture from him 'To Tom, love from Elton' you can see it plus other photos on my website: tomrussellrocks.com

Those few days still stick in my mind – it's an example of how much contrast there can be in life. On the Monday I was conducting surveys in the rain about womens sanitary products... on the Tuesday I was planting trees on a cold hillside... on Wednesday I was being flown to London to interview Elton John in a luxury hotel.

That trip definitely gave me a wee boost. I'd had such a great time. I'd been working for Radio Clyde for twenty or so years by then, and I'd met all these big stars. The shops were closed, but I'd had a great time running them. And most of all, I had a lovely wife and two wonderful kids.

I thought, 'If there's nothing as big or as grand as this in the future, I've still had a fantastic life.' Little did I realise that there was even more waiting ahead for me. You just never know what's around the corner... good and bad.

I eventually became aware of a slow change of ethos within the management at Radio Clyde. Along with having sold the record shops, it meant things were changing in my life. The original station was split in two: Clyde 1, the FM station, was aimed at a younger audience; and Clyde 2, an AM station, was aimed at an older audience. Even though a new AC/DC album might be loved by a sixteen-year-old as much as a fifty-year-old, the Clyde programmers decided the rock show should go AM.

Even though I went to AM, without the same stereo experience as FM, my show was still popular – mainly because there were still very few places to hear rock. If Iron Maiden brought a new single out, it wouldn't get on the BBC Radio 1 playlist, and it wouldn't be played on daytime commercial radio. So you'd put up with the AM signal to hear the music you wanted.

I'd had over twenty years of complete freedom to play whatever I wanted to play: local bands and obscure tracks as well as new singles from bigger bands like Aerosmith, Motorhead and Kiss. Once I had moved to Clyde 2, the shackles were put on. I had to submit my playlists to the head of music in advance for approval. If there was anything he hadn't heard of, he'd often take the easy route and tell me I couldn't play it.

'Why?' I'd ask.

'Not suitable,' he'd say – even though he'd never listened to it.

It was a far cry from earlier days, when I could argue my case and at least be given a fair hearing. I remember when The Beastie Boys' Fight for Your Right to Party came out of nowhere. It was a massive single all over the world. But the band had a reputation for being wild – it was part of their image, I suppose.

Alex Dickson was managing director at Radio Clyde at the time; he was a bit of a disciplinarian, old-school. Personally I got on very well with him. I liked him. If you treated him with respect, you got respect back.

It was a Friday night and I was in to do my show when we got talking about the fact that I had an interview with the Beastie Boys. I had it lined up the next day and I was going to put the interview out on the show the following week.

Alex had read the hype about their wild image and he said, 'The Beastie Boys? No. We can't allow that. This is a family station.'

No matter how much I tried to persuade him, he wouldn't budge. So eventually I said, 'I'll tell you what, Alex, rather than messing the record company about – why don't you let me do the interview, then I'll bring the tape back and you can vet it? If there's anything that's not right, we can edit it out.'

So I met the band, who were decent guys, and the interview went fine. No swearing, no insults, no fights breaking out. I didn't have to do a thing to the recording and it was broadcast the following Friday. It was all a bit of a storm in a teacup. (My favourite Beastie Boys a track is Sabotage. It's brilliant, and the Cancer Bats recorded a fine cover of it too.)

With the management changes, though, my show became more restricted; more mainstream rock and less left-of-centre. Safe stuff like the Eagles, Steely Dan, The Doobie Brothers and so on. My choice was: walk away, or stay on the radio. I had a mortgage to pay, so I stayed. It wasn't the happiest of times – until, in the summer of 2006, I got a call that changed everything. 'Hi, Tom, it's Jay Crawford here…'

Jay had worked for Radio Forth for about twenty years, during the day, playing pop music. But once a week he presented Edinburgh Rock, the station's version of the Friday Night Rock Show. Jay was a bit more traditional; I'm sure he wouldn't mind me saying that he was more into the established bands like The Who, AC/DC, The Stones and so on. He wasn't particularly open to a new band handing in a CD. That just wasn't his thing.

He'd moved from Forth to Clyde for about a year, then he'd gone back to Forth. Then he got a job with Real Radio, the station that had risen from the ashes of Scot FM. The Guardian newspaper had decided to get into radio and bought Scot FM, which had never really worked out, and gave Jay the head of music job. Jay knew his music and they marketed themselves well – soon Real began to creep ahead of Clyde in audience numbers.

Jay gave me a bit of small talk, then asked what I was doing. I told him I was on Clyde 2 and he said, 'I'm wondering if I can talk to you about something. Do you fancy coming into the office?'

For the next couple of days I wondered, 'What the hell does Jay Crawford want to talk to me about?' I surmised he was about to offer me a rock show on Real; and, sidelined on Clyde 2, he thought I was ripe for the picking. In my head, I wasn't keen on the idea. After twenty-odd years on Clyde I had a lot of loyalty. The show I had, plus my other bits and bobs, allowed me to pay the mortgage and look after my family. Taking all this into consideration, I wasn't sure about moving to Real.

I sat down in Jay's office and he said: 'Right, Tom, you probably don't know about this yet. The Guardian have bought the Paisley-based station, Q96. We're turning it into a rock station.' As you can imagine, my ears pricked up straight away. 'With the paper's deep pockets,' he continued, 'The plan is to build a similar model to America where, in any city the size of Glasgow, you have choices. On your car radio, you'll have button one for pop, button two for country, button three for talk, button four for news… and button five for rock.'

Every city in the States has that setup. As I've said, the American bands I met were always stunned that there were no rock stations in the UK – the home of Led Zeppelin, Deep Purple, Black Sabbath and so on. Real

Radio's owners wanted to change that; and they were going to kick off in Glasgow. They wanted me to be their first signing, for six shows a week of four hours a day.

I didn't even ask how much I was getting. 'What would I be playing?' I asked.

'You decide, Tom,' said Jay. 'Thin Lizzy, Boston, Van Halen, The Who, AC/DC. All the stuff that you play on the Friday Night Rock Show.'

I thought I'd died and gone to heaven. Of course, I said, 'Yes!' It was the end of September and Jay said, 'I'd like you to start at the end of October. I want you to help me programme the music we should play before we launch in January.'

I went home that afternoon with a rather large smile on my face. But then I had to endure one of the most unpleasant things that ever happened to me.

I wasn't on a contract with Clyde. I'd always just turned up once a week. There was no holiday pay, no sickness benefit, nothing like that; so I wasn't sure if I had to give any notice. The managing director of Clyde at that time was Paul Cooney, whom I'd known for more than twenty-five years, even before I started there. He'd joined in the station's early days, in a junior position. He was a hard-working, conscientious guy who was good at networking and worked his way right to the top.

I arranged a lunchtime meeting through his secretary. I was nervous – when you've been somewhere for that long and you need to leave, it's a bit of a leap in the dark. But when I arrived, Paul's secretary was full of apologies. 'Sorry, Tom. He's been called to a meeting in Edinburgh. If you really need to see him, we can rearrange. Or if it's something that can be dealt with by your line manager, just go and see him.'

I'd built myself up for a big meeting, so I asked to see the line manager. He'd been there less than a year and he was quite a quiet sort of chap. When I'd met him he'd been fairly cordial. The only conversation I'd had with him prior to that day was to do with my shops shutting down, when I'd asked if there was any chance of more slots on Clyde. His response hadn't been favourable. There just wasn't anything he could offer me, which was fair enough. Other than that, he just let me get on with my work.

When I went into his office he asked what he could do for me. 'It's a bit awkward,' I began. 'I've been here a long time, doing the one show a week. I've been offered full-time employment with a new radio station called Rock Radio. They've asked me to be on six days a week.'

There was a long silence – the kind of uncomfortable, embarrassing silence that makes cold sweat gather at the base of your neck. It probably only lasted for ten seconds, but it felt like an eternity. I'm thinking, 'He probably knew. There must have been rumours.'

Eventually he said, 'Is that it?'

'Well, yes,' I said, confused. 'I didn't know what the situation was. Do I need to work any notice?'

'No,' was all he said. I was struggling for a response and he told me, 'I'm busy. Is that it, or is there anything else?'

I said, 'No. That's it.'
I'll never forget him flicking his hand and saying, 'Well, there's the door.'

I felt the blood drain from my face. All those years … and that was it. I was shocked, and rather disgusted. He looked up and said in a very dismissive manner, 'Anything else?'

'Well,' I said, 'A thank-you for twenty-five years of loyal service would be nice.'

He just nodded at the door again and muttered, 'Bye.'

I thought, 'You're kidding.' Then I walked out of Radio Clyde for the last time, and that was that.

About a week later, I received a handwritten letter from Paul Cooney, MD of Clyde. It went something like this: 'Dear Tom, sorry I missed you the other day. I'd like to thank you for your years of service. You were a great member of the team, and a pleasure to work with. All your colleagues here at Clyde would like to wish you all the very best in your new venture. If you're ever in Clydebank, please pop in and say hello. All the best – Paul.'

As I read that I thought, 'That's how he's risen to be a managing director. That's the measure of the man – a decent guy.' I've never seen that line manager since. A few months after I joined Rock Radio he lost his job at Clyde. I didn't shed too many tears.

Proud Dad with Neil and Heather 1988

The Almighty present Tom with a guitar

Phil Collins and Mike Rutherford of Genesis visit Radio Clyde

Bon Jovi visit Radio Clyde's free festival at Kelvingrove Park

Ronnie James Dio – a man who loved his curries

Pete and Dan from Nazareth

Ozzy's front lawn, at his house in Buckinghamshire

Tom's two children – Neil and Heather

Tom with Ford Kiernan from STILL GAME

Judas Priest in Glasgow

Deep Purple – Edinburgh Playhouse

Dimebag, from Pantera's widow at Download

Steel Panther 2009 – the Garage dressing room

96.3 Rock Radio Studio

Tom with Dave Mustaine from Megadeth

Behind the AC/DC stage at Download with Paul Anthony

15. MUM AND DAD

Farewell to my parents ~ family values ~ murder suspect ~ Marillion, Linkin Park and Slash

My mum and dad were great parents and great grandparents. I've lost them both now, but I still think of them often. I look back at the times I spent with Dad when he had his card shop in my record store in Duke Street. It was great to be able to work alongside him. On one occasion Mandy Smith – once married to Bill Wyman of the Stones – came in on a promotional tour for a single she'd released on Jive Records. She was with her mother; and although Mandy must still have been in her early twenties, it was the older woman that caught Dad's eye: 'Tom, that lassie's mum is a cracker!' Samantha Fox also came in one day to promote a single. So there were a few nice perks for Dad in those days!

I mentioned earlier my rock night in Cumbernauld every Sunday, at a place called Sax. I was playing the tunes as usual, then there was a phone call – Dad was in the Royal Edinburgh Hospital because he was having bother swallowing. He'd had a triple-bypass a few years earlier after suffering badly with angina, but he'd come out with a new lease of life.

I was told: 'Your dad's not well. You should go through to see him right away.' The guys at the club were all really understanding and took over while I drove to Edinburgh. I sat with him for two or three hours; but even then I didn't think he was that bad. The next day, however, he got much worse, and he died later in the week. I was really shocked. I was so fond of my dad. He'd told me those great stories about his times in the RAF in North Africa, taken me to my first live gig… You just don't realise that it's 'the end' at the time.
He'd loved his last house in Anstruther, so we asked the local fishermen if we could go out and scatter his ashes in the sea. I was quite surprised

when I was told it was illegal. They said, 'We'd get the jail if we did that.' The coastguard were very strict about it.

Apart from sitting looking out to sea, Dad's big hobby was bowling. He went there every night during the summer. So we thought we might spread the ashes at Anstruther bowling green and spread the ashes there. I didn't want to them on the green itself, of course; I thought we'd put them on the rosebeds instead. We said the Lord's Prayer, but as I opened the box, there was a sudden gust of wind and it took his remains up into the air in a tornado of ashes that wafted in our eyes and down our throats. Poor Dad… he probably covered half of Anstruther. It was sad, but we all had a laugh about it and went back to Mum's for a cup of tea.

Mum carried on in Anstruther for a couple of years on her own, but then she developed Alzheimer's. We moved her to live close to us, but eventually she went into a care home. She was happy for a while, but over the months, she faded. She fell out of bed one night and broke her hip. Unfortunately, that was the beginning of the end. It was the Download weekend when it happened.

Rock Radio was heavily involved with the festival that year, and we were all down there for five or six days. It was hard going. It was on the Thursday that my daughter, Heather, phoned me at three in the morning to say that Gran had passed away. I was so upset. My mum, and I hadn't been there at the end. I'd been working.

I was due to come back up on the Friday anyway, because it was Heather's wedding on the Saturday. What a weekend. It was very emotional, being at my daughter's wedding, standing up to make the father-of-the-bride speech, and having to say a few words about my mother, who'd died only two days earlier.

I just hope that Mum and Dad are both up there looking down thinking, 'Imagine our boy writing a book!'

Weirdly enough, Mum's passing meant I wasn't able to set up a dream come true for Linkin Park – another band who gave rock a jolt when it was supposed to be 'on the way out.' They're not classic hard rock and they're very different from Slipknot; but their sound is still special. When I met two of them in London I found them very amenable. One of them asked, 'You're from Scotland – do you play golf?'

I said, 'Since I was twelve. Not fanatically, but now and again.'

They were both nuts about golf, and their lifetime ambition was to play at St Andrews. I told them, 'My mum lives in Anstruther, which is next door to St Andrews. As she's a resident, we can probably pull a few strings.' So it was all going to be arranged for me to play a round at St Andrews with Linkin Park. But sadly, I wan't able to make it happen in time.

Keeping in regular contact with the parents paid dividends for Jonathan Cain, one of the main songwriters in Journey, and before that, The Babys. I once asked him about the song Don't Stop Believin'. He told me the basics had been put down years before Journey recorded it. The core idea had come about when he was out on the road in America, driving hundreds of miles in the back of a van making fifty dollars a gig – just enough for some peanut butter sandwiches and fuel for the van.

He said it was really hard: 'A couple of us were at the end of our tether. We weren't enjoying it any more.' Jonathan used to phone home on a Sunday, to let his folks know how he was doing and check on them. One this particular Sunday he was telling them that he'd decided to wrap it and come home.

But his dad said, 'Look son, you've got the talent. You'll get there. Just carry on.' Jonathan protested that he was fed up with the whole thing. His dad replied, 'Don't stop believin' – give it a couple more months.'

That phrase stuck. A few years later he was in the studio with Journey, creating one of the greatest classic rock songs of all time.

Round about the mid eighties, my wife and I were thinking of moving house. We found a development in Cumbernauld, close to a golf course, so we put down a deposit which gave us six months to sell the place we were in. It sold quickly so it worked out pretty well, and we were looking forward to moving into the new one. As the entry date got closer it turned out that it was going to be a few months late. We had to move in with my mother-in-law. That was okay. We managed.

By the time the the house was ready, I was right into a Marillion song called Fugazi. I remember interviewing Fish before that album came out, and hearing this very powerful lyric: 'The whole world is totally fugazi.' It meant 'all fucked up' – during the Vietnam War, the South Vietnamese would come running in shouting 'Fugazi! Fugazi!' So I thought it would be fun to name the house after the song.

Quite early on, I got a knock on the door from the postman. He said, 'I always meant to ask you – are you the Tom Russell that does the Friday Night Rock Show on Clyde?'
I said, 'Yes, that's me.'

'What's the name of the house all about?'

I told him, and he had a good laugh. The last time I drove by I noticed that the people who live there now have changed the name to something much less inspiring.

In amongst all my rock'n'roll adventures, my life was just like any other guy's. My mother and father-in-law, Anna and Jack, were nice people, a family-oriented couple who went to church every week. They were quite straight-laced, so it's surprising in a way that I have a story to tell about them.

They loved going for a drive on a Sunday afternoon, normally to Callander. On one particular trip, when they got there the rain was bouncing off the pavements. They decided to have fish and chips in the car and watch the world go by. Fish suppers were bought, scoffed, and the leftovers were rolled up in the newspapers that they came in and dropped into the car park bin. After half an hour, it was obvious that the rain wasn't going to ease off, so they headed back to Cumbernauld.

An hour later they were home, shaking off their damp coats and putting the kettle on when Anna let out a shriek. Her false teeth were missing! Poor Jack was sent back to Callander, where it was still raining. Fair play to him: he rummaged through the bin, found the missing teeth, and delivered them back to his grateful wife in Cumbernauld.

My then-wife's sister was married to guy called Ian Smith, the younger brother of Walter Smith of Rangers. Ian, an engineer, emigrated with wife Anne to America in the eighties. We went out to visit one time, and the image of America in my head was that every girl was going to look like she was on Baywatch. The reality was rather different. They were all huge. They really can eat. My sister-in-law invited us to go power-walking with her.

Wearing all the gear, we jumped in the car, drove ten miles and then headed to the power-walking area. We did a few circuits of the park; then, halfway back, we visited the drive-in ice cream parlour. Any calories that had just been lost were immediately put right back on.
My big phobia is snakes. I've even had Alice Cooper try to put one round my neck, and I've had to say, 'Sorry – I just can't do it.' We were

in Atlanta visiting Ian and Anne, and I was going to be taken to my first baseball game. I was quite looking forward to it. The day before, I noticed the grass was needing cut, so I started on the job. As I got closer to the trees, however, I began to worry about snakes.

As I turned the mower round away from the trees, I stood on something and I felt a sharp pain in my ankle. I went down like a ton of lead. Nothing could take away the pain. I was writhing about, convinced I'd been bitten by a snake. I was screaming for help and eventually the girls came out and found me.

As it turned out, I'd stood on a stone, gone over on my ankle and torn a ligament. They had to take me to the hospital. I didn't quite believe them, I was sure I'd been bitten by something. Anyway, they strapped up my ankle and I got issued with a walking stick. I was able to hobble off to the baseball game.

I enjoyed the baseball, but the play only seemed to last a few minutes before the crowd all went for a hot dog. A few more minutes of play then they'd be off for a beer and a burger this time. Then they'd play for a full ten minutes. Followed by a popcorn break. It seemed to go on like that for three hours or so. No wonder so many Americans are overweight!

I'm fortunate to have two great kids. My daughter Heather was born in Rottenrow hospital, Glasgow, at about six in the afternoon of October 7, 1982. I remember looking at her and making a connection straight away – she was actually born with her eyes open. You weren't encouraged to hang about too much at that time; so as most dads do, I went to wet the baby's head. I did it in style: first, along to Lauder's Bar, then across to the Apollo to see AC/DC on their For Those About to Rock tour. Angus Young was playing like a demon, and my head was still reeling as I thought of Heather's wee face. What a night!

I've got grief off Heather for years, nicking off to see AC/DC like that, but it wasn't exactly a one-off. Thirty years later, we were all at Heather's birthday party. My new partner, Jean, was meeting the family for the first time, so we were all on our best behaviour. At six o'clock I made the announcement that I was going to have to leave a wee bit early – I had to go to the Corn Exchange in Edinburgh for a gig. Heather, well used to her dad, gave me a friendly bit of slagging, then told me to have a good gig.

The gig was a surprise to Jean. I'd forgotten to tell anyone. (You see, I'm far from perfect...) She didn't know anything about rock bands or gigs, so she asked me, 'Am I dressed okay?'

'Of course you are! It doesn't matter,' I replied.

'Who are we going to see?'

I told her, but it meant absolutely nothing to her. When we got to the backstage area at seven o'clock and I went in for my interview, Jean said, 'I can't come in.' She was out of her comfort zone, flappin' – but I didn't want to leave her hanging about in a strange place, so I persuaded her to come in.
We did the interview, which was fairly relaxed. In fact, most of the interview was about the new car the interviewee had just bought. When we'd finished, I decided it would be cool to get a picture with this guy. So I said, 'Do you mind, big man, if I get a picture with you?'

True to form, he replied, 'No problem, man.'

So I gave Jean the camera and she snapped a shot, then I said, 'I'll get one with you now, Jean.'

That's when she said, 'How – who is he?'

Flushing slightly, I told her. 'His name is Slash…'
Slash just laughed. 'So you're not a rock'n'roll chick?'

Jean replied, 'No – I'm just an old hen.'

My son Neil was born two years after Heather. They both went to Cumbernauld Primary school, and every year I'd get a really bad report about Neil. 'He's not interested; he just talks; he's disruptive.' He might not have been doing well academically, but by the time Neil was ten, he was doing really well at rugby.

At that time Stirling's youth rugby team were getting a great name so I took him for a look. There were about forty youngsters playing and they looked great. Stirling County training time clashed with his football training in Cumbernauld, but he picked the rugby and got really good at it. He was even talked about as a potential player for Scotland. But by the age of sixteen he'd discovered drink and women… so the rugby was gradually dropped.

Neil was still getting bad feedback from school. Most of the teachers told me that he was just a waster, so after second year we moved him from Cumbernauld High School to Dunblane High School. It wasn't that the school had been a problem; we just thought it might help because he was making lots of friends in Stirling. We'd drive him the twenty miles to school every morning and he'd come home each evening on the train. But within about six months of moving, the bad reports started up again. Nothing serious, just mischief. By the time he was eighteen he'd left school and picked up a job working in a restaurant.

As a dad, you can't help being a bit disappointed. You want better for your boy. He was happy as Larry for six months, but as time went on, many of his pals ended up at university. There was cheap drink and attractive women there, so he got the notion to go. He went to college and got an HNC. He got accepted by Stirling University and ended up with a first-class honours degree.

We went to the graduation ceremony and we were as proud as could be. At the end of the ceremony the rector announced that they had a special award for dissertation of the year. And it went to Neil! He got a cheque for five hundred pounds and he was put forward for a Carnegie Trust scholarship at New York University to do a masters. Later we went over for his graduation in New York, and again our hearts thumped with pride. When he came home, he told me he'd been accepted at Oxford University to do a second masters. Neil now speaks Arabic, and he's at Edinburgh University doing a PhD in Middle Eastern studies.

Heather was a steady worker who left school and got a job at the tax office in Cumbernauld. After a couple of years, she decided to move on, and got married to her boyfriend Richard. At nineteen we wondered if she was a bit young – but she went onto have three children: Emma, Rebecca and Peter. She went into business in the baby care sector and she's done really well. Then recently she opened her own shop selling children's clothes, toys, prams and bikes. Her shop is a not for profit business, which helps families starting out. People can donate clothes for the benefit of others. She runs her toddler sense classes and allows space for baby yoga and karate. Where possible, whatever is offered is at a reduced price. So I'm rather proud of Heather too.

A few years ago, when buy-to-let was all the rage, I borrowed money against the equity in my first flat, and went to see another place for sale. It was a repossession in a nice area of Cumbernauld. As we walked up the path of the semi-detached property, there were people coming out of the open viewing with real expressions of disgust on their faces. One guy was actually being sick. The place was absolutely stinking – a hovel, it was filthy and infested with flies. I don't think it had ever been hoovered. The windows were all rotten and the kitchen was a state. The bathroom was unusable and the bedroom ceiling was hanging down, just about to collapse. Yet the property was only about 20 years old. Unbelievable.

I spoke to the estate agent for a few moments before we went back to our car. Heather said, 'What do you think, dad?'

I replied, 'See all these people that came here thinking, "This is a nice part of the town," and then discovered what we discovered inside..? Most of them will never put a bid in. This may be an opportunity. Let's go for it." So we put in a low, silly bid – the bid was accepted.

Six weeks later when we got the keys, we got the overalls on and the family all piled in. The one worry we had was the ceiling. So I got a ladder and went up into the loft. The whole loft was piled to a height of probably two feet with magazines. Thousands and thousands of them. I picked the first one up – it was a Playboy. The next was a Penthouse. the next was a Hustler. The bedroom ceiling was about to collapse under tons and tons of porn! The dirty magazines filled two skips. We ran a relay until it was all cleared. The guys at the local recycling centre must have thought they'd died and gone to heaven.

I always wondered… what history was in that house? It was a family who had occupied the place, not some weirdo living on his own. Anyway, we got it to a habitable standard – new kitchen, new bathroom, new windows and a new ceiling. We rent it out to this day.

At one stage between the record shops closing and Rock Radio starting, my wife started doing bed and breakfast to help make ends meet. I chipped in to help when required, but it was mainly her business.

One weekend, she was going away and I was volunteered to look after a couple who were staying with us that night. I enjoyed the peace and quiet of the evening: a curry, a couple of cans and whatever I wanted on the telly. Then I went up to bed and fell into a deep sleep. My slumber, however, was dramatically interrupted in the weirdest way.

The light suddenly went on, and there were three guys and a girl at the end of my bed, shouting, 'Get up! Who are you? Are you alone?'

In shock, I jumped out of bed and stood there naked. I noticed the time was five o'clock in the morning, and I shouted back, 'Who are you? What are you doing in my bedroom?'

The guys got quite aggressive. They told me they were the police and insisted that I tell them my name, which I did. (The policewoman seemed pre-occupied with admiring the attributes of the poor old bugger, standing naked in front of her!)

It turned out that there had been a murder in Cumbernauld a couple of weeks previously, and the cops had received a tip that a suspect was living in a local B&B. After a cup of tea they rode off into the sunset, allowing me to get back to sleep.

In 2015 I was playing some tunes at Rockus in Glasgow when this guy came up and asked for a request. I said 'No problem' and he replied, 'You don't recognise me, do you? The last time I saw you, you were standing naked in your bedroom.' It was one of the cops from that night in Cumbernauld. We had a laugh about it – and, if my memory serves me correctly, he bought me a beer.

On another occasion when I was left to run things at the B&B, we had an older couple staying the night. I hadn't checked them in or even met them. The only information I had was a time for their breakfast and an indication of what they wanted. Around seven o'clock in the evening the phone went and it was a couple looking for a double room for the night. I said, 'No problem,' and they arrived about seven-thirty. They were in their early thirties and paid cash as soon as they arrived, declining any breakfast order, saying they'd be getting away really early.

Our house was in a rural area, next to a country park which, at that time, had a pack of wolves in a large run, so it wasn't a surprise when, around nine o'clock, I thought I heard one of them howling. But the howls got louder, so I went outside to see whether one had escaped.

To my surprise, the noises seemed to be coming from inside my house so, I ventured upstairs where the noise was getting louder. When I reached the bedroom area the howls calmed down a bit but were then replaced by a female voice shouting, 'Yes, yes, yes...' I realised then what was happening, but I wasn't sure what to do. They were at it, in my house, but I suppose they were allowed to be – they had, after all, paid their money. But they were making a hell of a noise and there was another couple to consider. I was just about to knock the door and ask them to quieten down a bit, when things came to a natural end, and a calmness overtook the house.

I went back downstairs and returned to my book. There was about half an hour of peace then the 'wolf' resumed howling again. It wasn't as bad this time, and ten minutes seemed to do the job. After that, I went to bed.

The next morning, I was up sharpish, but the young couple's van was well away. I got the table set for the older couple, but there was a frosty silence when they came downstairs. The silence continued when I served their fry-up. Then, I realised they thought the antics the previous night had been me. So I explained the situation to them. They relaxed – then laughed about it with me for half an hour.

Another family memory is my fortieth birthday – but not for the reason you might expect. We lived in Milton Of Campsie at the time, and my wife decided that a surprise party in the house was required. On the day, my neighbour, George, took me for a game of golf to get me out of the way. We played a round at Kirkintilloch Golf Club in the morning, followed by a tasty steak pie lunch, washed down with a single pint.

Heading off for the afternoon round, I started to feel a little bit queasy. By the time we got to the fifth hole, I was really unwell and had to return to the clubhouse. George drove me home around and I went straight to bed.

By seven o'clock I was no better, and the guests were beginning to arrive. There was nothing else for it – they came up to my bedroom in pairs to wish me a happy fortieth. The party, of course, continued downstairs, without the birthday boy. I heard later that a good time was had by all.

It's one of the few times in my life that the expression 'It must have been a bad pint' rang true.

16. OZZY AND ME

Bats ~ night-vision goggles ~ sneak previews ~ public kisses ~ the Prince of Darkness hides from a Beatle

The first time I met Ozzy Osbourne was in 1980, when his first solo album was about to come out. After Black Sabbath, people had been unsure what he'd come up with – but he silenced his potential critics with the superb Blizzard of Ozz album. Tracks like Mr Crowley and Crazy Train turned out be classics, and his new band, featuring Randy Rhoads on guitar, was the business.

It's changed days now; but back then, the record company said something like, 'Not sure if you'd be interested in this, Tom. We've signed this guy. He's a bit of a has-been. Used to sing with Black Sabbath… Ozzy Osbourne?'

I said, 'What do you mean "has-been"? He's one of the greats in rock!'
'If you say so. Anyway, we'll fly him up on Wednesday. He'll be staying at the Holiday Inn. Would you mind arranging a taxi?'

So Ozzy, along with Sharon, came to the Radio Clyde studio. It was long before their TV series graced our screens – he could probably have walked down Buchanan Street and nobody would have recognised him. We pre-recorded a smashing interview. In those days Ozzy had you on the floor in stitches; he told a great story. If he saw there was a twinkle in your eye he'd just ramp up the punchlines. He's a very funny and clever man. Sharon, even though she'd probably heard the same stories time and time again, kept laughing and egging him on. He told me about putting his band together with Bob Daisley on bass and Don Airey on keyboards. But he kept going on and on about guitarist Randy Rhoads.

After I recorded the interview with Ozzy, Sharon said, 'We're going for dinner now. Would you like to join us?' It was about eight o'clock at night, so we went to the Holiday Inn and got a table. 'What would you like to drink, Tom?' Sharon asked.

'A pint of heavy. That's my tipple,' I replied. (Just in case any of you are wondering…)

Sharon had a bottle of wine and Ozzy had a bottle of five-star Courvoisier brandy. We sat there having dinner, chatting away, talking about football, and Ozzy's drinking this brandy like it was wine. There was no effect, except that his patter just got funnier and funnier.

The second time I met him was after the first album had done really well. I think this was the time that he told me the bat story, which, at the time, I hadn't heard before. It hadn't hit the press yet.

I know told loads of other people since, but he said: 'Tom, I was pissed as a fart. I wasn't even sure where I was – Baltimore or Barnsley, and this guy throws this thing up onto the stage. I just assumed it was a plastic thing.'

Now, was it actually plastic? I wouldn't be surprised. Sharon was always very good at adjusting a story, slightly, to get the maximum impact. In other words, she's a great publicist. When I mooted the possibility, Ozzy said, 'No, no – it was a real bat.'

But think about it… you're dashing out the door to an Ozzy gig, and you stick a bat in your pocket, just in case? It leaves a wee bit of doubt dangling there. Anyway, Ozzy said that he'd picked this thing up off the stage and bit its head off. He told me how the blood and the guts were dripping down his chin, and the crowd went mental. The show came to an end and Sharon rushed him to hospital to get anti-rabies shots. The worldwide publicity did Ozzy's career no harm.

During our third interview he spoke about Randy's death. I know he's told the story again since, but I remember him telling it to me.

The band were out in America, in the middle of nowhere, when Randy Rhoads asked for some time off. He wanted to hire a plane as flying was his hobby. Ozzy said, 'No problem.' Randy went off to hire the plane. The rest of the crew were playing cards or sleeping in the tour bus. Ozzy remembered going out of the bus and shading his eyes as he watched Randy take off. He watched him circling round, then Randy did a dive-bomb run over the tour bus. Ozzy ducked down as the plane displaced the air above the bus.

It was either the second or the third time that Randy misjudged it and hit something. There was a terrible explosion and Ozzy's heart sank. Absolutely tragic. I could really hear the emotion in his voice as he talked about it. He loved Randy.

Around that time Ozzy was beginning to become a huge star in America. He wasn't just the ex-singer of Black Sabbath, he was now Ozzy Osbourne, shifting millions of albums and selling out big venues. Although in the UK he was still doing interviews with Tom Russell of Radio Clyde, in the States he was huge.

His second album, Diary of a Madman, was being launched in 1981, and he was at the launch party with Sharon. The record company suits were there, quaffing champagne, downing 'horse's doofers' and more or less ignoring the man of the moment. Ozzy was listening to all the business chat and beginning to get pissed off. 'Ooh yes, Claude. How's the new Madonna album doing? How many units? What's the projections?' The album he'd sweated over was playing in the background and no one was giving a shit.

There was a bird-cage in the room with two white doves inside. As the anger and the drink began to wash over him, he snapped. Ozzy opened the cage, grabbed a dove and shouted, 'Fuck the lot of ye!' Then he bit its head off. Definitely for real this time.

The first time I was invited to Ozzy's house was when I was working on the Hard'n'Heavy video magazine. He lived in Little Chalfont, Buckinghamshire, a place maybe forty miles from London, with money just dripping off of the trees. We pulled up in a car and passed through the electric gates. His personal assistant, Tony, a lovely guy, took us up to the house and into Ozzy's lounge, which was very Laura Ashley in style – the decor was sumptuous.

We couldn't have been made more welcome. We did the interview over an hour or so, then Sharon made us lunch. A nice salad, if I remember correctly, with a big glass of wine. There were three of us there from the magazine: the video director, Denis, the cameraman and myself.

Another time I was invited over to one of the Osbournes' parties. I went with a big Scottish lad called Robbie, from the record company. The party started at one in the afternoon. There was lots of food and drink but nothing too wild, and the thing was supposed to end around eleven. Changed days from Ozzy's wild years, but brilliant nonetheless.

It got to about four o'clock then Ozzy pulled me to one side and said, 'Have you got ten minutes?' He took me out the front door and we went round the back of his property. It was an old place, maybe two hundred years old, and behind the main house there was a big barn with the whole of the top floor converted into a den. He told me that was where he went when he fell out with Sharon. 'She's not allowed in here,' he explained. 'The cleaner comes in once a week. No one else gets in.' Inside there was the obligatory snooker table and beautiful, comfortable armchairs and couches. There was also a pair of the biggest hi-fi speakers I'd ever seen – they were taller than me. He said, 'Would you like to hear what I've been working on?'

Like I'm going to say, 'no thanks'! ... I was feeling so privileged to be up there, just about to hear some new material. He handed me a beer, put a cassette tape into the hi-fi and pressed the button. The track he played me was the title track of his next album, No More Tears; all seven minutes and twenty-three seconds of it, with Zakk Wylde on guitar. It was probably three months before anyone else in the media heard it. Again, I was thinking, 'How did I manage to get here?'

I told him, 'That track would make a great single.' Ozzy wasn't so sure. He told me the record company had said it was too long. I said, 'Ozzy, you should know by now – it won't get any airplay anyway, other than on the specialist rock shows. So just go for it!'
Six months later it came out as the single.

We went back to the party until about eight o'clock. Ozzy's guests weren't big stars; just friends and neighbours plus a sprinkling of record company people. Why was I there? I'm still not sure, but it was a great privilege and I wasn't going to question it. When it got to nine, Ozzy collared me again: 'Have you got another ten minutes, Tom?'

I said, "'Are you going to let me hear another track?'

'No, that's the only track we've got fully mixed. I want to show you something else.' It was dark by this time, so we went out onto the front lawn where he pulled out these night-vision goggles. He asked me to try them, telling me that they were the best things he'd ever bought. I put them on and it was just like you see on TV. You could see a blizzard of moths flying around the garden and the occasional, slightly nervous-looking bat. It was surreal. After a few minutes we trundled back into the house again. At eleven o'clock it was time to go, so big Robbie got me back to a hotel at Heathrow and then we flew back to Glasgow the next morning.

Hands up – I'm a lucky bastard.

Ozzy once told me a story about a time he came home from a tour while he was still relatively unknown, because the Osbournes TV show hadn't started. He was met at Heathrow by Sharon, who drove him home. She told him she'd arranged a breakfast TV appearance for the next morning. 'Oh, Sharon!' was the cry as an exhausted Ozzy complained that he needed rest. Sharon promised he would get rest, but that she just needed him to do this one show to plug the new album.

She woke him at five the next morning with a huge cup of coffee. He grumpily got dressed and headed out to the waiting taxi, clutching another coffee. A few miles into the journey, the coffee was finished and nature was starting to take its course; he was bursting for a pee. He asked the driver to keep an eye out for a toilet. Ten minutes later, with Ozzy increasingly desperate, he pleaded with the driver to pull over.

They were in a built-up area by now and it was hard to find a suitable spot. Then Ozzy spotted the big yellow 'M' of a MacDonald's, and the driver pulled into the empty car park. Ozzy ran over to the door but found it locked. Inside, a cleaner was sweeping the floor. Ozzy knocked on the window and asked if he could use the toilet. But the reply was 'We don't open till six – it's more that my job's worth to open before then.'

'It's four minutes to six,' Ozzy said, but to no avail. So he opened his coat, pulled down his zip and pissed all over the restaurant door. He shouted, 'Clean that!' then hopped back into the taxi and went on TV to plug his new album.

That story is on a par with another of Ozzy's more famous adventures, which he told me about in his own words. When he was touring Texas, the tour bus pulled in to refuel. He woke up and decided to stretch his legs, and wandered a few hundred yards until he came across an old wall. He needed a pee; no one was watching, so he did what he had to do. Just as he was finishing, a couple of security guards appeared and arrested him. Poor Ozzy was carted off to the jail where he had to spend the night charged with defacing a public monument. The old wall was The Alamo.

I saw him again at a Classic Rock Awards party in London. Rock Radio had been going for a couple of years and the bosses thought we should have a presence there, so the MD, one of the other jocks and I flew down. My job was to man the red carpet that led into the Park Lane Hotel.

Mic in hand, I went into the area that had been roped off for the press. I was taken to my spot, which had a wee sign on the floor with my name on it. On my left there were a Radio 1 presenter, a sound engineer and a flunky. On my right were a Radio 2 presenter, a sound engineer and a flunky. No wonder the BBC licence fee is a fortune! For Rock Radio there was just me with my flash mic – a great bit of kit. You press a button and it captures the lot.

It was interesting, overhearing the BBC guys saying things like, 'That Tony Iommi person; who is that? Does he play in one of the metal bands?' Or, 'Oh, Brian May. He was in Queen… Was he the guitarist?' It was that sort of level of chat, so I was being ignored, and getting the impression that the BBC guys were thinking, 'Who's this old codger?'

Then the stars began filing up the red carpet. To my surprise, my neighbours didn't even know who John Paul Jones was. They were fumbling at their press handouts in a panic: 'Now… who is he? Oh! Led Zeppelin! John Paul! Hi there, nice to see you. What about Led Zeppelin – are you going to reform?' Naff questions that he was fed up hearing. When Geddy Lee came along they really started to panic. 'Rush? who's Rush?'

I managed to catch some musicians' attention – they didn't always remember my name, but they knew the face, sometimes even the beard.

I asked Tony Iommi whether he was expecting an award or just a night out. He said, 'I'm nominated, but I don't know if I'm getting it. But, yes, it's a night out.'

I said, 'I see your old mucker in the vocal department is here tonight. Will you be catching up?'

'Of course!' he said. 'We're not at the same table, but I'm looking forward to seeing the old bugger.'

A few moments later a big limo arrived, and out popped Ozzy and Sharon. Radio 1 and 2 were on high alert because their TV show The Osbournes was really big by now. I was getting pushed to the side in the throng. As Ozzy approached, I noticed he was looking less stable on his feet than I remembered. Everyone was shouting, 'Ozzy! Ozzy! Is it true you bit the head off a bat?' Old news. He ignored them all, shuffling on with his John Lennon glasses on.

As he was pushing through, he looked up, caught my eye and shouted, 'Tom! You old bugger! I thought you were dead!' He came over and gave me a big hug and a kiss on the cheek. The BBC guys were staring at me open-mouthed.

It was lovely – we did a quick two-minute interview while everyone else looked on. That night, Ozzy got the Living Legend Award, sponsored by Marshall. Well deserved.

Ozzy once told me a story about flying on Concorde from America to the UK with Sharon. They were sitting in row fifteen having a drink, and as he looked around, he saw a head that looked familiar – someone he'd always wanted to meet. Using a visit to the toilet as an excuse, he plucked up the courage to walk up the aisle.

He told me: 'As I walked past, I glanced down. Tom… it was him!' Ozzy was talking about Paul McCartney, his hero.

He was too shy to look again on the way back, but when he sat down beside Sharon she told him, 'Go and introduce yourself.'

He got all flustered. 'No way! I can't just go up to him and start talking. He's Paul McCartney!'

She said, 'And you're Ozzy Osbourne – you're just as famous as him.'

'Don't be so ridiculous,' he told her. 'Give me another double brandy.' He spent the next hour knocking back the drinks, trying to get the courage together. He told me, 'I just wanted to say: "Excuse me, Mr McCartney. Pleasure to meet you. I've been a fan ever since I was a teenager." I just couldn't do it.'

With just twenty minutes until Concorde landed, Ozzy asked a hostess to take a menu over and have it signed. She asked who it should be made out to – and didn't recognise the name of Black Sabbath's frontman. When she spoke to Paul, though, he twisted round and glanced back at row fifteen. Ozzy gave him a wee nervous wave, then Paul signed the menu and nodded towards him.

I thought it was a lovely story. Everyone has their heroes. Perhaps Paul McCartney might have a similar story about Little Richard…

The last time I saw Ozzy live was at the Hydro in Glasgow with Sabbath when their last album, 13, came out. I was expecting him to be, you know, alright – but he was absolutely fantastic. I enjoyed the Hydro gig more that Sabbath's previous show at Download, probably because I had a seat. The problem with Download, at my age, is that you're on your feet all day. By the time it gets to nine o'clock and the headline act comes on, you're totally cream-crackered.

17. ROCK RADIO

The fun begins ~ the vibe builds ~ the arse is kissed

96.3 Rock Radio saved me from retirement. We launched in January 2006 with a big party in a marquee in the grounds of the Real Radio building. Lots of guests were invited, mainly potential clients; but I remember Dan and Pete from Nazareth turning up, as well as Ted and Chris from The Sensational Alex Harvey Band. The first record was played on air by my friend, breakfast presenter Kieron Elliot – it was The Beatles' track Revolution.

From early on the Rock Radio jocks and producers used to sit round a coffee table, trying to come up with wacky ideas that would help sell the station. One of the first belters we came up with (and it's one of the things that people remember the most) was the Five Word Weather. One of the 'suits,' even before we started broadcasting, said: 'We have to do the news and weather together, but I think we should call the news something different. How about the Rock Report? And we need something for the traffic and travel. How about Roads, Rails and Runways. We need a catchy name for the weather too.'

Straight away, somebody piped up, 'Five Word Weather!' It was as simple as that. Some of the laughs we had with that were brilliant: 'It's pure pishin' doon again!' 'It's a smashin' day today!' So many people used to count the words; and, yes, sometimes it was more that five. Then they'd phone up and say, 'Ah! I got ye!' I even used to get email suggestions. One guy sent in a cracker one cold winter morning – 'Brass monkeys have fallen off!'

Jay Crawford hadn't done any rock shows for a while. For the first few months, when we were building our playlists, I'd go in with Metallica, Guns N' Roses, Iron Maiden, Soundgarden, Nirvana, Peal Jam and so on. Jay, who'd lost touch a bit with the rock scene, wasn't convinced those bands would be good on the radio. He was fine with Led Zeppelin, but Metallica were a different prospect. I had to fight quite hard to keep the station from becoming too lightweight. I'm glad to say I won him over in the end. I like to keep up to date with bands that are even coming through right now – rock is always evolving.

Jay told me he wanted daily features on my show, so I came back with the idea that listeners could get to choose a playlist. People could pick three songs and we'd play them at noon – and nothing too obscure unless it was sandwiched between well-known tracks. We had to make it worth their while, so I asked Jay if we could afford to give away a Rock Radio t-shirt to whoever got their pick.

Later that day I bumped into Gavin, the station sales manager. He asked me, 'What is it they call you after all your years on radio?'

'Quite a few things,' I said, 'Some people call me The Godfather of Rock.'

Gavin said, 'Why don't you name your feature after that? The winner can be Godfather or Godmother of Rock for the day.' So we tried it, and it stuck. It became one of the station's most popular features.

Another of the wee ideas we came up was called Rockin' All Over The World. I'd invite any listener who was going on holiday to take a photograph wearing a rock t-shirt, preferably a Rock Radio t-shirt. But it had to be somewhere interesting – in front of the Eiffel Tower or something. The winners would go on the station website. (It was before the big days of Facebook.) There was a cracker that came in from St Petersburg in Russia: a guy was standing in this huge square holding a Rock Radio car sticker. Radio Clyde had used car stickers very effectively back in the seventies and eighties, so I'd suggested the same for us, and it really took off. You still see cars going around with Rock Radio stickers today.

The atmosphere at the station was amazing. All these marketing ideas came out of a real desire by the whole team to raise the station up as high as we could. We were all genuinely proud to be there. Some ideas would come from chatting round that coffee table. Others would just pop into your head.

I was down south in a pub one time where there was karaoke, but with a live band rather than just a backing track. I thought, 'How could we use that?' Back in Glasgow we found a karaoke place that was also an Indian restaurant, down by the helicopter pad near the SECC. We couldn't get a band sorted – but we did put on some successful nights there. We couldn't make up our minds whether to call it 'rockaoke' or 'curryoke' but the name didn't matter. It was great fun, and the more the beer flowed, the funnier it was. Some of the guys trying to hit the Bon Scott, Meat Loaf and Robert Plant notes were just priceless.

I used to get the big artists to record a wee liner for me when they came into the studio – you know, 'Hi, this is Ozzy Osbourne here. You're listening to the man who rocks Glasgow... Tom Russell!' Or Bruce Dickinson from Iron Maiden saying, 'You're listening to Tom Russell on Rock Radio.' Some of them were game for a laugh: Gene Simmons said, in his big deep voice. 'This is Gene Simmons from Kiss, and I'm sitting here next to a nude Tom Russell, and you're listening to him on the radio!' ... some of these, you can hear on my website: tomrussellrocks.com

Our sales rep Angela would take our wacky ideas and turn them into something that could make the station a few quid. She had a chat with Paradise Crazy Golf at Braehead, so we ran a competition over a few days and took prize winners for a few rounds. It was Tom's team against Ted Rock's team. It was great interaction for the listeners, it was good fun for the presenters, we made some money for the station, and it was good advertising for the Paradise crazy golf. A win, win, win, win!

We did the same thing with paintballing, once at East Kilbride and once at Cumbernauld. Listeners won prizes and we divided into different teams. Billy Rankin took a slagging at the Cumbernauld event when he refused to change into overalls for the paintballing. He said he was only there to present the prizes – the big fearty!

And there was our long-time advertising arrangement with SJ at Snooks in Barrhead. We did a Christmas party in June, the whole shebang, with muggins here as Santa Claus, handing out the presents. Tinsel, a tree, Christmas music, all in June. Wacky, but great fun. We also did the Legend at Lunchtime with Snooks on air – the first person to identify a band from a series of clues, won a meal for two.

For Rockin' or Shockin' we'd play a brand-new song and listeners would text in with their opinion. The Bit that Rocked gave people the chance to win a wee bit of rock for being first to identify a snippet of a song. We had Rock Times, the day in rock news for years gone by, and Rock Buzz, covering what was happening at that moment. Septembeer gave people the chance to win a crate of beer every day of the month, and that was followed by Rocktober, with prizes given away an all thirty-one days.

The Tuesday Takeovers were very successful. We'd have an artist choose around twenty songs and talk about why they'd selected them. A lot of the results were fascinating – there's a list at the back of this book.

I'd kept lots of the memorabilia, posters and displays from my record shops, so when we got our studio I brought some in, and so did the other DJs. Someone brought in a tailor's dummy, which we dressed in a Rock Radio t-shirt, a red wig, green wellies, a green hat and a pair of skiing goggles. He looked wonderful. Soon the whole studio was covered. We fought a daily battle with the 'suits' to keep it all in place. Their excuse was the memorabilia 'caused audio interference.' A lot of shite! But many of the big stars who visited would often comment on the decor – Meat Loaf, Slash, Alter Bridge, Alice Cooper, Airbourne, Dream Theater, Halestorm and Thunder all complimented our studio, saying it made them feel more comfortable.

I kept spinning the songs on Rock Radio and interviewing the greats – and now I began to enjoy a new lease of life at the rock festivals. There was a band called Papa Roach playing Sonisphere one year. I hadn't seen them live before. Last Resort was a huge single for them and they were fairly high up the bill, maybe third from top. It's really hard to balance the time watching artists with the time you spent talking to them, but Papa Roach was one of the bands I wanted to see. I was blown away. They were fantastic.

I did an interview with the singer, Jacoby Shaddix, A very distinctive guy who wore black eyeliner. When I walked in he said, 'Are you from Scotland, man? Do you know our buddy, Donald McLeod?'

'Yeah, I know Donald,' I said. 'I've known him for thirty years. He used to come into my record shop as a kid.'

With a big grin, Jacoby said, 'You tell Donald the next time you see him that he's a bastard! We've only ever cancelled one show, and it was his fault.'

'Why's that?'

'We played Glasgow and Donald was the promoter. After the gig he invited took us to the Cathouse for a "couple of drinks." We ended up rat-arsed at three in the morning, with Donald still going strong. We were all so ill that we never saw any of the next day. We were supposed to play Newcastle but there was no way we could even walk on stage, never mind play.' I passed on the band's regards to Donald the next time I saw him.

As I told Jacoby, Donald used to come into my Bishopbriggs shop about once a week as sixteen-year-old. He was in a band called First Priority for while. After some years he appeared on the scene again when, along with a few others, he opened the Cathouse.
Donald was one of the guests at the Rock Radio launch party and he got up to make a speech. He was always a bit of a bear. He started up, sounding a bit like Billy Connolly, saying, 'This is gonna be fucking great. I see Dan McCafferty from Nazareth, I see Ted McKenna, I see the local MP and I see Tam Russell there. Hello, Tam! You're lookin' cool. I remember Tam used to have a record shop in Bishopbriggs.

'He had a bloke called Allan working in that shop. Me and Allan were in the same class at school and I never liked the guy. One day I went into the record shop and he was cheeky to me. Tom wasn't there, so I kicked Allan's cunt in!'

Everyone was decking themselves – but a few of the 'suits' were a bit taken aback, thinking, 'Is what Rock Radio's going to be about? Bad language?'

Donald is always a good laugh; one of the real characters on the scene that I'm proud to know. (The wee ditty he composed for the start of this book was too good to leave out.)

One of the bands who always make me laugh are Steel Panther. They have a wonderful sense of humour. I heard the song Death To All But Metal then saw them in Glasgow before doing an interview with all four of them in their dressing room. I don't usually like doing an interview with a full band – you end up jumping all over the place with the microphone. Steel Panther were very professional however, and I joined in with the fun rather than trying to rein things back in.

At one point I asked, 'Well, being so successful now, how long is the queue of girls waiting to meet you after a gig?'

Singer Michael Starr said, 'Last night in Newcastle, I had seventeen. What about you, Satchel?' Most of the rest was totally unfit for broadcast. Their single at the time was Community Property, so I asked, 'Which one of you came up with the lyric "my dong is community property"?' Again they all joined in; but again it was unfit for broadcast.

That reminds me of Poison's song Unskinny Bop. I interviewed them a few times and I always found singer Brett Michaels an extremely affable, friendly guy. When I asked Brett about the lyrics he laughed and admitted that it had been written about guitarist CC Deville, who, at a band video shoot, had become very friendly in the back of the tour bus with one of the more rounded catering ladies. Hence the title.

As a rock jock you can be asked to do all sorts of things. When I had the lunchtime show on Rock Radio, I was contacted by a young lady – let's call her Lindsay. She wanted to a look round Rock Towers, our studio. As an added inducement, Lindsay said she'd always wanted a tattoo of my lips... kissing her arse. Of course, I agreed.

When the great day arrived, Lindsay, her husband John, and various members of her family appeared at the station. I was still on air as they plastered my lips with bright red lipstick and placed me in the ready position. Lindsay, with her man holding her hand, dropped her drawers and bent over the mixing desk. I very cautiously, kissed her left cheek, leaving the red lipstick marks. Great hilarity ensued as the drawers were carefully pulled back up, then the whole family headed off to Coatbridge, where a tattoo artist had been briefed. He did a fine job, and from that day on, Lindsay has proudly gone about her daily life with my bright red lips tattooed on her backside.

I'd never got round to getting a tattoo myself, but that gave me the notion. One afternoon after my show, I headed to a tattoo parlour in Partick that had been recommended to me. It took half an hour to have the Rock Radio logo put on my left arm, where it still has pride of place. People said, 'What happens if the station closes, or you get sacked?' My reply was that the station had been a huge part of my life and I'd be proud of my tat, no matter what.

A few months later I met the artist who'd tattooed Lindsay's bum. He had a look at my arm and offered to improve my ink. It was risky, but the result was excellent and I'm still proud of it.

18. CAN'T WIN 'EM ALL

Mick Hucknall ~ Dave Mustaine ~ Tom Petty ~ Courtney Love ~ and the brighter side of the job

Not every interview is a dream come true. I've had the odd sticky moment in my time. I'm often asked, 'Who's the worst person you've ever had to interview? What are these big stars really like?'

Well, the answer to 'what are they like?' is that they have their ups and downs, the same as the rest of us. They're normal people that happen to play in a rock band. Now, pop people... some of those guys are a different breed.

My boss at Clyde once said, 'Tom, we have the offer of an interview with Mick Hucknall of Simply Red. Could you go down to London and and sort it out?' As usual it was the BA shuttle to Heathrow, collection in a taxi and a journey to a hotel. I went in, got a sandwich, and after an hour it was my turn. I walked into a plush room and found the great man sitting in wait.

A girl from the record company said, 'Fifteen minutes, okay, Tom?' Then she turned to Mick and told him, 'This is Tom Russell from Radio Clyde in Glasgow.' He looked away and shrugged his shoulders.

We did the interview, but it was uncomfortable. I don't think I was screwing things up with my questions; he was just uninterested. To be fair, he'd probably done ten interviews already that day with a lot of the same questions.

Now, if you do an interview with Jon Bon Jovi, and it's his tenth interview of the day, it would go something like: 'Hi Jon. This new album, how pleased are you with it?' Jon would smile and get stuck in with a hundred and ten percent enthusiasm. He's fully aware that what he's doing is selling his product. He's been given an opportunity to talk about his album to more than a hundred thousand potential buyers. That's part of the game.

Mick, however, sat there, uninterested and non-responsive. At the end I still said, 'Thanks very much for the interview.' He just grunted, stood up, and walked over to the window, (which looked out over Kensington Palace, home of Princess Diana). That was me dismissed.

At the end of my interviews I tend to put people into one of two categories: great and not-so-great. Dave Grohl is a perfect example of the first category. I talked to him once in Edinburgh when he was playing with Them Crooked Vultures at the Corn Exchange. Josh Homme, also of Queens Of The Stone Age, was sitting reading a book in one corner and John Paul Jones, of Led Zeppelin, was in the other corner strumming a guitar.

Dave is the most genuinely interested guy you could wish to meet. At the end of the interview, you reach over and you press 'stop' on the tape recorder. With Dave, the conversation carries on. This time John and Josh joined in too. They were asking, 'What's the Scottish rock scene like at the moment – any bands we should be looking out for?'
Josh piped up, 'Last time we played Glasgow the support band was so-and-so and the drummer was fantastic. What's he doing just now?'

John Paul Jones asked about this and that too. The conversation carried on for another fifteen minutes until the tour manager said, 'Sorry guys, but we need you for soundcheck.'

Dave turned to me and said, 'Enjoy the show, Tom, and pop backstage for a beer afterwards. Point out all my mistakes.'

Josh shouted over, 'There'll be plenty of them!'

It was four rock fans sitting in a room talking about where the music was heading. Some of the biggest rock stars are actually the biggest rock fans. Nice, down-to-earth, real people.

I interviewed Tom Petty once. He has the reputation of not suffering fools gladly and doesn't particularly like doing interviews. In 1989 MCA Record flew me to London to talk to talk about his album Full Moon Fever. In another posh hotel we were taken into the interview room one at a time. The girl from the record company said, 'Don't ask him this. Don't ask him that. Don't upset him.'

I was thinking, 'I'll ask him what I ask him – if he doesn't like it, fuck him. Who does he think he is? I've come all the way down from Glasgow to interview him, yes, to make my show better, but also to plug his album.'

So I went in, pretty much ready for a fight… but it was all, 'Scotland, Glasgow, yes! Nice to meet you!' You couldn't have met a more co-operative guy. He talked about I Won't Back Down, Runnin' Down A Dream and Free Fallin, with no problems whatsoever. We talked about his time with the Travelling Wilburys, working with Roy Orbison, George Harrison and Jeff Lynne. It was a joy. It just shows you – sometimes you get all these warnings and the artist turns out to be brilliant.

Courtney Love wasn't brilliant. Her record company wanted me to interview her band Hole (who were never that big and possibly trading on her name as Kurt Cobain's widow a bit). Her management wanted a list of the questions in advance. I said, 'I don't know what I'm going to ask her yet.'

The record company girl said, 'They're insistent. You're allowed twenty questions and they'll decide the ones you can ask and the ones you can't.'

As calmly as I could, I replied, 'I've interviewed Robert Plant, Angus Young, Jon Bon Jovi, Axl Rose, Elton John, Ozzy Osbourne...I've never been asked to submit questions in advance.'

She said, 'I quite understand, Tom. I'll ask them again, and get back to you tomorrow.' They came back the next day with the same pish, so I declined the interview. That was one of the few times I ever did that; but I thought it was the thin end of the wedge. I thought, 'If they're starting to do this, what next? Where does it go? Record companies giving you a typed sheet with the questions to ask?' I still think I was right, and I've never been asked to submit my questions in advance since.

Switching back, I'd have to cite Chad Kroeger of Nickelback as one of the true professionals. I think they're are a good pop-rock band, similar in a way to Bon Jovi. The rock snobs (of which there are a few) sometimes snub them, calling them shite. I don't think that way. They have a very distinctive sound and they write good songs and put on an entertaining live show. And Chad has a great sense of humour: he tells funny stories. I've interviewed them three times, and each time it's been an absolute pleasure.

I really liked Jethro Tull back in the day and I enjoyed playing their tracks on the radio. I'd say their later material wasn't as strong as it was back in the seventies – Aqualung is still my favourite Tull album.
When I was working in London, we all got invited to a barbecue at Ian Anderson's place, a lovely old farmhouse in Berkshire with a bit of land. The only problem was Ian himself. He's an alright guy, but I find him a bit difficult to talk to at times. Maybe it's just me? The last time I interviewed him was probably 2009. It was actually on the phone and he was a bit more relaxed that time.

Dave Mustaine, the leader of Megadeth who was first in Metallica, is sometimes a bit difficult. I've probably interviewed him ten times over the years; he can have a twinkle in his eye one moment, then the next he'll hit you with some awkward answers.

Sometimes you have to ask a question you already know the answer to, because you're making a radio programme. You'll say something like, 'The new album's out next month, Dave – can you tell us a bit about it?'

Instead of taking the chance to sell the album, he might come back with, 'Why? What do you want to know?'

'Can you tell me the title?' I'm there with the CD in my hand. I know what the title is; I just want the artist to tell the listeners.

Dave might say, 'You know the title. You've got a copy right there.' Sometimes he's like that. Other times he's fine.

Every time I got a new Megadeth album it would disappear. I'd go to pick it up from my desk at home to take it into the radio station, and it wouldn't be there. 'Neil! Megadeth album?'

'Sorry, Dad!'

I'd got Dave to do a wee autograph, 'To Neil' on something, which he loved. He was about eighteen by this time, and Megadeth were playing the Barrowland. I said, 'Do you want to come to the interview and meet Dave?'

Neil is thinking, 'Maybe my dad isn't an arsehole after all… this is cool.'

So I took him along – but I said, 'Look, no gushing. Just sit and wait quietly and you can get a photograph after.'

As soon as I walked in I could tell Dave was in one of his moods. I did the interview, but it really was hard work. It was doubly hard because I was struggling with a guy that my son actually worshipped. On reflection I should have just got up and left, but I was trying to be professional.

After the interview was finished I introduced Neil and said, 'I know everyone tells you this – but he's a big fan. He pinches all your albums from me and comes to all your concerts. Would you mind if I take a picture of the two of you?'

'Hmm…' Dave grunted.

Neil came over and I introduced them, 'Neil Russell – Dave Mustaine.'

Again: 'Hmm…'

I took my picture anyway. Neil was awestruck and didn't pick up on the atmosphere too much, thank God. But the whole thing was just a bit sad. That's the reason that, a few years ago, Megadeth were playing at a festival but I didn't even bother asking for an interview. It got me uptight thinking about it and I had another thirty interviews to worry about. But Danielle from the record company came up to me and said, 'Tom, you're not down to see Dave. I've got a slot free at three-fifteen.'

I said, 'To be perfectly honest, I didn't enjoy the last one. You know what he's like – it was really hard work. I could only use about half of it last time.' She persisted and I said, 'Okay.'
But I was dreading it.

I went backstage to the dressing room at my allotted time and Dave looked up and said, 'Hi, Tom. How are you doing?'

I got my microphone out and I'm thinking, 'Fuck it.' So I said, 'I hope you're in a better mood than the last time we met.'

He said, 'Oh… yeah.'

'Yeah. What was all that about?'

He said, 'I'll tell you what it was all about. I flew in the night before. Practically no sleep. I had a pinched nerve in my shoulder and I was on painkillers. Sorry about that.'

I shook his hand, and we sat down and did a great interview.

At the top end of my adventure list is the time I was asked to go to Mike Rutherford's house, when he was doing his Mike and the Mechanics project with Paul Carrack. A few years earlier I'd been approach by Genesis's record label and I agreed to interview them. Even they found it difficult to get mainstream airplay in those days. Phil Collins and Mike came to the studio, live on the Friday night; they were pleasant and mischievous, and we had a great chat. Not just about their band, but about rock music in general.

So I flew down south and I was picked up at Heathrow and chauffeured to Mike's house. We listened to his new songs in the studio in his barn. It was also the Genesis studio, where they rehearsed and recorded. One of the songs really stuck out: The Living Years. I was probably one of the first media people to hear it. Then we had lunch in Mike's dining room, and I'm sitting pinching myself, thinking, 'This is bizarre. Wonderful, but bizarre.'

I must have interviewed Alice Cooper six or seven times over the years. Down south, at the Edinburgh Playhouse, in the studio, in Glasgow itself; I've even interviewed him in America, in Philadelphia, when I was with the video magazine. We went over to cover a show in a huge sports arena with Alice, Judas Priest and Motorhead. (That was the time Alice tried to get me to put his snake round my neck, and I politely declined.)

It's well known that Alice plays a lot of golf, but he doesn't like talking about it. In interviews he'll there's nothing off-limits in terms of music and touring, but he's not keen on chatting about golf. Maybe it would dilute his wild rock image – fair enough, I suppose.
I last met him in 2011 was when he was promoting his Welcome 2 My Nightmare album. He came in to Rock Radio, on his own, to record an interview. No big fuss. We walked through the studio complex together and no one batted an eyelid. No one realised the guy with Tom was a rock legend! We played the single, I'll Bite Your Face Off, a lot on the station, but my favourite track on that album was the epic I Am Made Of You.

Recently, Alice has been recording and touring with Johnny Depp and Joe Perry as a member of the 'Hollywood Vampires'. That's a gig I'd like to see.

Another guy who came into Rock Towers alone, without a minder or a promo person, was Tom Morello from Rage Against The Machine and Audioslave. Again, when I met him at reception and escorted him through the building into the studio, no one turned a hair; no one had a clue who he was.

Tom has a degree from Harvard and he's right into politics as well as music. So before the interview, I asked my son Neil, who was studying for his masters in politics at the time, if he could suggest any interesting questions for Tom. After bringing up his Harvard days, I added 'Can you tell me Tom, do you think economic development leads to democratisation?' He burst out laughing and said that these days, he was more into political activism than academic questions. It was probably just as well, as I barely understood what the question meant to follow on from it. When the interview was over, he was happy to sit for a while, off air, just chatting about music and the state of the world. Then to cap it off, he played me an acoustic song live in the studio, which I recorded.

When I think of bands that really got me excited early on in my career, I have to mention Cream. The only band I was ever in had been named after their track Strange Brew. I still play their album Fresh Cream and I continue to appreciate the raw energy that a top class three-piece can produce.
My first record shop was in Bishopbriggs, and that's where Cream bass player Jack Bruce came from. He was only around sixteen when he moved to London and played with: John Mayall, Alexis Korner, Steam Packet and the like. He then did the whole Cream thing and then, after everything had died down, he worked on solo albums for years.

In 1994 I got another of those calls, from Virgin in this case, asking me to come to London and interview a band they'd signed. They were named BBM after members Jack Bruce, Ginger Baker and Gary Moore. Obviously a great lineup, and they made a class album in Around The Next Dream. I'd met Gary a few times, so when I sat down with him and Jack there was a wee bit of recognition. With Jack it was, 'Glasgow? Where are you from?' so there was a wee bit of connection there too. The interview was standard enough and I saw them at the Barrowland a few months later – an excellent gig.

I always loved Van Halen's raw bass, drums and guitar sound; and of course they had David Lee Roth, the frontman who carried them on to greater heights. I never got to interview David when he was with Van Halen, but I did when he released his solo stuff, Eat 'Em and Smile' and then Skyscraper. What a character – totally over the top, overpowering and yet so likeable. He was great fun to interview.
I remember him telling me that he was excited about the Skyscraper sleeve. I only had the white label, but he said, 'Wait till you see the

cover! I flew down to South America and went up this mountain with a cameraman. I hung off some precarious precipices and he took some shots. It's all real, Tom… it's all real!'

When I saw the finished album sleeve, I wondered if it was actually a staged shot. But then again, the power and the energy of the guy lead me to believe that the pictures are legit.
David is larger than life and a hard act to follow, so when Sammy Hagar stepped into the breach, I wasn't so sure it would work. It did – but in a different way. I still prefer the original lineup though. (I don't understand why, when David got back together with Van Halen, they never came over to the UK. There must be a huge following here, even now.)

19. SCREAM SENSATIONS AND BALLAD BOYS

From Bruce Dickinson and Brian Johnson to Extreme and Foreigner ~ reflections on fame ~ David Coverdale, Robert Plant ~ a go-kart race

Stadium shows aren't my favourite kind of gigs. You can find yourself looking at a wee dot in the distance, without much atmosphere. but I've seen some of the greats at Hampden, Ibrox and Parkhead – and Parkhead is where I saw Extreme one time in 1992.

I'd interviewed them previously, first when their album Pornograffitti came out. Get the Funk Out – good song. My interview was with guitarist Nuno Bettencourt and we just hit it off. He autographed one of his signature guitars for me; I've still got it.

After More than Words had become a worldwide smash, they came to Parkhead, supporting Bryan Adams. Despite my stadium concerns, Extreme nailed it. I happened to get Nuno for that day's interview. The sad thing was that after More than Words a lot of rock fans turned their backs on them: 'You're a sell-out… you had a hit!' It wasn't their fault people liked the song! And of course the pop fans who'd bought it moved on to the next thing five minutes later.

Gary Cherone, their singer, went on to join Van Halen, and Nuno did some solo work as well as production. He formed a band with Perry Farrell of Jane's Addiction called Satellite Party, who played Download in 2007. I interviewed them both and Nuno told me he was happy and busy, and he'd even done a couple of pop tours, which paid the bills.

Next time I heard of him he was playing the SECC, with pop star Rihanna. I thought Nuno would be perfect for a Rock Radio Tuesday Takeover – but Fergie, my producer, said, 'Nuno who?' Fergie wasn't a huge rock fan, but he was a great producer. I explained who he was and it soon became The Extreme Tuesday Takeover.

The next problem was that Nuno refused, explaining that all interviews on the tour had to be done by Rihanna. I told him, 'I'm not interested in her in the least. What I'm looking for is for you to pick twelve of your favourite songs and tell me about them.' We did the whole recording at the SECC and it was a excellent selection. We've included a few of the artist Tuesday Takeover selections at the back of the book.

Gary Cherone came back from Van Halen and Extreme returned to Glasgow in 2009. I contacted Nuno and he asked me to come along. (By this time record companies no longer existed the way they used to – for all those years at Clyde, I'd have to phone the label and ask for an interview, or perhaps they'd approach me. That was almost gone.)

We did the interview in the Carling Academy dressing room. Just as we finished, Gary came in and Nuno said, 'Hey Tom, you know Gary, don't you?'

I said, 'No, I've never met him.' Nuno was shocked. I told him, 'Over all these years I've always been landed with you.' He laughed, 'No luck, Tom!'

Gary was very easy to talk to; we chatted away for a few minutes before the guys went for their soundcheck. The gig was excellent as usual – but the support band, Hot Leg, who were led by Justin Hawkins of The Darkness fame, went down like a lead balloon with the Extreme audience.

So many American lead singers seem to be able to reach those crazy high notes. Is it the weather out there? The genes? Lou Gramm of Foreigner is an example: in songs like Juke Box Hero and Urgent he really goes for it. (Lou, who released his solo album Midnight Blue in 1987, is another decent bloke to interview but I met him only once.)

Mick Jones, the leader of Foreigner, kept the band on an even keel after Lou left. The current singer, Kelly Hanson is also a great frontman. As you can imagine, not many people out there could fill Lou's shoes vocally.

I Wanna Know What Love Is and Waiting for a Girl Like You are probably the tracks the'll be remembered for most, but they had so many other great rock tracks too. Cold as Ice, Feels Like the First Time, Hot Blooded... But when they were at their peak there was little chance of a rock band getting mainstream airplay. So record companies would push bands like them to write a ballad. It also happened with Extreme, Journey, Heart, Styx and REO Speedwagon. 'Get a ballad out there, rake in the bucks' – but potentially lose credibility with the rock fans. It's a gamble.

You could argue that all those high-voiced American rockers are trying to emulate the British singers like Robert Plant. One of my favourites to this day is Bruce Dickinson of Iron Maiden. He's an interesting guy. I first met him when he was still in Samson, who were with Polydor. I met him later on at Donington, at the Monsters of Rock Festival. He wasn't even playing that day, but it had just been announced that he was to be the new singer in Maiden and that they were recording an album called The Number of the Beast.

I was in the backstage area and I saw the bold Bruce sitting on his own. Nobody was bothering him, because very few people knew who he was yet. I went up, re-introduced myself, and asked him to do a few minutes on the mic. We must have ended up doing forty minutes. He was loving it – it was all still new for him. He told me about his sword-fencing, his pilot's licence; all that stuff. As the years went on I interviewed Bruce quite a few times. He's one of these guys who's totally multi-talented. But, most of all he's one of the best rock singers ever.

Sometime vocalists are born here and then end up somewhere else. A lot of people people still don't know that Bon Scott was actually born in Scotland. Everyone knows Angus and Malcolm Young were brought up in Cranhill, Glasgow before heading off to Australia as kids. Bon was from Kirriemuir. There's a photo of a painting of the Young's house at: tomrussellrocks.com

I only met Bon once, at the Apollo, but I've interviewed Brian Johnson, his replacement, and Angus, four times. I'm sure Angus told me that Bon didn't actually play bagpipes in the local pipe band, but played drums instead. The first time I spoke to Angus I asked him about the schoolboy outfit and the satchel. 'That was my sister,' he told me. 'Right back in the early days she decided I should wear a school uniform; shorts, socks, blazer, shirt, tie and cap. Later, she even brought a satchel home, which she'd bought in a local shop for me. So, it's all her fault!'

Angus was one of the first to fully utilise a cordless guitar. I reckon he may have put the electronics in that satchel back then. I still remember him duck-walking round the balcony of the Glasgow Apollo, soloing like crazy, with no guitar lead!

AC/DC drummer Chris Slade once put a band together with Chris Glen of The Sensational Alex Harvey Band, and they did a show at Oran Mor in Glasgow. This was before he rejoined Angus and the boys. The Chris Slade Timeline played a few songs, then he came forward and told some of his stories. He'd played with Tom Jones in the sixties, then with Manfred Mann's Earth Band when they had the hit Blinded by the Light. He also drummed with Frankie Miller, The Firm, Uriah Heep, Dave Gilmour, Gary Numan and Asia. He also played to four hundred thousand people in Rio with AC/DC. To hit that bass drum and have so many people feel your power in the pit of their stomachs must have been fantastic. It was a fascinating night in Oran Mor. Earlier in the day, Chris put on a drum clinic at a Glasgow drum store called Rhythm Base, and my pal Chris Glen invited me along to compere. I did a wee interview and chatted away, taking questions from the audience and so on. Being up close to this small, bald guy with glasses, and then later feeling the sound he got from his kit, was unbelievable… A few months later, Chris got a call from Australia and he was back in AC/DC.

Slash is a great guy to interview. He's so open. I suppose he's made a bob or two and he lives in LA. I still have great memories of all the cars I saw on Sunset Strip during my Rick Rubin trip, I once asked Slash what kind of car he drove.

'Why do you ask?' he said.

'I just thought it might be interesting for the listeners.'

'The reason I'm asking,' he said, 'Is that on Friday last week, I took delivery of my new car.'

'So what did you get?'

'The same as I got last time,' he said. 'A different colour, bigger engine, slightly updated Aston Martin.'

The James Bond car! I'm trying to imagine Slash sitting in this thing, the pinnacle of English refinement. At that time the new F-Type Jaguar had just come out, so I said, 'The Aston Martin is lovely, but I've always been a fan of Jaguars. Would you not fancy one of those, Slash?'

He said, 'I had a look, but I'm an Aston Martin man, through and through.'

Open, natural, easygoing – a great interviewee.

It's funny how people outside the business have a certain image of an artist. Part of it is internal, but part of it is reading interviews and seeing them on TV. Thirty years ago you would never see David Coverdale on your screen. (Things changed when MTV kicked off.) So my image of him, before I met him, came mainly from written interviews – and it was a bit negative. He didn't seem to be especially loved by the London journalists. After I met him, I was totally surprised by that. He's always polite, well-spoken, and generous with the information and time he gives me. He's a Yorkshire man who developed a bit of a 'hello darling' posh voice. Whether that pissed some people off, who knows? It's just a persona he developed. In every interview I've done with David he's always friendly, and even flirtatious. Not with me, but with any female company that happens to be about.

I took my then-wife to one of his record launches. What a ladykiller – a handsome man with good manners. He smiled and kissed the back of her hand. 'Well, hello darling…' That kind of thing. She, of course, melted.

In 1990, when I was working with Hard'n'Heavy video magazine, Whitesnake were headlining Monsters Of Rock at Donington, along with Aerosmith and Poison in support. We usually went down the day before the festival to do the interviews, with the bands all lined up in a schedule. On this occasion it got to six o'clock on the Friday evening, our allotted slot with Whitesnake, but the record company said, 'He's running late. Can you make it 6.30?' Then it was, 'Ah – can you make it seven?' He was the headline act so we waited politely. You just accept it. You just wait. When it got to seven-thirty, the record company said, 'We're going to have to blow this out. He's been running late all day. We're really sorry.'

You can kick up hell and get the reputation of being an arse, or you can just say, 'Ach well. Shit happens.' I actually said, 'I don't suppose there's any chance of getting something with David tomorrow – on the actual day?'

'Tom, you're on tae plums,' was the reply from EMI rep Steve. 'David doesn't do interviews on the day. One, to protect his voice, and two, to relax. He's going to be performing in front of a hundred thousand people.' He added: 'But I'll ask the question.'

When I bumped into Steve the next day he said, 'I don't know what swing you've got – but I asked the question and David said, "Yes, Seeing that it's Tom." He was full of apologies about last night. He just wanted to eat and then get to bed, with Tawny.' His then-wife, Tawny Kitaen, was a charming American girl who seemed to quite fancy me, or perhaps that was just my imagination. Still, who could blame David?

At six o'clock we were the only interview of the day. David, who was sitting with guitarist Steve Vai, said, 'Tom, it's lovely to see you. Sorry for keeping you waiting last night. There was Spanish TV and then the BBC, and Tawny was giving me grief about wanting to get back to the hotel. How long do you need? Sit down. Have a beer.'

To me, that was the measure of the man. He didn't need to do that. But he did.

I don't often take someone along to meet one of the rock legends. I feel it's imposing. But my son Neil is well into the music and there was someone I wanted him to meet, so I broke my own rule with Robert Plant. Robert loves Scotland – he'd often tell me how he wrote this track or that track when he was in Oban, Fort William or Thurso.
Robert was due to play at the Barrowland and when he came in for an interview, I asked the tour manager for two tickets. I'd rather be invited

backstage than try to blag my way in, but this time I said, 'Is there any chance we could say hello to at the end of the show?'

The tour manager told us to hang on until everyone was away. But hanging back when the bouncers are telling everyone to get out isn't easy. I explained that I was waiting to see Robert.

'Have you got a backstage pass?' a bouncer asked.

'Naw…'

'Well, shift.'

'Aye, but the tour manager's coming back out to get us.'

'Have you got a backstage pass?' he persisted.

I had to say 'no' again – but luckily, just as we were about to be physically ejected, the tour manager appeared and flashed his badge. 'They're with me.'

He stood us right in front of the stage and brought Robert out. Neil was delighted. Robert was charming as usual. 'Nice to meet you, Neil, did you enjoy the show?' Neil and Robert then chatted away, firstly about Robert's son, who had taken up music, busking on the streets of Cardiff. 'Does he play your music?' Neil asked.

'I hope not' came the reply. 'He plays Jeff Buckley mostly. Jeff fucking Buckley!'

Before turning to leave, Robert looked at Neil and said, 'Hey Kid. Remember this. Life is like a box of chocolates. You never know what you're gonna' get. Just make sure you have a good time living it.' A great moment. (People don't always realise that the artist's head is still buzzing after a show. They're drenched in sweat. They need an hour to chill.)

Iron Maiden always put on the best album launches. Manager Rod Smallwood is always generous – no expense spared. I think the launch I'm thinking of here was for Powerslave, in 1984. We were flown to London, picked up and taken to a nice hotel. We had interviews all day, and then, about thirty of us piled into a bus. (Remember, there weren't that many outlets on radio for Maiden airplay in those days.)

We were taken to bass player Steve Harris's house for the party. He's a huge West Ham fan and he still plays football himself; in fact, there's an Iron Maiden football team and a Def Leppard football team. Steve had a football pitch, a tennis court and a barn beside his house that had been converted into a pub. It was like MacSorley's in Glasgow: a proper pub with jukebox, pool table, loads of different beers and whiskies. What a night that was...

A few years later, when Maiden singer Bruce Dickinson released his solo album Tattooed Millionaire, EMI invited us to a launch party in London. After the reception, we all went to a go-kart track. Johnnie Walker of Radio 1 was there – he has great style on radio, but he came third in the tournament and he wasn't very happy because he's a very competitive guy. Of course, Bruce was one step ahead of everyone and ended up winning the thing. I'm pleased to say that your old Uncle Tom came second. I have a photo of Bruce and me on the winner's rostrum.

Tom at full draw

Two of Biffy Clyro

Alice comes into Rock Radio for a chat

The Two Rivers Festival - It's a hard job sometimes

Father and Son at Download

David Grohl of the Foo Fighters

The Download stage before the gates opened

Five Finger Death Punch at a Secret Session

Geezer Butler of Back Sabbath

Meat Loaf in his Glasgow hotel room

Lindsay about to get Tom's lipstick on her bum before her tattoo

Myles Kennedy from Alterbridge

Rock Radio paint balling day

Airbourne at King Tuts

Listener wins AC/DC tickets by kissing Tom's bare arse on air

Slash

20. THE WALL

More tips for blagging interviews ~ life backstage ~ my favourite shows ever ~ Aerosmith, Avenged Sevenfold, Rammstein, SAHB, The Who

Despite the 'big wall' around the huge rock acts, I've sometimes managed to get a wee interview in here and there. In 1994 I was at the Monsters of Rock festival and Aerosmith were headlining – but the record company didn't want any interviews the night that the band were playing. I was working backstage, interviewing bands lower down the bill when I saw this guy walking towards me. I thought, 'I saw you the other night at the Marquee.' I would have recognised Joe Perry or Steven Tyler straight away, but I couldn't quite place him, and anyway he was able to stroll around on his own. I thought it must be rhythm guitarist Brad Whitford. We got talking and I told him I'd seen the band play a couple of nights previously at a Marquee warm-up show. I commented on how Aerosmith had brought Jimmy Page on for an encore and he said, 'Yeah, that was special.'

I said, 'Look, I know the record company has said no interviews. but is there any chance five minutes?'

He replied, 'The record company said that, did they? I'll be having words with them. It's no problem at all.'

So we just stood in the middle of the field and did a wee interview. I asked him how three hundred or so at The Marquee compared to 90,000 at Donington. I'll let you decide how he answered that one…

I did interview Steven Tyler when Aerosmith did the TFI Friday show on TV. We spoke in the early afternoon, as TFI Fridays was recorded live between four and six. Up close, Steven looked even more like Mick

Jagger than in the photographs. I just couldn't stop staring at his lips! He was dressed up like a gypsy, with the scarves and stuff.

The last Aerosmith interview I did was with Joe Perry. The album was Nine Lives and the single was Falling In Love Is Hard On The Knees. Joe was in one hotel room and Steven was in another; you just took whichever one you were given. Joe was dead laid-back and cool, 'man'. He said, 'Have a seat, man. You're from Glasgow? Wow!' Sometimes it helped to come from Glasgow – it gave you a bit of an edge. A lot of the American bands love Scotland.

There was also a 'wall' around Avenged Sevenfold when they were given special-guest billing at Download – a billing that caused a bit of controversy. Some people thought they'd got there too early in their career. I wasn't so sure – they'd sold a ton of albums and they were very good live.

As I've said, the managers of a band near the top of the bill might decide 'no interviews.' The rule of thumb is, if a band's on their way up it's 'yes please!' If they're at the top, it's 'no thanks!' Then when they're on their way back down, it's 'yes please!' again. So Avenged Sevenfold's people said 'no thanks,' and I thought, 'Fair enough – there are plenty of people to talk to on their way up.'

Around three in the afternoon, while I was backstage, I bumped into one of the girls from a record company I hadn't seen for a few years. She told me, 'I'm working with Avenged.'
With a wry smile, I said, 'You can't be doing much then. They're not doing any interviews.'

'I know,' she said. 'It's a pain in the arse trying to convince the American management that the band aren't quite household names over here.'

Then she said, 'Tom, do you have your recorder with you?' I did. 'Even the band are complaining about not doing interviews, come with me…'

There are usually three backstage areas at these big festivals. There's one that any Tom, Dick or Harry can get into. There's the one we call the working area, which the journalists, stagehands and up-and-coming bands frequent; and then there's the inner sanctum, reserved for the big acts.

She took me inside the hallowed area and right into the Avenged Sevenfold dressing rooms. She then had a wee word with the guitarist – Synyster Gates. He looked across at me and said, 'Yeah, great!' So we sat down to do the interview – but not before the rep told me not to talk about The Rev, the band's late drummer, who'd died of an overdose the previous year.

During the conversation Synyster himself brought up The Rev. I said, 'Well, it would be nice to toast the man.'

'You're from Scotland, aren't you?' he asked.

I narrowed it down. 'From Glasgow.'

'Are you fond of a whisky?'

'I'm rather fond of a malt.'

He nipped into his dressing room and came out with a bottle of single malt. He poured two large ones while the interview was still running and we toasted The Rev. That's another video that got thousands of hits, and it's still out on YouTube.
https://youtu.be/DF72e42CeDM

I'm often asked about my favourite live performance. I've seen so many great shows, but one stands out from 1976 for so many reasons. The Sensational Alex Harvey Band were at their peak – they remain the best rock band to come out of Scotland by a mile, in my opinion. The Who were also massive at the time: Tommy, Quadrophenia and Who's Next were all terrific albums.

I'm not sure if three UK dates count as a tour, but that's what The Who were doing, and I wanted to be there. Luckily for me, the third date after Charlton and Swansea was at Parkhead in Glasgow. The big sales point was that The Who were going to be using lasers in their light show for the first time. The support lineup included a band called Streetwalkers (formed by Roger Chapman and Charlie Whitney from Family), Little Feat, The Outlaws and The Sensational Alex Harvey Band.

So I got a ticket and went along early. The sun was shining. Everyone was drinking and getting chilled. The first few bands went down okay – but around seven o'clock, SAHB came on stage to thirty thousand people. Alex Harvey had an unbelievable stage presence. He had a wonderful band, but the man himself was just off the scale. He started things off with: 'Good evening boys and girls! My name is Alex Harvey. Let me introduce you to my band: The Sensational Alex Harvey Band!'

I bet a good percentage of the crowd hadn't seen SAHB before. They were there to see The Who. They must have been thinking, 'Who is this guy?' But then the band hit it – and it was totally brilliant. It must have been one of their best shows ever. They owned that stadium. They played for an hour or more and the place went mental. By the time they went off, everyone was buzzing, looking forward to the main event.

We waited. Half an hour went past, then an hour, then an hour and a half. You could actually feel the atmosphere changing. Not everyone's got a car; they're like, 'I've got a bus to catch…' Finally, The Who came on, but instead of. 'Yes! Fantastic!' there was a rumble of discontent. Half the crowd were booing.

The band got started and won the crowd back after the first few songs. Towards the end of their set, though, people were wondering about the amazing laser show they had been promised. Around round ten-thirty, at encore time, right round the top of Parkhead, these wee green lights come on. A few pathetic beams, about six yards long, flickering about for a bit and then they died. And that was it.

What did the Who's promoters forget? Well, you can play in London or Swansea at ten at night, switch on the lasers, and it looks spectacular. But in Scotland, in summertime, and if it's not raining, the sun is still shining at that time. It emerged later that concern over it being too light for the lasers was behind the delay to the start of the set. Bad planning.

When I saw Rammstein at Download, they were absolutely superb – they put on a really entertaining show. Towards the end of their set, their roadies pulled on a big vat of burning oil. Singer Till Lindemann and guitarist Richard Kruspe ran across the stage, grabbed keyboardist Christian Lorenz, lifted him up and dropped him into the vat. Then they each got a massive flame-thrower, and, standing at either side of the stage, they directed them at the vat – and poor wee Christian was roasted alive in the pot!
The crowd was going wild. Ninety thousand people were demanding an encore. About two or three minutes later Rammstein came back; but before they started, their crew appeared in the security pit at the front of the stage.

They'd carried a huge inflatable boat with them, so Till and Richard grabbed Christian again (he was obviously still alive!) and dumped him in the boat. They turned it around and pushed it onto the crowd. Christian sat up, and a paddle miraculously appeared in his hand. He paddled from the front of the stage at Download right back to the mixing desk – probably a hundred yards. Everyone pushed him back over their heads. He went right round the mixing desk and came back, lit up by spotlights all the way.

Some people might say, 'What's that got to do with anything?' I'd respond: 'It's entertainment, it's pantomime, it's fun – it's rock'n'roll.' People sometimes say Germans don't have a sense of humour... if that's true, Rammstein are the exception. Even their lyrics bring a smile to my face. For example: 'You've got a pussy, I have a dick... So what's the problem, let's do it quick!'

From greatest gigs to greatest guitarists... When I joined my one and only band, Strange Brew, I was a budding guitarist, but I never came close to reaching the dizzy heights of some of the people I've seen.

I met Mark Knopfler twice. The first time was early in his career, when Dire Straits' Sultans of Swing was in the charts. I was in Newcastle at a filming of The Tube, the TV series presented by Paula Yates and Jools Holland. I was actually there to interview Bryan Ferry – one of those interviews Clyde asked me to do. It was fascinating to see The Tube being made, and Bryan was a real gent, suave, well-mannered, and surprisingly good fun to talk to. That same day I was introduced to Mark in the green room, and during a wee chat I found out he'd been born in Scotland.

A couple of years later, just as Brothers in Arms hit the streets, I got a proper interview with Mark. I asked him about the track Money for Nothing and he told me he'd been in New York doing some press. Fed up and a bit homesick, he went out for a walk and ended up in a big electrical store, where he overheard two guys moaning away about their lot in life. They were saying, 'We've got to move these colour TVs. We've got to move these refrigerators. This is a shit job!' As they moaned away, the screens in the store were playing a music video. It was someone like David Bowie. 'Look at him,' they continued, 'He gets money for nothing and chicks for free! And look at us...'

I only interviewed Rory Gallagher once, when he played the Glasgow Pavilion. He came into the radio station and he was a lovely, gentle wee guy. I liked him. I went to the Pavilion that night and he was astonishing. What a player; and actually, what a singer. He really nailed that whole blues-rock groove with that beat-up Stratocaster of his. Songs like Shadow Play and Laundromat blew the roof off as he played for two and a half hours. It was so sad to hear that he'd passed away in 1994, at the age of just forty-seven. I believe he'd had a liver transplant and complications set in.

Gary Moore was another great loss. He had a very successful solo career after Thin Lizzy, first with was G-Force and then with his blues-rock period. I interviewed him a few times, but I noticed he changed over the years. The first few times he was shy, but co-operative. As the years went on the shyness increased. I remember asking him what he thought of the new widdly-widdly style of guitar playing by guys like Steve Vai, Joe Satriani and Yngwie Malmsteen. Gary said, 'Tom, I can do that stuff if I want to. I've done it sitting about in the rehearsal studio. But I think you can say more as a guitarist with one note if it's played with feeling and love, than you can with a hundred, if they're just being played to show how technically good you are.'

I last saw him at the High Voltage festival in London in 2010. Emerson, Lake & Palmer were headlining and Gary was playing around tea-time. I asked for an interview but his record company said he wasn't doing any. (Sometimes there's a good reason.) He was back playing rock. He'd had his jazz-rock time with Colosseum II period, then his first rock period and a long blues period heavily influenced by Peter Green. In fact, he owned Peter's 1959 Gibson Les Paul guitar and often played it. At High Voltage he was rocking again, and I loved it.

Maybe two hours after he played, I was rushing backstage to meet Kelly Hanson from Foreigner, and I noticed two guys with someone in between them, who was being carried towards the exit gate. He was out of it and his feet were dragging along the ground. I thought, 'That poor bugger isn't looking so good.' Then I looked again. I'm sure it was Gary.

A few months later, in February 2011, he was found dead in Spain. It was reported that he died of a heart attack in his sleep. He was just fifty-eight.

(Kirk Hammett of Metallica now owns Peter's Les Paul, the very one that Gary played. A massive fan of both Gary Moore and Peter Green, it's reported that Kirk paid around two million dollars for it.)

Queen's Brian May is another unique guitarist. They were quite a heavy band in the early days and I was into tracks like Liar and Ogre Battle. When I was working for Hard'n'Heavy in 1992, Brian had brought out an album called Back to the Light, that included a great track called Resurrection, featuring Cozy Powell and Jimmy Page. I went backstage to meet him after his show at the Hammersmith Odeon, where I met his missus, Anita Dobson – a little bit of me was star-struck to meet Angie from EastEnders.

Last time I interviewed Brian, we didn't talk about music; it was all about animal cruelty. He wanted to discuss the plight of hedgehogs and badgers. I thought, 'Why not?' He's an absolute gentleman.

I once asked him if he still used the guitar he'd built with his dad out of an old mantelpiece. 'Yes,' he replied, 'Not all the time, but as much as I can.' I know his technique is key to his sound – but I wonder how much of it is down to that very unique guitar?

I remember interviewing Yngwie Malmsteen for the Metal Hammer Video Magazine. The cameraman followed us as we walked past guitar shops in Soho, London. I was asking the usual questions when he stopped dead outside a shop and said, 'Woah! I need to try that one!'

Can you imagine the sales assistant looking up and seeing Yngwie Malmsteen standing there? He said, 'Can I try that white Strat?' The assistant, happy as a pig in shit, handed him the guitar and watched as Yngwie started playing all these Paganini riffs.

As he handed over his gold Amex card, I asked, 'What made you buy that one?'

'It's the look and the feel,' he said, 'and the tone. And it's a certain year of production.'

'How many Strats do you have now?' I said.

He thought for a moment, 'This will just put me over the two-hundred mark.'

Two hundred Fender Stratocasters… and he had to buy another one?

There's a similar story about Joe Bonamassa. The first time I met him he was playing the Renfrew Ferry. The second time he was at the Arches in Glasgow and he gave us a signature model guitar for a Rock Radio competition. The listener who won it came to the station and had photos taken with Joe and the guitar.

Next time he was playing the Royal Concert Hall, and after that it was the Edinburgh Playhouse. By this time The Ballad of John Henry had sold amazingly well – number one on the US Billboard blues album chart for 2009. I got a slot to see him at six o'clock in the Playhouse, and I arrived about half-five. I was shown in but there was no sign of anyone. Eventually a member of his crew came back and told me, 'Joe went out in Edinburgh and he's not back yet. If he doesn't make it in time, can we do the interview after the show?' As I've said before, shit happens; best to go with the flow.

Two minutes later Joe arrived, guitar case in hand, and apologised for keeping me waiting. In his dressing room I switched on the recorder and started the interview, 'Here we are at the Edinburgh Playhouse with Joe Bonamassa… who kept me waiting for twenty minutes.'

He laughed. 'I couldn't resist it,' he said. 'I just bought myself a guitar.'

I said, 'How many bloomin' guitars do you need, Joe?'

'It's not about how many. This one is special.'

I looked at it. 'It's just a red Strat,' I said.

'Ah,' he said. 'But it's the exact same model as the one Hank Marvin used to play.'

'Hank Marvin? You rate him then?'

He replied, 'Totally! Hank Marvin of The Shadows was a pioneer of guitar.'

Hank was also a huge influence on Michael Schenker, Brian May, David Gilmour, George Harrison, Tony Iommi, Pete Townsend, Peter Frampton, Mark Knopfler, Steve Howe, Ritchie Blackmore, Jeff Beck and Eric Clapton. A real guitarist's guitarist.

21. GIVING BACK

The Rock Radio Birthday Bashes ~ the Tartan Clef Awards ~ Biffy Clyro, Joe Elliott ~ been caught stealing

Jay Crawford called us all into his office about six months after Rock Radio started on air. He told us that our owners, the Guardian – who'd really done a good job of promoting us – were in turn owned by a trust, and part of the arrangement was that all its companies had to do an annual charity event. Jay wanted suggestions.

I said, 'Why don't we have a birthday party?'

'Already?'

'Yeah,' I said. 'Let's get some local bands to play it. We can charge at the door for charity. And it would be good publicity – newspapers and magazines might pick up on it.'

So we started work on the idea. At that stage there weren't many presenters who knew the local bands. Kieron Elliot came from an acting background (he'd worked on River City). David Grant came from pop radio. Father Ted wasn't from the area, and it was a year or so before Billy Rankin joined us.

So I thought bands who might pull a crowd. The Sensational Alex Harvey Band were doing a few gigs again so I asked Ted McKenna if they'd play, telling him it was for the Nordoff Robbins Music Therapy charity. There would be a bar tab, but that was it. Ted said 'yes.' Then I bumped in Giuliano from Gun and asked what he was doing. He said, 'We had a good time, but the band's finished. I'm working in the family restaurant.'

'What's your brother doing?' I asked.

'Dante's in another band, El Presidente.'

I said, 'How about doing a wee charity night for us?'

But he said, 'The guitar's up in the loft, Tom.'

'Come on,' I said. 'Just you and Dante – not Gun. A one-off. Just do Money, Shame On You and Better Days. It's for charity and there'll be a few drinks at the bar.'

Then I phoned Doogie White, who was singing with Yngwie Malmsteen. Doogie had been impressed with what we were doing at Rock Radio, but he was worried about the expense of getting the whole band to Glasgow. I suggested that he come on his own and do a few acoustic classics, and he replied, 'How about if I have a guitarist with me?' I told him we'd give them a hotel room for the night. Doogie phoned Chic McSherry from his La Paz days – but Chic said he hadn't played in years; and anyway, he was a very successful businessman. But Doogie persuaded him.

I met my friend, an agent called Martin Jarvis, who said, 'Why don't you phone Toby Jepson from Little Angels?' After the band had split Toby had become a producer, but I called him anyway. He had an acoustic album out so a charity date in Glasgow suited him. We had a birthday bash lineup!

On the day of the show, during soundcheck, I introduced all the bands to each other – and specifically introduced Toby to the Gun brothers. They'd toured together years ago, and that led to them agreeing to play a couple of songs together. And that led to them working together as Gun featuring Toby Jepson for a few years.

The night was a great success; we raised a few thousand pounds for a worthy charity, and actually the only negative was the number of local businesses that were short-staffed the following day. There were a lot of hangover sickies...

The Rock Radio Birthday Bash became a fixture on the Glasgow scene. The third one featured an unusual moment I'll never forget. I'd made contact with Dan Reed, who'd first risen to attention with the Dan Reed Network in the eighties. They were on the same label as Bon Jovi and their albums were neck-and-neck in sales for their first few years.

Dan had beautiful long hair – but, tiring of girls coming to see him for that rather than his music, he shaved it all off. Almost immediately, the band's popularity began to fade. It was a bit of a Samson and Delilah moment, which was a shame because they were a great band.
Around 2008 Dan decided to get back into music and I interviewed him during an acoustic tour. We instantly hit it off again. So when we were putting the bill together for the third birthday bash, I told Dan about it. There was no fee, as usual, but we offered to pay his flight from his home in Prague, and give him a night in a hotel, and he agreed.

We had him picked up at Glasgow airport on the afternoon of the show, but when he arrived at the Garage he told me there was a problem. The customs people had pulled him up for planning to work without a permit. Even though it was a charity show for Nordoff Robbins, they classed the trip as work, meaning he needed a visa. They let him into the country – but if he performed they told him they'd put him in jail and issue a massive fine.
There was nothing we could do. On the night, around the time he'd been due to perform, I went on to the stage and told the crowd, 'Dan Reed has flown in especially —' lots of cheers — 'But he's not allowed to play.' Lots of boos. 'But he is going to come and say hello.'

Dan walked on to a huge cheer. He told the crowd what had happened, and that he'd be back soon for a tour. Then he asked them to sing Dan Reed Network track Rainbow Child for him, because he wasn't allowed. The audience began singing, and it was a fantastic moment.
(I remember talking to Dan about Rabbie Burns one time. I was surprised that he hadn't heard of our national bard. So I gave him a book of Burns poetry as a wee gift.)

The Ultimate Rock Chick was an event that we ran, only the once, on 96.3 Rock Radio. It was Father Ted's idea and it proved to be a very popular, albeit non-PC concept, which we got around by promising a future Ultimate Rock Guy event. Funnily enough, we never did get round to that. The Ultimate Rock Chick was held at Apollo 23 in Glasgow, a venue in the basement of Cineworld, built on the site of the old Glasgow Apollo. Father Ted and I had the honour of conducting onstage interviews with about twenty entrants, and judging the winner. All assets were taken into account, including rock knowledge and singing voice. The venue was busy that night.

Then, of course, there was the famous Kiss video. In 2010 the band announced they were going to play Glasgow for the first time in ten years. (Around 1995 I did an interview with Kiss on Radio Clyde, and at the show that night Paul Stanley dedicated a song to me, which was embarrassing and humbling at the same time. Great guys.)

When they came back in 2010 we wanted to celebrate. It just so happened that the husband of Steph, one of our production assistants, owned a video production company. They kindly shot the video for us, while some of the Rock Radio girls dealt with the required makeup. A few of us dressed up as members of Kiss and mimed to the song I Was Made for Lovin' You. It was great fun, and another good way of raising awareness about the station. That's another video that you can still see on YouTube:
https://www.youtube.com/watch?v=q06nY7LNjtg

Biffy Clyro were one of the first bands to take part in a Rock Radio Secret Session. Kieron Elliot had introduced me to them and took me to see them at the Barrowland, where their talent was obvious.

Their manager, Dee, who worked wonders with them, asked if they could do a live interview with me around the release of 2007 album Puzzle – the one that really broke them. They seemed nervous, but they had that very out-there Scottish-type vocal. It's kind of brave: they must have decided, 'Stuff it. We're Scottish. Why not sing that way?'

We staged the Secret Session at Sloans in Glasgow by candle light and it's another video you can still see on YouTube. These days, of course, They're headlining big festivals all over the world. 'Mon the Biffy! https://youtu.be/23izHnsKW2o

Nordoff Robbins Music Therapy hold the Tartan Clef Awards in Glasgow every year – it's designed to raise money for the charity's important work. They've found that severely handicapped kids, many of whom can't see or hear, respond to the use of music and instruments. There's a connection that sparks their psyche. The Rock Radio bosses sponsored the Scottish Rock Band of the Year award five times, as another way of showing support. My job was to present the award on the night, about six months after we'd nominated an artist.

The left side of rock – Simple Minds, Hue & Cry, Franz Ferdinand, The View and so on – got lumped into the pop category. So once we'd been through Nazareth, Biffy Clyro and Big Country there weren't that many more to choose from, especially since bands like The Sensational Alex Harvey Band and others had received awards before our involvement.

So in our fourth year, I went to the committee and asked if we could expand the criteria a bit. I told them that I could contact Def Leppard, who'd had a massive year, sold millions of albums and would add a bit to the night. The committee said 'yes,' because the more bums on seats, and the more businesses who attended, meant more could be raised for the charity.

I got in touch with Joe Elliot, Def Leppard's singer, and put it to him. He said, 'You're lucky, because we're on downtime just now. Will any of the Alex Harvey Band be there?'
I replied, 'I can try and get them there.'

Joe said, 'Here's the deal, Tom. I'll buy my own plane ticket from Dublin. Get me somewhere to kip, and I'll come over – on the condition you get Chris Glen, Ted McKenna and the boys to appear on stage with me, and we do a couple of songs.'

Of course, the boys in SAHB were delighted to help, so Joe flew over and we brought him to The Old Fruitmarket, that year's venue. They rehearsed for half an hour, which was all they needed to sound great.

Joe is a huge SAHB fan. When he was about fifteen, SAHB was one of the first-ever rock gigs he went to. During the Sheffield City Hall show, Ted was battering away at his kit, and one of his cymbals came off and rolled across the stage. Joe, who was at the front, reached out to grab it – and it sliced his hand. He got carted off to first aid, and that was his gig over.

That night they played Faith Healer, and Boston Tea Party. I actually wanted them to do Delilah, because it was more of a pop audience, but there was no need to worry because they were simply amazing. My fellow rock DJ, Billy Rankin, guested on guitar.

As Joe recounts at the start of this book, I once spoke to him about their song Women, saying, 'There's a line in the song that puzzles me. I don't know how you got away with it.'

'Which line?' he asked.

'You know – "What's that smell?"'

Joe started laughing. 'It's "What's that spell?"!'

After forty-five years of rock my hearing isn't one hundred percent. But any time I bump into the Def Leppard guys, the urine is definitely extracted for that one.

I've been friendly with the band since I interviewed them in Sheffield in 1983, when their Pyromania album was released. Their label had asked me to do it, but they didn't have the budget to bring the band to Glasgow, so I took a train down to them.

When they played the SECC in Glasgow about ten years ago, I did an interview in the afternoon and they said, 'Pop into the dressing room before the show, Tom, then come back afterwards as well.'

So, I was in the dressing room, where the rider is laid out – a stack of provisions the band have asked to be laid on as part of their contract to play. I was told, 'Help yourself, Tom,' just as wee Mal, their tour manager, told them to get ready to go onstage. I was alone in the room when I spied a basket full of Earl Grey tea bags. 'Yes!' I thought, in a bit of a drunken state… and I stuffed loads of them into my pockets.

When I went back later for a nightcap, I had to confess. To be honest, I think one of them pulled me up after seeing all the tea bags hanging out of my pockets. 'What's this, Tom?'
'But,' I protested, 'You can't get Earl Grey in Scotland!' A load of nonsense, of course…

Everyone has misconceived notions about what it's like backstage and in dressing rooms. I'm sure in some cases it really is all sex, drugs and rock'n'roll – but in the vast majority of cases it's people doing their day's work. There are truck drivers trying to catch a few hours' sleep, roadies waiting to lift all these speakers back onto the trucks, sound and lighting technicians milling about... There's work to be done.

When you go backstage at a festival, however, it's almost like stepping into a mini town. As I've said, these are working areas; there are stalls geared up to supply the bands with Guitar strings, amp repairs, drum gear, laundry places with all their prices up on a big board. (T-shirt fifty pence, pair of jeans two pounds, ironing included). Even massage tents – a lot of big touring bands have a massage every day. One year at Sonisphere I said to one of the massage girls, 'Any chance I can get a freebie? We'll video it and put it on the Rock Radio website.' I know what you're thinking: 'That sounds well dodgy!' But it wasn't. It was actually agony; she really put me through the wringer.

The bands use Portacabins for dressing rooms. Inside there's usually a table, a TV, a few soft armchairs, some normal seats, and maybe a fruit machine, plus whatever's on the band's rider: usually crisps, sandwiches, fruit, nuts and beers; with a few bottles of Jack or vodka thrown in. Of course, at a festival the Portacabins are used by different bands throughout the day, which means different riders have to be set up continuously.

It's quite unusual to get on stage with the headline band, but one year, Def Leppard were at the top of the bill at Download, and I got the okay. It was fantastic to see a band like that perform from just yards away from me. They were playing to ninety thousand people, and I was right there with them. That's a memory and a half! My photos weren't great, but I remember appreciating the view from the band's position when the crowd were asked to raise their arms in unison, like a great rock army. It was mind-blowing.

One year, backstage at Sonisphere, I went past an articulated lorry and I could hear the thump of drums from inside. I stood listening to a Metallica song, For Whom The Bell Tolls, followed by Creeping Death.

Suddenly the back door of the truck flew open and out came Lars, James and the rest of the guys from Metallica, who were headlining that year. It was their warm-up room – they took all these trucks on tour with them and one was just for rehearsing, and they only used it for about twenty minutes a day.

I was once asked to interview a Greek guitarist called Gus G from a band called Firewind, who were way down the festival bill. As usual, I said 'yes'… You never know where these bands will end up. Gus was a good, honest lad, but I didn't see his performance that time. Firewind never quite made it – but then, a couple of years later, there was a wee bit of a stir in the press about Zakk Wylde, who'd been Ozzy's guitarist for years. Zakk had gone to concentrate on his band Black Label Society, and had left – or been kicked out of – Ozzy's band. Then Ozzy announced he'd found a new guitarist, and it was Gus G.

A wee bit later on I got another interview with Gus at the Cathouse. By this time his head had got a bit, you know, bigger! He was suddenly a 'star', which was a shame. One minute you're a hard-working young guitarist, and the next you're a big name. But watch out: take the wrong turn and you're suddenly back down a few rungs of the rock ladder and fighting for your life against the snakes. The music business can be so fickle. Zakk Wylde is a case in point… in 2011 he was playing the Academy with Black Label Society, and I asked for an interview. The record company said 'no problem,' and told me he was staying at the Travelodge in the Gorbals, and even asked if there was any chance I could pick him up instead of them paying for a taxi. So there we were, just the two of us, driving to Rock Towers. At least the interview turned out to be very interesting.

22. SECRET SESSIONS

Up close and personal shows ~ archery ~ fire alarms ~ Black Stone Cherry, Airbourne, Skunk Anansie ~ The mystery of Schenker's broken guitar

As I keep saying, it's lovely to see a band that you've got behind in the early days go on to do well. Usually they're the ones who work hard, play well, write great songs, maintain the same lineup as much as possible and hire good management.

I remember standing near the front of the stage at Download one year with Paul Anthony, breakfast DJ on Planet Rock, watching Black Stone Cherry for the first time. You could see the class literally oozing out of them. They were nice, modest, humble guys, who were delighted to be there, and thankful that people were interested in doing interviews with them.

They were also impressed that I was from Glasgow – you see, the Kentucky town they hail from is actually quite near the American Glasgow. Deep in the heart of bourbon country, they rehearse in a studio that belongs to drummer John Fred Young's dad Fred, who drums in a band called the Kentucky Headhunters.

Now, in this studio there's an old battered drumkit, with hens nesting in the bass. Fred picked it up at a jumble sale, and the reason he was attracted to it was because it actually once belonged to Darrell Sweet of Nazareth. Many years ago, Nazareth were on tour in America when their record company went bust. They got plane tickets to come home, but they couldn't afford to take all their equipment. So John Fred's dad picked the kit up for a song.

The night before Black Stone Cherry played in Glasgow in 2014, I happened to be going through my record collection when I found an album by the Kentucky Headhunters. I was talking to John Fred Young the next day and I said, 'Do you have any vinyl of your dad's band?' He said he didn't, so I pulled the album out of my bag and slid it across the table. The wee present left him stunned – had had tears in his eyes.

Another time, I picked up John Fred and guitarist Ben Wells from the Barrowland, and took them to Rock Towers for an interview. I was supposed to take them back to their hotel... but I had another idea. During the conversation it had come out that the guys loved archery. Bow-hunting seems to be a big thing in Kentucky. I'd mentioned that I did archery too. Not animals, but targets.

I'd taken it up around 2003, mainly because my then-wife was keen. She was really good at it, and being very competitive, she ended up a British champion. I was not nearly as committed; I did enjoy it, but it was more of a hobby for me. The good thing about it was the opportunity to travel to all the European and world championships. You didn't need to be Robin Hood to go – they were seeded, and you could shoot with people at the same level as yourself.
The championships tended to be over five days, and I had the pleasure of shooting in Portugal, Switzerland, Estonia, the US, Finland and Namibia, which was a fascinating country.

Shooting targets was anathema to Black Stone Cherry – they couldn't understand how you could be bothered going out with a bow unless it was to shoot something for your dinner. But I said, 'Do you fancy a wee shot at the archery range I use?'
We spent an hour or so at the range. They were, of course, shit-hot. I remember thinking what might be said in the unlikely event of an accident: 'Black Stone Cherry gig cancelled after band member gets shot with bow and arrow in Glasgow...'

Another band I met on the way up was Airbourne. They are, of course, heavily influence by AC/DC and even though they were just playing King Tuts, they were excited to be playing in the town where Angus and Malcolm Young were born.

The interview I recorded during the afternoon wasn't the best in the world – they were a bit inexperienced and slightly overawed by the whole thing. When they went on stage that night, it was busy without being sold out, but as soon as they started, you just knew: they had it. The energy, the musicianship, the synchronised headbanging. They'd played for about an hour and fifteen minutes when one of the King Tuts staff got up on stage and told them to stop, then told the crowd: 'Stay calm, but the fire alarm has gone off. We need you to vacate the premises.'

Of course, the whole place started booing; but sensibly, we all filed out onto the street. A lot of people thought, 'Ah well… night over,' and headed up the road. But about ten minutes later, after two fire engines had turned up, we got the all-clear. One of the Airbourne guys said to me, 'Do you want to see if these people will come back in again? We'll finish the set.' I shouted out the message to the few people who'd stayed around, and we filed back in again. The band went back onstage and did the best, rocking, last three songs you could imagine. A great gesture from the band that left me with a lot of respect for those guys.

As predicted, Airbourne reached Barrowland level within a couple of years. They sold the place out. It was, as usual, a fabulous performance but the memorable highlight for me was when frontman Joel O'Keeffe went into a guitar solo, and, while playing, got onto the shoulders of a big roadie and started moving through the crowd – just like Bon Scott used to do with Angus thirty years previously.
The roadie finally made it to side of the hall and Joel jumped up on to the bar, still playing his solo. He demanded an empty glass from a stunned barmaid, poured a pint, and downed it. He didn't miss a note.

Then he climbed back onto the roadie's shoulders and they went back to the stage, where he finished the solo. Rock'n'roll entertainment at its best.

After the success of our first Rock Radio Birthday Bash, we tried to think of ways to involve the audience more. Our trips to Download meant I'd met up with old contacts again, so I called a few of them and said, 'If you have a band coming to Glasgow, how about we run a competition on my lunchtime show? The prize can be the chance to meet and greet the band.'

Our sales rep Angela and I extended the idea into having the band play two or three acoustic songs, in an authentic Glasgow pub. We wanted to use the Saracen's Head or the Scotia Bar – you don't get many pubs like that in America, full of character and history.

The arrangement went like this: we ran the contest on air, without telling anyone where the show would be held. Our office assistant Lisa phoned the forty or so winners, the day before the show and told them where it would take place. The band arrived at six o'clock; doors opened at six-fifteen; the band went on stage at six-twenty; the meet and greet started at six-thirty. The winners all got a picture with the band to go on the Rock Radio website, and the band were clear by seven o'clock. We then plugged the event and the venue for a few days after it had happened.

It was a win, win, win. The record company got great exposure, the listeners got to meet their idols while the band got to meet their fans and promote their single. All in less than an hour.

One of our managers, Gavin, had come up with the Godfather of Rock feature title, so I talked him through the concept. He said, 'Aye, I get it – it's an acoustic session, but the venue is a secret. Call it the Secret Sessions.' I didn't like it at first, but it grew on me.

The first band we had for a Secret Session was Shinedown (at the time they weren't the massive band they are now). That first event was downstairs at The Solid. The second one was with Biffy Clyro, in Sloans. When we went to look at the venue, it was missing something, so it was suggested that we do it by candlelight. It looked incredible.

We also did one with Skunk Anansie, featuring singer Skin, who's openly bisexual. At the end of our interview I said, 'Last question – how much do you long for an interview that doesn't mention your sexuality?'
Skin and drummer Mark looked at each other then she said, 'You were so close to being the first interview that didn't. But you blew it!' She was okay about it; she said, 'I like a bit of both, but it doesn't make me a bad person.'

We did that Secret Session at Pivo Pivo. Skin is slim, quite petite, her head is shaved and she's quite demure. But when they went on she just seemed to explode – she became a six-foot-six Amazon. It was an astonishing transformation.

When Def Leppard guitarist Phil Collen formed a side-project, ManRaze, with Sex Pistols drummer Paul Cook, not many radio stations were interested. I, of course, said 'yes'. They came into Rock Towers and we got them to play a live song in the studio. There was an old battered acoustic guitar amongst our memorabilia, and a forty-quid toy drumkit – but they sounded great, good players can make anything sound good. Afterwards we had a Secret Session in Rockers in Midland Street. They played semi-acoustically and they sounded terrific. After the Session, just as I'd told the winners that we were going to set up the photo session, Phil caught my arm and said, 'See this gear behind me? What's this?'

There was a full backline including amps and drumkit. H, who owned Rockers, played in a band and it was his own gear. Phil asked if he could have a shot, and H, delighted, went off to get his Les Paul. After the photoshoot I went back on stage and said, 'Look, ladies and gentlemen, if you're not in any big rush you can stay and hear Phil and Paul having a jam.'

Sometimes people just get lucky. Those guests got to see some really special playing. The guys launched into half an hour of electric covers and blew the roof off. Who would have thought that a Sex Pistol and a member of Def Leppard could sound so good together?

Other Secret Sessions featured Stone Sour, Black Stone Cherry, The Virginmarys, The Temperance Movement, Coheed and Cambria, The Answer, Rival Sons, Five Finger Death Punch, Thunder, Halestorm, Gun and The Quireboys. We didn't get every venue that we asked for, but we did visit The Hard Rock Cafe, The Solid Rock Cafe, Rockus, the Classic Grand, The Box, Apollo 23, Cottiers Theatre and others. Rock Radio production assistant Steph McCrackin and her hubby Alistair filmed a few of the sessions for the website and you can still find them on YouTube.

Chris Glen, of The Sensational Alex Harvey Band and the Michael Schenker Group, is one of the many pals I've made over the years in the music business. He often tells the story of the moment he decided to wear his underpants over his trousers in SAHB, to be as distinctive as guitarist Zal Cleminson, who used to paint his face as a clown. Chris tells some of the best rock stories I've ever heard. Many are unrepeatable, but even some of those are in his new book Chris Glen: The Bass Business, which you should buy.

One of those stories involves yours truly... When Michael Schenker of the Scorpions and UFO formed his own group, he turned to one of the tightest rhythm sections on the planet, Chris and SAHB drummer Ted McKenna. One time, the band finished a soundcheck, but Chris and Ted stayed behind to work on something. Michael had left his treasured Gibson Flying V on its stand – and Chris stumbled over it, knocked it over, breaking the neck in two. He thought, 'I've just been hired by this guy, and now I'll be out on my arse. He loves that guitar!'

No one had seen Chris break the guitar, so he put it back on the stand, fixing the neck back in place as best he could. Then he legged it. Later on, Michael caused a big scene. He was absolutely livid because no one would own up, threatening all sorts of action. The whole band and crew were going to get the sack!

Many years later I was interviewing Michael and I happened to say, 'Do you remember back in the early days of MSG, when one of your Flying Vs had a bit of an accident?' But even as I said it, I was thinking, 'Oh shit – Chris never told Michael it was him!'

But the genie was out of the bottle. A suspicious Michael said, 'Of course I remember. But how do you know about it?'

I was all, 'Eh… eh… Chris told me.'

'Chris!' he blasted. 'I always suspected it was that bastard!'

A few months later, Chris caught up with me. Luckily for me it had all turned out okay – Michael had phoned him and said, 'Chris, you are the one who broke my guitar. You bastard! By the way, I'm putting MSG back together. Would you and Ted play Japan with me?'

(I've had the pleasure of interviewing Michael several times. He's got a great sense of humour; but he's one of these guys that, after you ask a question, you can go for a pee, have a three-course lunch, two glasses of wine and a snooze, then come back just as he finishes his answer. You say, 'Michael, what do you think of your new album?' And you get his life story…)

23. DOES A COW MOO?

Meeting Meat Loaf ~ sniffing Bon Scott ~ backstage with a bell ~ Bon Jovi, ZZ Top and more arse-kissing

Sometimes I just sit back and smile as I think about the new lease of live Rock Radio gave me. Among my absolute favourites are the adventures I've had involving Meat Loaf, AC/DC and Bon Jovi – and all those experiences were completely different.

Meat Loaf is a strange character. Sometimes he's great fun, other times he's not. One time in Glasgow, I had to go to his hotel for our interview, and I took a huge record shop display poster and a press photo with me. He was on good form that day, so, after the interview, we posed for a photo and I asked him to sign the press picture for my daughter Heather. He happily signed it, but complained that his record company didn't even know his name. They'd printed it 'Meatloaf' instead of 'Meat Loaf'. I also asked him to sign the poster, which he did, with the message: 'Meat – does a cow moo?' When I asked him why, he just smiled.

I've interviewed him eight times, firstly on Radio Clyde, then in the dressing room at the Apollo; we also did one in a hotel in London. He did seem to be rather bitter about Jim Steinman. I remember him telling me that he was singing in the Rocky Horror Show in New York when he got a knock on his dressing room door. Jim had written a bunch of songs but couldn't sing them the way he wanted them, so someone had suggested Meat Loaf. Jim gave Meat a card, they met up a couple of days later and did a deal.

In 2010 he brought out an album called Hang Cool Teddy Bear, and I asked his record company if he'd do a Rock Radio Secret Session. They said his songs were too big to be done acoustically, and he didn't play and sing solo. So I suggested a special Secret Session – instead of a live performance, a 'Meat Meet and Greet' where we open the floor to fan questions. To my surprise his people said 'yes'. We arranged for him to give us an hour at six o'clock on a Tuesday afternoon.

Rock Radio sales rep Angela and I put our heads together over a venue, and she came up with MacSorley's. I thought, 'Yes! That's what makes our station so special. Meat Loaf walking into MacSorley's Bar? Magic!'

I think most of the forty ticket winners believed it was a wind-up – but at five to six a taxi pulled up. No limo, no company rep. Just Meat on his own in the cab he'd ordered. He'd brought an advance CD of his new album, so we put it on and I introduced the great man. He sat on the stage and chatted about the songs. After forty-five minutes, I remember saying. 'How are we doing for time?'

He said, 'I'm enjoying myself! Let's keep going.' So we opened it up to the audience for questions, which worked well, because they could get away with asking things that maybe I couldn't. Meat stayed for almost two hours, and we had a wonderful night that everyone who was there will remember.

One of my regrets is that, over the years, I didn't get more things signed. I tended to think it was a bit naff, asking for autographs. However, I do have a twelve-inch live single of AC/DC's Dirty Deeds Done Dirt Cheap, signed by Angus Young and Brian Johnston. It's a prized possession, as Angus has signed it with: 'Nice working with you Tom'.

I once interviewed them in a posh place called The Chelsea Harbour Hotel in London. They appeared in the lounge bar, decked out in their usual scruffy jeans and t-shirts, while we were surrounded by clean-cut businessmen. That pair probably had more money than the whole lot of 'suits' put together. It was long before the smoking ban, so Angus lit up and puffed his way through the whole chat. He called over a waitress and ordered a nice cup of tea. Brian had a coffee and I had a beer. I just thought, 'Woah! Rock'n'roll!'

Paul Murdoch, who persuaded me to write this book, went with me to see the bronze statue of Bon Scott in Kirriemuir. It's a wonderful memorial to the late, great icon. And it reminded me of the AC/DC exhibition in Glasgow's Kelvingrove Museum in 2011. I'd been invited along to do the official opening. It was well-posh – the lord provost was there, along with an assortment of high-heidjins, and an AC/DC tribute band playing in the foyer. The organiser had toured the exhibition all over Australia before deciding it should be seen in the city where Angus and Malcolm Young were born. There was everything you could possibly imagine: cannon from the For Those About To Rock tour, guitars, photographs and all sorts of amazing artefacts.

I found it quite sad to look at Bon Scott's passport and some of his t-shirts. On the other hand, there was a fun picture of wee Angus, around three years of age, sitting on Santa's knee at Lewis's in Argyle Street. Just like any other kid in Glasgow in those days, his mum and dad had taken him along for Christmas.

I remember asking Angus about his childhood memories of Cranhill, before his family signed up for the ten-pound emigration package on offer in the sixties. He told me: 'I remember playing in front of the close – it was a relatively modern block we stayed in. But my main memory is that my brother and I shared a bedroom, and from the bedroom window, lying on the bed when the curtains were open, we could see the big water tower. Any time I think of Glasgow, I think of my family that are still there and that big water tower. Every time I'm back I take a taxi round Cranhill.'

The water tower is still there; but the last time Angus visited he found that the block of flats he'd been brought up in was gone.

Another favourite from the exhibition was a photo of Bon backstage in New York. A stunning blonde is standing with her back against a wall, and Bon, with one hand on the wall over her, a drink in his other hand, is obviously in full chat-up mode. What he doesn't know is that the girl is actually a guy – transvestites were seemingly pretty common in the Big Apple in those days. It turned out that everyone in the room knew the truth, except Bon. I wonder if he found out... and at what stage in the evening?

The curator told me that he'd managed to find out where Bon's mum lived, and had gone to ask if she had anything for the exhibition. A pleasant wee woman, she said, 'Come on in, son. Do you want a cup of tea?' He explained his plan and she took him through to Bon's bedroom. He'd been dead for twenty-five years by this time, but his bedroom was still just as he'd left it. She went to a chest of drawers and pulled out his passport, and said, 'I'll give you this but I want it back.' Then, from another drawer, she took out a supermarket bag which was falling to bits, pulled a couple of t-shirts out of the bag and handed them over.

The curator then said, 'Look, Tom, since it's a special night...' He opened a glass case and handed me one of the shirts. 'Have a sniff.' It still smelled of sweat and beer – Bon Scott's sweat and beer.

In 2009 AC/DC set out on their Black Ice world tour, and included a show at Hampden Park. Rock Radio got an allocation of press passes, and we had a pair left over. On the day of the gig, I mischievously asked listeners to text in what they were prepared to do to win them. A judging panel of me, producer Fergie and Father Ted sorted out the contenders, and we picked a guy who said he'd kiss my arse live on air. Lisa called him and he was at Rock Towers within the hour.

Because it was the day of the AC/DC show, I was wearing my kilt, true Scotsman style. I bent over the mixing desk, lifted my kilt and presented our worthy listener with a target. Fair play to him – he got down to the task with gusto, kissed my arse and was presented with the passes.

The following year, AC/DC wanted their own stage at Download. I was there with Paul Anthony, who worked on Rock Radio at the time before moving to Planet Rock. We were backstage the day before the festival opened, about nine in the morning, so we were able to chance our arms and go places where our passes wouldn't normally take us. The AC/DC crew were already setting the band's stage. It was great; but the best bit was seeing the big bronze bell lying on the ground, waiting to be hoisted onto the stage… I can exclusively reveal that it's not made out of bronze. It was big though, so Paul and I took each other's pictures standing beside it. We felt like a couple of naughty schoolboys, so I think Angus would have approved.

During my fourth year with Rock Radio, Bossman Jay (as we now called him) asked if I'd like to take an unpaid day off to go on a trip. I said it would depend on what the trip was. He said, 'We've got an opportunity for Real Radio, but I'd rather you did it for Rock Radio. You've to go to Madrid to interview Bon Jovi, then see them play in a really small showcase venue.'

Does a bear shit in the woods? I said, 'Of course I'll go!'

There must have been about forty of us from press, radio and TV. We were taken to the Spanish tennis academy, about an hour out of Madrid, It's huge: dozens of tennis courts, all full of young folk learning the game. I got to interview Richie Sambora and Dave Bryan – the same guys who'd helped push that minibus in the snow all those years ago. It was quite a coup, getting to meet the guys again. As I've said, it's hard to get access to the big bands once they're really up there.

I wanted to know whether a band like Bon Jovi really needed a wee radio station like ours. Richie, who still had his feet very much on the ground, explained his position, saying that, the bigger you got, the more press you had to deal with. You just had to cut it down; you had to leave it to the management and the record company and there wasn't much the band could do about it. I thought he explained it really well; then he said, 'It's not that we don't like you any more, Tom.'

Later there there was a mass press conference for those who hadn't got one-to-ones. There must have been ten different TV stations from all over the world, and dozens of microphones spread over the tables. I hadn't seen Bon Jovi for about ten years until the band swept in – it was strange to see them like that, after knowing them as a wee rock band who'd been so happy to grab any publicity they could.

After about an hour it started to quieten down, and the MC said, 'Are there any more questions?' The place fell silent, so I thought, 'Fuck it!' I put my hand up and I got the nod. I said, 'The European tour you're doing doesn't have any UK dates. Could you tell me if there are any UK dates planned?'

Jon Bon Jovi looked over and said, 'I know that voice! Scotland, isn't it? Yeah, we'll be back soon, and I guarantee we'll come to Glasgow.' That was so cool – because for years I'd been thinking that he'd turned into a bit of an arse. I hadn't been able to get near him for ages, but he was still alright.

After the press conference, I went back to the hotel for a couple of drinks, then got on a bus to the gig. It was terrific: there were only around four hundred people in the place, but it was packed. Bon Jovi are a band at Hampden Park level when it comes to Scottish gigs, so it was great to see them in such an intimate venue.

It had been a fairly early show, and now it was a case of making our own way back to the hotel. Some people were going for meals, some were going clubbing. I decided to walk to the hotel with a few of the guys I knew, and grab some chips on the way (though they don't tend to sell chips in Madrid). I got back around ten o'clock – not late. Then, while I was having a nightcap, something bizarre happened.

A couple walked into reception to check-in. I recognised the guy straight away; I knew him, I'd been out drinking in Glasgow with him. But would he remember me? I wandered over. 'Billy Gibbons! How you doing?'

He said, 'I know that beard!'

I replied, 'I know yours!'

He didn't remember how he knew me but he told me, 'We're here on a few days' holiday. We've just finished a tour in Moscow.' He was there with his missus. He would have been in his sixties and she wasn't much older than forty. Lucky man – she was gorgeous.
I asked him if he fancied a beer. His wife wanted to have a bath, so he told her he'd catch her upstairs later.

I walked back to the bar with Billy Gibbons from ZZ Top. The two lads I was with couldn't believe it. We must have sat there until half past one in the morning, just blethering. We only had a couple of beers, nothing heavy, but we had a fantastic conversation. I remembered he had a museum somewhere in Texas, and we talked about that and blues-rock till bedtime.

24. ROCK IS DEAD?

Slipknot ~ Still Game again ~ a radio wedding ~ veggie haggis

On Rock Radio we tried so many daft ideas; some worked, some didn't. Talk Like A Pirate Day really did work. It was Father Ted's idea and instruction came from Bossman Jay that every presenter must do his show using a pirate voice. It was hilarious, but it was actually bloody hard work. I searched online for 'How do pirates talk' – and there it was, a wee site with all these sayings. Before long I was giving it, 'Shiver me timbers, that were Rock an' Roll by Led Zeppelin. It be Talk Like A Pirate Day on 96.3 Rock Radio, ahaar!'

You had to do it non-stop, so after a four hour show your voice was totally gubbed. Father Ted, Billy Rankin and Phil were brilliant at it. I'm not sure how I was, but I did my best. The worst was The Captain, David Grant – he tried, but he couldn't get away from sounding like a Devonshire farmer. It was more like Talk like a Wurzel Day… Can you imagine Radio Scotland, Radio Clyde, Capital or any other big radio station doing that? No way. It was silly, knockabout frivolity; pure magic, and the listeners loved it. We even got Fergie to make up wee sea-shanty jingles. The whole station rallied round the idea and made it work.

At the first birthday bash, I met up with a guy called Greg, who played the bagpipes, and so was known as Greg the Piper. I thought it would be fun to invite him to teach me the pipes live on the radio. Everything started well: Greg brought in a chanter and showed me how to produce a tune. I think it was Three Blind Mice. But it all went downhill when I insisted on progressing to a full set of pipes. It's really hard work! I barely had the puff to blow up the bag, never mind keep it up while concentrating on Three Blind Mice. It descended into a lovely, live, on-air farce.

Charity work and motorcycles often tied together at the station. (Not every biker likes rock, but a good few of them do.) One day Angela came in after visiting a motorcycle shop in Renfrew and said, 'I'd like you all to wash motorbikes on Saturday, two hours each.' So, that day, when someone came in and wanted their bike cleaned, it was down to us – Phil McCrackin, Billy Rankin, Father Ted, The Captain or I would scrub up their bike. The owners were all very generous with their donations.

Later we got involved with a group of bikers raising cash for Yorkhill children's hospital, who held an annual Easter egg run across the city, ending at the hospital, with a band and burgers at the finish line. Every biker who took part brought bring an Easter egg for the sick kids. In the early days there had been maybe fifty or sixty bikes; although, bikers, being generous, would bring three or four Easter eggs each. After a few years there were hundreds of people and something like four thousand eggs, so they started sharing them out to other hospitals and charities.

They asked me if I'd represent Rock Radio and start the run off from Kelvingrove bandstand. They put me on the back of a trike, surrounded by about a thousand other bikes; I blew a horn and off we went. When the run finished I noticed that a lot of bikers would hand over five, ten or twenty pounds along with their eggs. So the next year, we took on more help and gave them collection buckets. Between us all we raised thousands of pounds – a success story that continues to this day.

I didn't stop supporting up-and-coming artists either. A case in point was progressive rock band Pallas, from Aberdeen. They'd been signed to EMI and their first album had done well years earlier, but then they fell out with singer Euan Lowson and faded away. Then they got a new singer, Allan Reed – formerly of Abel Ganz – and did well again. They're still going, with another singer, Paul Mackie.

From time to time you hear people saying rock music is finished, that it's had its day. Then a band like Slipknot come to the fore. They had an amazing sound and a unique image that appealed very much to teenage kids at the start – people who probably hadn't even thought about rock music before that. Slipknot transcended the downward spiral.

I went to see them at the SECC and the vast majority of the audience were teenagers. The whole place was bouncing up and down to these guys in masks and their energy, was astonishing. I'd taken my son Neil along; he was maybe seventeen, and he was looking down his nose at the rest of the crowd. But I said, 'See these ten thousand people? Maybe nine thousand of them will be into whatever the latest fashion is next week... but a thousand of them will become diehard rock fans for the rest of their lives.'

I met Slipknot frontman Corey Taylor with his other band, Stone Sour, when they played the Carling Academy. What a lovely guy! He smoked like a lum, though – you'd be doing an interview with him indoors, then, ten minutes in, he'd say, 'Can we stop for a few minutes while I nip out for a fag?' A year later, when Stone Sour were promoting their second album, Come What(ever) May, they did a Secret Session, just two of the band, three songs, then met all the fans.

A couple of years after that, Slipknot were headlining Download. When a band get that big everybody wants a piece. All these radio stations that would never have played Slipknot in a million years wanted interviews. Of course, the record companies tend to take the easy way out and say 'no interviews' full-stop. That was the situation at Download. As a compromise, Corey was going to give a fifteen-minute press conference, which was no real use to us as Rock Radio. I went along anyway and there were perhaps a hundred journalists from all over the world trying to get his attention: Corey! Corey!' He was doing his professional best when, ten minutes into the interview, he happened to look up and catch my eye. I think it was the beard. He shouted out: 'Tom! How are you doing, pal?'

I said, 'Hi, Corey.' All these journalists turned round thinking, 'Who the fuck is he?'

He mimed across to me: 'Cigarette, round the back, once this is finished?' I gave him the thumbs-up.

I went to the side, and there's Corey: 'Hi Tom, nice to see you.'

'Have you not given up those fags yet?' I said.

'Oh no man, I'm addicted,' he told me. 'I need them for the voice.'

The beard does have its advantages now and again.

Round about the second year of Rock Radio, I'd just finished my show when a chap appeared at reception to see me, with a great big parcel under his arm. Obviously a rock fan, he said, 'I've listened to you for years, I love the music you play, I do a bit of painting – so this is for you.' I opened the parcel and inside was a five-foot high painting of me, standing with a guitar, in my Rock Radio t-shirt.

I was absolutely flabbergasted. What do you say to someone who's done something like that for you? I stuttered, 'How much do I owe you?'

The guy said, 'Don't be silly. I did it as a token of appreciation.'

Still in a state of shock, I took it through and showed it to the boss. It resided in the studio for a while, then the boss decided, 'That picture should be in the green room.' So for six years it hung in pride of place over the area where all the visitors to Rock, Real and Smooth Radio waited.

Most of the interviews we did on Rock Radio were with rock bands, for obvious reasons. But one day I was told to speak to Ford Kiernan and Greg Hemphill, the stars of Still Game. I've told how I did a bit of work on the show, although by this time it had finished. But I was told the subject of the interview was a possible reunion of the cast.
As soon as they came into the studio they started to rip the piss right out of me. They remembered my wee stint in Navid's shop, when I walked in and asked for the Big Cocks magazine. 'Hi, Tom – are you still a dirty bastard?' That kind of thing, all great fun.

The series had ended because the pair had fallen out, but it was obvious they were back to being best pals again. More importantly, they announced they were getting back together and had booked the Hydro for five nights. That soon became sixteen, then twenty-one nights as ticket sales got more and more out of control. Everyone in Glasgow wanted to see Still Game Live.
I asked about a new TV series but they were cautious, saying they'd wait and see how the Hydro went... Aye right. It was a total success, there's another TV series, and there's another live run at the Hydro.

Within Temptation, a rock band from the Netherlands, are massive in Europe and getting bigger here in the UK. When they played in Glasgow in 2010 we invited singer Sharon den Adel and guitarist Ruud Jolie in for a chat. It happened to be Burns Night, and the station bosses had sent out for haggis, neeps and tatties, along with a few bottles of Irn-Bru. (It was the sort of thing the bosses did – just wee freebies that encouraged good staff relations.) Sharon and Rudd arrived just as the haggis was being served, and they were offered a plateful. Rudd was delighted and tucked in, but Sharon, a vegetarian, was not impressed. She asked us to explain what was in this strange dish. When we told her, her face was a picture. The day was saved when a portion of veggie haggis was sourced. Sharon tucked in, live on air, and cleared her plate. A couple of years later I was interviewing her at Download and she still remembered her lunch in Glasgow that day. When I asked her if she'd tried haggis again, she politely replied, 'No…'

Madina Lake were local favourites even though they came from America. The band were led by two brothers, Nathan and Matt Leone, nice lads, and they played one of our birthday bashes. I was sad to hear about an incident in their home town of Chicago that nearly left Matt dead. He was walking home one night when he came across a domestic, a man and a woman having a fight in the street. He bravely intervened, but the guy turned on him, gave him a serious kicking, and finished things off by taking a brick to his head.
Matt was at death's door for weeks and spent months in intensive care. He pulled through in the end, but it finished the band.

When Rock Radio's Phil McCrackin announced that he was getting married, he asked me to be his best man. I was honoured. He was marrying the lovely Judith down near Gretna, in a castle that had been converted to a wedding venue. It was to be kilts and the whole shebang, and we were to head down on the Saturday morning before the ceremony at two o'clock.
My then-wife had everything ready in the hall of our house to load into the car. She was going down to pick something up from the village, so she asked me to load up the car. I got everything packed, she came back and we got underway. We reached the hotel in good time and we'd started to carry the stuff into our room when she said, 'Where's my dress?'

I said, 'I don't know.'

'It was hanging up on the on the dining room door.'

'I never saw it!' I protested.

Yes – my fault. You can imagine the grief I got; it was an hour before the wedding and she had no dress. Luckily we found a charity shop with a selection of wedding-type attire. Nothing was particularly suitable but we got something.

Then it was back for the ceremony, in the old stone keep of the castle. Weathered old flagstones and high turrets – a magical setting. When it got to the bit where the minister said, 'Have you got the ring?' that's when the next near-disaster kicked in. I handed the ring to Phil, but as I passed it over, it dropped onto the ground, rolled across the flagstones with Judith scampering after it, she grabbed it just before it disappeared down a drain.

Then it got to the best man's speech. I started with: 'Ladies and gentlemen, I'm very proud and honoured to be here at the marriage of my good friend Phil, and the lovely Judith. But before I get on with it, can I ask you to be upstanding? I'd like to propose a toast to the two most important people in the room... the bar staff!'

It was all downhill after that.

Phil McCrackin's real name is Phil Reed, a great guy from the south of England. He'd done a bit of DJ work in the Portsmouth area, and after two years at Rock Radio, he was desperate to get on air with us. But the bosses weren't keen: 'No, you're the engineer. Just stick to that.' He finally got his chance when somebody was off sick; Phil stepped up to the plate. He didn't want to call himself Phil Reed on air, so decided he'd just be Phil. But the rest of us thought it was a bit boring and had him announced as Phil McCrackin. And it stuck – he still calls himself that.

Every Guy Fawkes Night the bosses would put on a fireworks display and order in fish and chips for us. Phil, along with being chief engineer, was also the company's health and safety officer, so he got the job of setting off the fireworks. He'd always appear in statutory safety helmet, goggles, hi-viz vest – the full jobsworth uniform. We all had a great time taking the piss out of him.

25. STEVIE NICKS AND ME

A moment of ecstasy ~ an afternoon with crumpet ~ a move to the country ~ an attack on Status Quo

Rock Radio probably had the best atmosphere of anywhere I've ever worked. They put a great team together at Baillieston. If you go along the M8 from Glasgow to Edinburgh, you'll see a big metal horse on your right. Rock Towers was tucked in behind that horse in a small industrial estate.

In our first couple of years there was a lot of media coverage for our new radio station. Quite often, the press would come and take photographs of us in the studio. They'd come in, set up big lights, flashes and umbrellas and shoot us using a huge assortment of lenses and filters.

One day I got a call from a student who was studying photography, asking if he could come in and take a few pictures for his college course. He was a nice lad, with just one camera and two lenses. He shot six photographs in ten minutes and said, 'That's it – thanks very much, Tom.'

I asked, 'What about all the white umbrellas and flashguns?'

'No,' he said, 'I think I've got what I want.'

A few days later he emailed me a black-and-white photo, and I thought, 'What a picture!' That's the one on the cover of this book. He was delighted when I chose it. A big hats-off to John Morrison.

As the business developed our owners launched a Rock Radio in Newcastle and then a bigger station in Manchester. That led to quite a power struggle. In the early days the Glasgow team assumed that, because we'd compiled a multi-thousand track playlist, developed the Five Word Weather, Godfather Of Rock and Septembeer concepts, that the additional stations would follow the blueprint. That didn't happen – Manchester took the bits they liked, then added bands like Oasis to their playlist for obvious reasons. They had a licence to broadcast to a bigger audience, and the Guardian headquarters were there too, so, gradually, Glasgow became marginalised.

The year after Rock Radio Manchester gained control, they decided to have a Halloween fancy dress party. Since my Friday Night Rock Show was also broadcast in Manchester, I was invited down for the party. It was a superb night. I dressed up as a character from Beetlejuice, and mingled with about five hundred rock fans in fancy dress. At the entrance we were welcomed by a couple of models from the Sport newspaper – they made every single guy feel especially welcome since their outfits left very little to the imagination. The event was in a venue called The Ritz, which had the sticky carpets and cobwebs that gave it that special atmosphere, just like The Barrowland or even the Apollo. A rock venue needs to be like that in my opinion; it felt like it hadn't been cleaned since the sixties, when it had been the Manchester venue. The Who, the Small Faces and the Beatles had all played there.

My producer, Fergie, had really bad eyesight, but compensated by having fantastic hearing. He's a superb operator. I remember the day he told me he had some very important news for me, concerning Stevie Nicks.

Back in the late sixties, I loved the original Peter Green's Fleetwood Mac. They were great, but they only went global when they brought in Stevie Nicks and Lindsey Buckingham. Rumours is still one of the biggest-selling albums of all time. I saw them at the Apollo in the seventies and I instantly fell in love with Stevie Nicks. I sat there mesmerised, with my tongue hanging out – she had a sensuous sex appeal. Despite being in my thirties I had a poster of Stevie on my wall.

My then-wife would kid me about her all the time; I still have a crush on her.

So when Fergie asked if I could stay late the next afternoon to interview her, my heart nearly jumped out of my chest. 'Is it live in the studio?' I asked.

'No, it's a phone-in from California.' That didn't matter. I went home and prepared all my questions about Stevie's new solo album and the band she'd put together for a tour.

The next day, I finished my show, had a coffee, then sat down as Fergie set up the equipment and left the studio. Then I heard the voice in my headphones. 'Hi, this is Stevie. Is that Tom?'

'Yeah...' I mumbled like an embarrassed schoolboy. I started with a few standard questions about the album and the tour, which was to include a show at Glasgow's Royal Concert Hall.

All the time I'm thinking, 'I'm actually talking to Stevie Nicks. God, she sounds so sexy...'
Then, in her sultry American accent, she said: 'Tom, are you the one with the beard? I'm looking at the station website right now.'

I said, 'Yes, that's me.'

'It's not all that well known,' she told me, 'but I have a thing for men with beards.'
I'm thinking, 'She what? Oh, yes! I'm beginning to melt into my seat!'
Flushing, I said, 'I've had it for a while.'

'It's an absolute beauty,' she said in an even more flirtatious voice. 'It's so long, and so thick.' Then she asked, 'When I play the Concert Hall, would you like to be my guest?'

Breathlessly, I replied, 'That's really nice of you, Stevie.' I wasn't going to tell her that I'd be chaffing the record company up for a ticket anyway.
She said, 'I don't suppose you'd fancy joining me for supper after the show?'

I thought I was going to have complete cardiac arrest. I was in heaven! 'That would be really nice, Stevie.'

'I'll be staying at One Devonshire Gardens. Do you know it?'

'Yes – just up Great Western Road.'

'I always stay there any time I'm in Glasgow. I just love that little hotel. I'm in the room with the four-poster.' Was Stevie Nicks flirting with me? I didn't know, but I was loving it. 'Are you a wine man?' she asked.

It was still all part of the interview, so I said, 'Aye, I'm fond of a wine – but I prefer a pint of heavy.'

'A pint of heavy? what on earth is that, Tom?'

'It's ale, but I can also force down a JD & coke.'

'I like a red, as long as it's strong and hard.' said Stevie.

'Oh,' I said, turning a little crimson, 'I can drink a red, no bother.'

'Fine,' said Stevie. 'I'll get a bottle of red with supper. I'll look forward to seeing you. We can continue our conversation then.'

Just as she said those words, the studio door burst open, and in came Fergie, half the office staff, my wife and two or three others, all shouting: 'Wind-up!'

'Stevie' was an American actress in the next studio. She was at the Glasgow College of Music and Drama, a friend of a friend. Bastards! To this day, I've never met the real Stevie Nicks. There's no fool like an old fool…

Speaking of old fools, I'll never forget I was offered crumpet on a plate at Hard Rock Hell. The festival was set up by my friend Jonny Davies, who came up with the idea of hiring out a holiday camp during the winter and filling it with bands. People laughed at him, saying, 'Rock festivals take place in summer, Jonny. People stay in tents and drink beer outside. You're mad!'

The first time he ran Hard Rock Hell the attendance was okay. By the third year he'd moved it to Wales and it was selling out in advance. People liked the quality bands and the friendly atmosphere as they stayed in chalets, with toilets and heating.

It was customary to meet Jonny during Hard Rock Hell to have a few drinks, down a midnight kebab and stagger the four hundred yards to bed, drink a half pint of water and then collapse for a well-earned sleep. In 2010 we met around three in the afternoon, and I'd partaken of a couple of cans, but not too much because I'd been doing interviews. That was when two ladies approached me and said, 'Tom Russell! Great to meet you. We listen to you on Rock Radio Manchester.' We chatted away for five minutes and they began to get flirty. 'Are you getting up to any mischief when you're, here, Tom?'

I played a straight bat, saying, 'No, just work, bands and beer.'

One of them snuggled up close to me, thrust her groin against my leg and said, 'We're just heading back to our chalet... would you like to come?'

I shyly replied, 'I'm actually doing a show later and I have a few interviews to do.'

She persisted. 'Come-on, Tom, come back to our chalet. Just you and the two of us.' I hesitated, then she added, 'Wouldn't you like some crumpet?'

I'm such a silly old git. 'Crumpet?'

'Yes, the two us and you. Some crumpet back at our chalet.'

Well, my feet were sore because I'd been standing about for hours. I didn't plan to get up to any real mischief. I thought, 'It can't do any harm. I'll go back, just to be sociable. I know how to behave.'

So I set off back to the chalet with them and they were whooping and laughing. When we got there I settled down on the settee – and then I got this wave of trepidation. One of the girls gave me a triple rum while the other got a frying pan out, put something in the pan and went to the cooker. She poured what she'd cooked onto a plate and placed it on my lap.
She'd handed me a plate of crumpets with butter and maple syrup. The two of them were in fits of laughter at the silly old fool with the big beard.

We ended up having a jolly nice spot of tea. I still see them every now and again, and they never fail to remind me how easily I fell into their trap. I suppose it was a fair cop...

Still on the 'old fool' theme, another band who have broken through in recent years are Halestorm, fronted by Lzzy Hale, who's a great rock singer fronting a hard-working group. I first interviewed them at the Carling Academy in Glasgow when they were supporting Shinedown.

Lzzy is a lovely girl, with the knack of making an old man like me feel like I'm the centre of attention. Her brother Arejay, the drummer, is a smashing bloke too. Since I've started interviewing them, they've become more and more well known. The last time I saw them they were headlining at the Barrowland. The gig was totally sold out, but they still had time to give the likes of me an interview. Watch out for them – they'll just get bigger.

As a married man with two children, I decided to move to a bigger house, and I found one I liked just outside Cumbernauld, set in its own piece of land with very few neighbours. It was out of my price range, but I loved it, and I thought it would be great for the kids. So I totally overstretched myself to buy it. Luckily the bank rate came down over the next few years, making the mortgage payments just about manageable.

Sadly, after a number of years, my marriage came to an end, and I had no choice but to sell the place to help with the settlement. The most difficult thing about moving out was dealing with the massive collection of memorabilia and rubbish I'd collected over the years. Hands up, I'm a hoarder – but I had to face up the fact that I wasn't going to have room for everything any more.

One of my biggest regrets was giving up my Afghan coat. I'd bought it in the late sixties and I found it again when I was clearing out the loft for the removal. My daughter Heather said, 'Dad, Chuck it in the skip.'

'No way,' I said. 'It brings back so many great memories.'

'Take a picture of it and then chuck it,' she said. 'Where else are you going to put it?'

That was the killer. Where was I going to put it, and all the rest of the artefacts I'd accumulated over the years? Heather said, 'Are you ever going to wear the coat again?'

'I might,' I tried.

'Let's see you in it.'

I got one arm in. It must have shrunk in the wash, because that was as far as I got. Or maybe I'd put on a pound or two? I turned my back for a second and Heather threw the coat in the skip.

Six months later the guys from The Temperance Movement were in at Rock Radio for an interview, and one of them was wearing a sixties Afghan which he'd bought in a retro shop for three hundred pounds… I miss my coat.

I have fond memories of that house. The land that came with it had a few mature trees dotted about the place. There was a big storm one time, and one of them was blown over. So I bought myself a chainsaw and started the massive job of cutting it into log-size chunks for my lounge fire. When I relayed my woodcutting exploits to Gavin, now the RealXS managing director, he said he'd use a log as a footstool. I happily obliged the next morning, and he placed it behind his huge desk. Two years later, when he was leaving the company in the changeover to XFM, he returned the log with a nice little message: 'Giving this back to you, Tom. It kept my feet firmly on the ground for the past two years.'

Next to the driveway up to the house there was a pond that filled with frogspawn every spring. We never saw any frogs, but the pond was literally filled. The first year we were there I saw a couple of big white birds near the pond. I thought they were seagulls, but they turned out to be herons. They were there every day for about a fortnight, standing in the water, motionless apart from the odd jab down with their long yellow beaks. No wonder we never saw any fully grown frogs. There was also a badger set somewhere near the house. Occasionally when I was driving home after a late night, I'd see a badger crossing the road. He'd just turn his head, look at the car and carry on, no doubt thinking, 'Who's this, invading my space at two in the morning?'

We had two neighbours in a nearby smallholding, Brian and Raymond. They made us very welcome and were great company. Brian was a big fan of Dusty Springfield – in fact, he was totally obsessed. He had an autographed photo of her in his bathroom, just above the taps.
One Saturday afternoon, he was in the bath having a long soak in preparation for his Saturday night out. Goodness knows how, but he inserted his big toe into the tap and it got stuck. He tried everything, pulling, pushing, twisting, but it refused to budge. Then it started to swell. Poor Brian was there for an hour before Raymond came home and heard the shouts. He made the call to the fire brigade, who arrived fairly quickly. Brian lay quietly, stark naked in a cold bath, with no bubbles to hide his modesty, gazing at Dusty's photo and casting an occasional glance at the fully uniformed fire men freeing his toe. Brian is, of course, gay… and often looks back on that Saturday afternoon with a glint in his eye!

When my daughter Heather was sixteen, I got a phone call from Scottish Television who were doing a late night series called Trial by Night. They picked a subject each week and held a trial, with one expert speaking for the prosecution and one for the defence, in front of a studio audience of about fifty people. They wanted me to appear, and although I'd never seen it, I went along for the recording anyway.
The host, Bernard Ponsonby, (now one of STV's main political correspondents) was a cool guy. The subject was 'Status Quo: should

they just pack it in?' I spoke for the defence; I can't remember who spoke for the prosecution, but they claimed the band had only actually written one song, and just kept reusing it – which, as any rock follower or half-decent musician knows, is complete bollocks. You go to a Status Quo concert and you get two hours of hit after hit after hit. They've always put on a great show.

Heather came along to the recording, which I'd thought would be find. But, my God, the whole thing was a complete nightmare. I hadn't realised there would be a baying mob there, all on the attack, as I tried to defend Status Quo. It was very stressful.

I tried to say, 'You don't have to listen to them if you don't want to. But why deny the band a living, if people still want to go to their concerts? Frank Sinatra played into his eighties, Paul McCartney is still doing it, and so is Keith Richards.'

They just booed and moaned at me all the way through the recording. It wasn't my best experience – and unsurprisingly, I was never asked back.

My Aunt Betty, one of my mum's sisters, did well in life. She and my Uncle Bill worked hard, made a few bob and retired to Cyprus, where they built a lovely house. They used to come home to Scotland regularly to visit family, and the family returned the compliment, going over to Cyprus for a visit.

One year, Betty, my mum and a couple of cronies flew to Cyprus for a holiday. The plane was delayed and arrived in Limassol fairly late in the evening. The girls, with a couple of airline whiskies in them, were waltzing through customs, when Betty was pulled over. An examination of her case revealed a substantial amount of black pudding, square sausages, plain bread and Scottish lamb chops – all strictly banned items.

Well, threats were made, prison sentences were mentioned and tears were shed. But Betty stepped up to the plate, demanded to speak to a supervisor and disappeared into the customs private office for ten minutes. Afterwards the girls' cases were quietly closed, complete with the offending items, and they were waved through to their awaiting taxi. Betty, to this day, has never revealed what went on in that Customs office. I suspect a few banknotes changed hands… but you never know.

A lot of my older relatives have passed away, but Betty is still going strong. She recently celebrated her ninetieth birthday and I was delighted to receive an invitation for Jean and I to attend her birthday dinner at the very posh Culcreuch Castle in Fintry. It was a smashing night: great food, a lovely setting and a chance to re-acquaint with family I'd not seen for some time.

At the end of the night, Betty and Bill's taxi was first on the scene, so they were seen off in good style. Just as they disappeared down the tree-lined drive however, the hotel manager appeared and chased after them, waving the bill. They'd forgotten to settle up. Luckily, Betty's son Alastair was still around, so I was able to point the worried hotel manager in his direction… and make a swift exit myself. All was fine, of course. Alastair put it on his credit card and an embarrassed Uncle Bill squared up the next morning.

In 2015 Jean and I went to Dubai for a week, to celebrate her birthday and to visit her son, Colin, his wife, Esra, and grandson Zac. Colin is a civil engineer and he's been working out there for a few years. As a nice birthday surprise, they gave Jean afternoon tea for the two of us at one of Dubai's poshest hotels, The Ritz. We got done up in our finest, and we were feeling very grand after being shown to our table in this opulent setting.
Just after the first helping of no-crust cucumber sandwiches, this gorgeous model-standard, beautiful woman, walked past. She was on

the phone and wearing a long black cocktail dress with a sexy slit right up the side. I had a quick glance, then pretended I hadn't noticed.

Two minutes later, the woman walked past again, still on the phone,. Jean leaned over to me and said, 'Hooker.'

I had a good look this time, and quietly thought to myself, 'How much?' Over the next fifteen minutes, she must have sauntered past six times, with Jean and I deeply discussing whether she was, or not…

Towards the end of afternoon tea, the truth was revealed. Two of the hotel staff appeared, carrying a huge harp, and set it up in front of our table. The 'hooker' hitched up her cocktail dress, sat down and proceeded to serenade the birthday girl with a beautiful rendition of Happy Birthday To You.

Jean, as you can imagine, has never been allowed to live that one down.

Left: John Fred of Black Stone Cherry gets a copy of his father's album
Right: Beetlejuice at Manchester Halloween party

Carnage and Tom after a night out

Standing on the right side of Guns N' Roses man, Duff McKagan

Def Leppard's Joe Elliott's backstage at the Hydro

Tom introduces Corey Taylor to Rival Sons

Temperance Movement visit the Rock Radio studios

Within Temptation sample haggis

My partner, Jean

Grandson, Zach, in Dubai

The three grandkids: Becca, Emma and Peter

Gene Simmons of Kiss

Interviewing Gary Numan

Ozzy in his Lennon specs

Rock Radio Launch Party

Phil's Wedding

Blackberry Smoke

26. I WAS THERE

Apollo musical ~ Two River Festival ~ a lifetime achievement award ~ Andy Fraser, Justin Hawkins and The Temperance Movement

Free were unstoppable for four or five years in the 1970s – they were blues-rock at its best. Guitarist Paul Kossoff (son of David, the British actor) passed away in 1976 of a heroin-related heart disease, so I never got to meet him. I'd interviewed singer Paul Rodgers a couple of times and I always found him great to talk to. But I'd always wanted to meet bass player Andy Fraser. He'd started out when he was sixteen and wrote a lot of the Free songs, along with Paul.

In 2012 Andy came into Rock Towers with a guy called Tobi, the singer in his new band. Andy was fascinating; he talked about the seventies, touring with Free, and even remembered the Sunderland gig where I'd seen them play.

It was no secret that he was gay and that he had AIDS. By the time I met him, he also had lung cancer. He'd lived in Los Angeles for years making a living as a producer, and he'd decided it was time to have one final crack at putting a band together.

I played the interview on the radio, and about six months later, tour dates were announced. Amazingly, they only had one date in Scotland, at Greens hotel in Kinross. It's a smashing wee venue – the first time I went there was to see Debbie Bonham, late Led Zeppelin drummer John Bonham's sister; she's a very good blues-rock singer.

Backstage in Kinross the band and crew were milling around getting ready, and I saw Andy, sitting in the corner like a wee wizened old man. It was so sad to see him like that. He really didn't look well. His skin was grey. However, he looked up and recognised me right away: 'Oh! Glasgow! how are you doing?'

We chatted away for a few minutes but I could see that he was tired, so I said, 'Have a great show,' and left him to it.

I was worried about him performing that night, but he walked on to the stage with his Fender Precision bass, which was bigger than him, plugged it in... and I couldn't believe it. He grew two feet taller and exploded into a six-foot giant who pranced about the stage for an hour like a true rock god. The place went mental. I was gobsmacked. What a pro!

Sadly, Andy passed away in California on March 16, 2015. A great loss to music and the world in general – a lovely guy.

In 2008 I got a call from a guy called Tommy McGrory from Paisley. He did a lot of work with youngsters in the area who hung about on the streets and didn't have many prospects. His project was called Loud'n'Proud – The School of Rock. It offered kids the chance to learn guitar, bass, drums, violin, keyboards, production or singing. I was impressed, and I told him I'd do anything I could to help.

Tommy said, 'It's not that. You see, I've written this musical, and it's going to be performed by the youngsters from Paisley. I got a grant from Paisley council and the Scottish government, and I've hired the Armadillo for five nights. But I'm hoping to make the grant money back, or at least break even.'

I admit I was flabbergasted. I said, 'The Armadillo? That holds three thousand people. Five nights?' I'm thinking, 'Is this guy the full shilling?' I asked, 'What's your musical about.'
'Well,' he said, 'It's about the Glasgow Apollo. It's called I Was There.'

Tommy worked hard to make it happen, and Rock Radio helped with some free plugs. I think he actually bought some advertising. The show didn't sell out every night, but the first night and the Saturday sold out and the others did okay.

I have to say, it was absolutely brilliant – full of all these funny stories centred around the Apollo. There were wee sketches interspersed with songs by The Who, Roxy Music, AC/DC, Thin Lizzy, Bon Jovi and so on. One particular sketch comes to my mind, set in the Apollo toilet. Wee Johnny and Wee Wullie are in for a slash and Wee Johnny says: 'Anybody watchin'?' Then he takes his ticket out of his pocket, puts it in an envelope, ties something round it and slips it out of the window. It floats down to Wee Shug, who's waiting outside in the street. You see, even although the Apollo held three and a half thousand people, it would have about four thousand in there some nights.

Another sketch featured the notorious bouncers. Wee Malky and Big Jimmy wander into the venue, steamin' after a session in Lauder's bar. The bouncer shows them their seats and they sit down. Two minutes later a different bouncer cames up, looks at their tickets and says, 'There's a problem with these tickets, boys. Come with me.'

'Aw, but mister,' the boys say. 'The band's just about to start.'

'It's awright, come on and we'll get it sorted.' He takes them to the side door and hurls them out into the lane, their tickets safely in his pocket. Then he heads to the front door and re-sells them.

The Apollo was created by Frank Lynch, who owned Unicorn Leisure, the firm that managed Billy Connolly, Christian and Slik back in the day. He'd sold up and moved to Florida, but Tommy had invited him to come and see I Was There. Frank flew over for a night, and watched, possibly with a tear in his eye. At the end, Tommy got up on stage and rattled off a list of thanks including the cast, their parents and Frank.

Then he said, 'There's one other person I'd like to thank – he's about halfway up the auditorium.'

Suddenly this big spotlight came on and he said, 'Tom Russell, would you please come up onto the stage?'
I was totally shocked. I went up, and with a lump in my throat, I stood there and was presented with a plaque from The Loud'n'Proud Orchestra, for services to rock music.

Talking of lumps in throats and tears in eyes…
In 2011 I was invited to the Scottish New Music Awards in Glasgow. I was told that I'd been nominated in one of the categories, so I was chuffed to bits. It was usually the big names like Dougie Donnelly, Robin Galloway or George Bowie that got these plaudits. On the night, it was the Radio Show of the Year award – and to my utter astonishment and great joy, they named me the winner.

I was invited again the following year, and told I'd been nominated again. I thought it was unlikely I'd win, but there was a free bar so I thought I'd go along. You could have knocked me over with a feather when my daughter Heather appeared on the stage, and did a wee speech about her dad, while a video screen dropped down behind her. All sorts of people – Ian Gillan, Joe Elliott, Joey Tempest from Europe, Spike from the Quireboys – all these amazing artists said nice things about me. Then I was presented with a lifetime achievement award. You can see a video of that on my website: tomrussellrocks.com

Tommy McGrory was also responsible for putting another big initiative together in Paisley. He thought the town was in a bad way; the massive shopping centre at Braehead was turning the town centre was into a ghost town. The youngsters didn't seem to be getting a chance in life. Tommy came up with the idea of an open-air music festival in the centre of Paisley. Over a weekend he'd have up-and-coming bands in every pub, and on the Saturday he'd have a big stage in the town square. I said to Tommy, .Why don't we get a couple of well-known bands to attract more people?'

He replied, 'Tom, we can't afford to pay for big acts.' But he let me see what I could do.
The first year of the Two Rivers Rock Festival we managed to get Gun to headline. The next year we got the Quireboys, and for the third year we got The Union, formed by Luke Morley of Thunder. We did it all with no contracts; just a few phone calls and a whole lot of trust and goodwill.

The festival was a great success and the demographic was different from your usual show – whole families, maw, paw and the weans, right in Paisley town centre. After the third year the council pulled the funding. It was hard to justify giving thousands of pounds to a music festival when they were having to cut back on schools, libraries and home helps. Still, it was great at the time.

I only met Justin Hawkins after The Darkness had split up. He and his brother Dan, along with the rest of the band, enjoyed so much success between 2003 and 2004; not only on rock stations but on mainstream channels too. Things went pear-shaped, Justin went to rehab, then he formed his own band Hot Leg, and that's when I arranged to interview him. I thought, 'He's going to be an arse.' But he wasn't. He was a smashing bloke.

In 2011 The Darkness got back together again. They were playing at Download and I was doing my usual, wandering about, interviewing as many people as I could, when I bumped into Justin in the backstage area.

He'd grown a thin, waxed moustache and had a well trimmed goatee beard – he looked just like a baddie in a silent movie, like one of those guys who ties a helpless maiden to a railway track. So I said, 'I see you've grown a moustache… are you trying to keep up with me?'

He laughed and he told me how things were going. I said, 'How do you get your tache to stick out like that?'

'I use wax,' he said.

'I've tried that and it doesn't work.'

He shrugged. 'You must have been using the wrong kind of wax,. Come with me.' I followed Justin to his dressing room and waited util he'd dug out this tin of wax.

There I am, standing with Justin Hawkins of The Darkness, and he's dabbing this wax all over my face, trying to shape my beard. People are walking past, staring at us, as if we're mad. The incident was filmed – I've been told it's on YouTube, though I've never found it.

I've always liked putting on new music. Rival Sons are a very good example. I heard of them from their record label, Earache, which are best-known for the growling style of metal. A journalist called Talita, whose taste I respect, sent me a Rival Sons demo and said, 'Tom, this is a bit different from Earache's usual signings, but have a listen.' I did, and I thought, 'This is really good.'

I met them at the High Voltage festival in London, and when I watched them live they confirmed my suspicions. Singer Jay Buchanan has that one-off mystical thing that means you can't take your eyes off him. He reminds me of Jim Morrison.

The Temperance Movement are another fabulous band. When I had the record shop in Bishopbriggs, this young lad used to come in from time to time and buy an album, usually things like The Rolling Stones. He would tell me he was a singer-songwriter and that he was hoping to make a career in music. I'd wish him all the best. Then he came in one day and told me he'd been signed to EMI.

His name was Phil Campbell and the record label pushed him for a few years, but it didn't happen and he was eventually dropped. A good while later he came into the shop and asked if I was still doing discos. 'I'm getting married,' he said. 'We'd love it if you could do the wedding, play a bit of rock for us and a bit of ABBA for the mums and dads.' The night went well and I never saw him for a couple of years – then, lo and behold, he was signed by Virgin. Unfortunately after an album and a couple of singles he was dropped again.

I was in Argyll Street a couple of years later when I bumped into Phil again. I don't know if he had a drink in him that day, but he really looked down-and-out, quite depressed. I thought, 'This guy has had two bites at the cherry and he still has nothing to show for it – career over.' I was still convinced he had lots to offer, so I said, 'Look, you write good songs and you can really sing, Keep going, Phil.'

Driving back from Manchester one day the following year, I was playing a new bands compilation CD. The first band was okay, the second was poor; then the third track came on and I nearly veered off the road. It was an absolute stormer. And more than that, there was something familiar about the voice. I couldn't put my finger on it, but I played the song, which was by The Temperance Movement on my Friday Night Rock Show that week.

When I was sent their album about a month later, it all went 'click'. They played Nice N'Sleazy in Glasgow, I went along and saw Phil fronting this superb rock band. Then they came back and played Oran Mor, then the Queen Margaret Union. Then the ABC and then the Barrowland. The band is just what Phil needed – his songs, his fantastic voice, his perseverance and unquenchable talent got him there in the end.

There are so many band stories I could tell that would fill this book, but I've kept it to the ones that I can clearly remember... and that I won't get sued over.

Around 2005, a band I won't name were playing Glasgow as part of a UK tour. They were staying in a less fashionable hotel, and, after the gig, held court in the bar for a handful of friends. The drink was flowing freely, but around two in the morning the hotel staff announced curtly that the bar was shutting – much to the annoyance of the bass player and the drummer, who hatched an ingenious plot for revenge. After breakfast the next morning, just before checking out, they unscrewed the back of the old-style TV in their room, took a dump into the works, then screwed it back on the TV.

I can only imagine the reaction that evening when the next residents thought the room had a funny smell, until they switched on the TV and had to vacate the place. Silly and immature, yes – but perhaps a lesson to all late night hotel staff: don't upset your guests.

Something similar took place in the late eighties, when a big American band were starting a European tour at the Apollo, and staying overnight at the Albany Hotel. One of their new roadies was a big Glasgow guy who had a reputation as a bit of a drinker. I was in the hotel bar with them all when, around two in the morning, the roadie challenged the band's singer to a drinking contest. Since the singer was known for holding his drink, I stayed to watch the fun. By four o'clock they were just about keeping the game going, and then the big roadie collapsed. The singer blurted out, 'Thank God! I don't think I could have managed another drop!'

The handful of us left standing were saying our goodnights when the singer said, 'Wait a minute.' He turned the blacked-out roadie on his side, undid his belt and pulled his jeans down. He went into his pocket and pulled out a Durex – or, as he called it, 'a rubber'. He rolled it onto his finger and inserted it where the sun doesn't shine. Then he extracted his finger, leaving the rubber in position, pulled the roadie's jeans part-way-up and staggered off to bed.

I never did hear what happened in the morning, but you can just imagine around six in the morning, when the hotel cleaner was running the hoover through the lounge bar… The poor roadie, wakened by the noise, must have thought, 'Oh, my head!' Then, soon afterwards, he'd have thought, 'Oh, my arse!'

27. ROCK OFF

The end of the dream ~ my struggle to survive ~ new interests ~ thanks to the team

Radio Clyde never revealed exact audience figures for their shows. They'd just say they were 'good' or 'bad', full-stop. Managing director Alex Dickson was a shrewd man – he knew that if a DJ thought he was doing well, he'd knock the door looking for a few more pounds a week. So Alex preferred to keep us in the dark.

Rock Radio was much more open, as part of the 'one big team' feel. We were kept informed about our figures. We started off with thirty-five thousand listeners and it kept creeping up until we got to seventy thousand, which was pretty good given the coverage we were allowed. Ofcom, the government body that controls the use of radio frequencies, issued different types of licences. Rock Radio's coverage was very limited.

An analogy might be that you can have different sizes of PA system. A thousand-watt PA will push sound further than a fifty-watt PA. When it came to radio transmitters, Clyde was five kilowatts; Real Radio was ten kilowatts; Radio Scotland was twenty kilowatts. Rock Radio was only one-and-a-half kilowatts, and the government wouldn't change it.
That meant a lot of Glasgow and the surrounding area couldn't hear us, and that advertisers didn't always want to come on board. But we were stuck with it; the government wouldn't change it.

I'd meet people, even a few years into doing Rock Radio, who didn't realise I was still broadcasting. They'd say something like, 'Tom, I saw you back at the Apollo. I used to listen to you on Radio Clyde. What are you doing now?'

I'd say, 'I'm doing lunchtimes on Rock Radio.'

They'd ask, 'What's that?'

So there was plenty of work to be done when it came to spreading the word – or the sound, in my case.

On the other hand, I'd sometimes meet a guy at a gig with a well-worn AC/DC shirt, who'd tell me: 'I used to listen to you on Radio Clyde when I was seventeen. I went to university, qualified, got married and the t-shirts and the jeans got lost in a drawer somewhere. I had a couple of kids, stopped going to gigs, wore my suit every day… Then one of my pals told me about Rock Radio.'

That would reignite his interest in rock music. Before you knew it he was digging out the old shirts, going to gigs, and getting his old friends – who might be bank managers, dentists or lawyers – to come with him. Then, at the gigs, he'd start meeting people he hadn't seen in years. A lot of guys like that might stand in the queue to get in feeling a wee bit embarrassed, out of place, around the younger folk; but by the time they're inside watching the show, they've forgotten any worries about being outsiders.
That scenario has happened to me loads of times. And you know something? It's wonderful. Rock is a family.

The next step is embracing new, young bands. It annoys me when I wander into a gig with a great new band on, and they're brilliant, but there's only about fifty people watching them. I know fine well that you can go round the corner to a rock pub and find another fifty people, having a couple of pints, and asking for Ace of Spades to be played – instead of supporting a new band. It's great when you can combine those two audiences.

It was a terrible disappointment in my career when the Guardian decided to rebrand Rock Radio. Some of the senior management were made redundant and they decided to launch a station of their own. I was sad that I wasn't asked to be part of it. I don't know why; perhaps I was too old, or perhaps, as happens in my life, my face just didn't fit.

Radio is a funny business; it tends to be run by accountants. In fact, if you ask some people at the top of these stations who Ozzy plays with, they wouldn't have a clue. Not their strength, perhaps.

The accountants knew that Real Radio was their pop station that was doing well; Smooth Radio was easy-listening and made a lot of money; and Rock Radio was this bastard child with DJs who wanted expenses for going to a festival to interview people with names like Axl Rose.

Big advertisers would sometimes be reluctant to advertise on a rock station. It wasn't the right demographic. 'Long-haired layabouts wearing Led Zeppelin t-shirts and jeans? That's not the sort of crowd we're after for our product,' they'd say. Of course, just because someone has long hair and jeans doesn't mean they're a layabout!

The Guardian had found that the internet was reducing newspaper sales, so the planned Rock Radio expansion – that aim of putting a rock station in every UK city, like they have in America – was put on the shelf. The Newcastle station was closed, then, despite some flawed logic, they changed the remaining stations' names to Real XS. That meant it could be more readily associated with Real Radio, so a sales rep could go to a customer and say, 'We've got a special package: for twenty thousand you can get five spots a day on Real; and for an extra five you can get the same on Real XS. It's the same thing as Real, only we play a bit more Eagles and Bon Jovi.' It sounded easier to pitch.

Things improved financially, but that meant the 'suits' wanted us to lose the Metallica, Motorheads and Megadeths of this world. We'd argue that they were some of the biggest rock bands in the world. The answer was: 'It doesn't suit the advertisers.' Soon we were left with Steely Dan, Bon Jovi and Journey – and inevitably, a percentage of the listeners disappeared.

It was even more frustrating when, after two years, the Guardian decided to sell their radio division to Global, who already owned dozens of stations, mostly in England. As far as Scotland was concerned, they wanted Real and Smooth because they made money, and they turned Real Radio into Heart FM. They didn't have a classic rock brand, but they did have XFM in London and Manchester. So Real XS Glasgow became XFM, offering three-city coverage to advertisers.

I knew my coat was on a shaky peg. XFM plays indie music with just a smattering of classic rock. When the boss came up from London and asked me in for a chat, I thought my P45 was on the way. So I was surprised when he said, 'We want to keep you, Tom, but we'd like to move you to weekends.'

I had a choice to make. I still had a mortgage to pay and I was already in my sixties. Should I take a gig that my heart wasn't a hundred percent into? Or should I say, 'The music's shite – I'm off.' I could leave with my head held high, but I'd be struggling to make ends meet.

Looking back, I'm not sure if I did the right thing, but I decided to give it a go.

Global were keen on networking. They could see a way to maximise profits by merging output across multiple stations. Rather than having fifty DJ's working away in local studios, one DJ could do it all from one place, usually London with the obvious savings in wages. Some of us threw our hands up and said, 'What about the whole point of local radio? How does a guy in London know what's happening in all those other places?'

To me it was total anathema. I remembered what it was like before there was any local radio – you had Radio 1 with some presenter saying, 'Oh, we've had a request from Mill-in-gavie, up in bonny Scotland, hoots mon, it's a braw bricht moonlit nicht. Here's Diana Ross and the Supremes with Baby Love.' No disrespect to those guys, but they generated a huge feeling of condescension. When Radio Clyde kicked off in Glasgow it was wonderful: you could listen to Tiger Tim and Tam Ferrie, local guys that were talking about Argyle Street, Dumbarton Road or Motherwell in your own accent. They were speaking to the people in the area. Global planned to take us back to the bad old days, undoing all the good that had been done, just for profit.

The government body, Ofcom, resisted networking for a while. They came up with the rule that, in a different country (and Scotland was classed as such) there should be seven hours of locally-made programming every weekday, and four on Saturdays and Sundays.

So, the only reason I was kept on at XFM was that I ticked the box for the required four hours at the weekend. Through the week, Fraser Thompson did the breakfast show and Jim Gellatly did the drivetime show. And that was it.

I found myself going into the studio in Baillieston, which had been a hive of activity and excitement for seven years, where we'd made fun and creative radio. Now I was there at weekends from six until ten in the morning. There were only two people in the entire building – me and the newsreader – and, as you can imagine, there aren't a lot of listeners around at those times.

I know you have to make money or cut costs but the balance didn't seem right. That was XFM. I did it; but every record I played had been pre-programmed by some young chap in London. All I had to do was talk in between the tracks, limited to the amount of time I could speak. Sometimes it was just 30 seconds. It killed spontaneity.

Jim Gellatly is a well-respected presenter, and although his main love is the indie scene, we get on fine. He was covering T in the Park when I was on XFM, and I was told he'd do a live interview with me on Saturday and Sunday, setting the scene at the festival. On the first day he told me about who he'd seen, who he was going to see, and the interviews he'd done that he'd play on his show through the week. It was all relevant stuff and we did it in five minutes.

Well, what a bollocking I got from the boss: 'Tom, five minutes of speech? You should know by now that two minutes is the max!'

So on the Sunday Jim came on again, and we ended up talking like Pinky and Perky on speed, just trying to cram it all in. It was even more ridiculous when you considered that the show after mine was hosted by some comedian in London who talked non-stop mince for at least five minutes between every record.

Over the years I've had a few minor altercations with bosses at Radio Clyde, Rock Radio and Real XS. They were mainly about the length of interviews. The standard practice on commercial radio has always been that an interview should only be two to three minutes long, at the most. The theory is that the listener gets bored after just a couple of minutes of speech. My argument has always been that the most listened-to shows on radio are the football phone-ins, which are two hours of non-stop talking. I reckon, if the speech is interesting, it doesn't matter whether it's a football manager or a singer in a rock band. If the listener is interested and the chat is engaging, then it's good radio – whether it's two, three or five minutes.

On XFM, I was seriously frustrated. All I could do was say what the next record was, plug the next show and tell the time. The pay was okay, but there was no fun, and no sense of doing anything useful. XFM was just too different from Rock Radio. The station lasted less than a year and Global handed the licence back, saying they couldn't make it work.

A new DAB station had started in Scotland called Rocksport Radio. Based in Glasgow, it played some rock music and covered all the sport, not just football. My friend Ian Martin was working there, so I called to see if there were any openings. The boss, Bill Young, offered me a couple of weekend shows. It was a new challenge – interviewing football managers, golfers, tennis and ice-hockey players, along with helping to expand the range of rock played on the station. It was just what I needed. I was back working with local, like-minded people and I thoroughly enjoyed my year there. Sadly, the station went out of business in 2016.

Just when I'd started to slow down a bit, I got a call from one of the bosses at RealXS Manchester, which had continued as a standalone station after the buy-out. He asked if I'd be interested in doing some shows for him. I thought he was maybe talking about a couple of weekend shows; but he offered me six nights a week on a six-month contract. After a bit of thought I told him I didn't fancy all the travel. He said they were prepared to hire a studio in Glasgow for me. So of course, I said 'yes', and off I went on another hectic six-month stint, busier than ever.

Regrettably, at the end of the six months, they changed the station format at RealXS Manchester, and I was replaced by a football phone-in.

I started doing the film extra work again, and I landed a couple of weeks' work on a film called Tommy's Honour, about golf in St Andrews in the 1870s. The star was Glaswegian Peter Mullan, who was a joy to work with – no airs and graces, just one of the boys. (During the shoot I got talking to Paul Murdoch, a fellow extra in top hat and Victorian coat. He persuaded me to write this book and he was instrumental in making it happen.)

I also worked on the remake of Whisky Galore, starring Gregor Fisher and Eddie Izzard. I played an islander, helping to steal cases of whisky from a wrecked ship. It was a lot of fun.

The older I get, the more interested I get in Scottish history. My pal Gordon has a lot to do with that. He really knows the subject and he's right into traditional music. I enjoy going round the old castles and stately homes. I love reading about the Scottish enlightenment, the clan system, and the influence that this wee country of ours has had on the world. In 2015 I started reading a series of books called Outlander by Diana Gabaldon. I found them fascinating – so, as you can imagine, I was disappointed not to get a job as an extra on the Outlander series, which is mainly filmed in Scotland and set in the 1740s, the time of the Jacobite rising and the Battle of Culloden. I think my beard may have been too long to play a Highlander!

(One of my favourite stories about my pal Gordon took place at a folk festival in the north of Scotland, where, admittedly, strong drink had been taken. A few of the musicians were staying over at a local hotel, and around two in the morning, only the last few diehards were still standing. The word went round that one wee fiddler had retired early, in a bad way (an alleged bad pint was the cry), so the rest of the team managed to get into his room, where they found him fast asleep. It was a budget hotel, so the bed was not substantial; and the lads managed, without waking the fiddler, to unscrew the legs from the bed, and manoeuvre it down the corridor to the deserted reception area. They just left him there, in the middle of reception, snoring his head off.)

The staff at Rock Radio were second to none. Some real stand-out people for me were: Angela, LJ, Father Ted, Fergie and young Lisa.

LJ (Laura Jane) was the events co-ordinator, the merch' girl, whatever was needed – she usually stepped up to the mark. A lovely girl, her mother-hen qualities really came into play with all us rascally DJs. I would stay sober all day when I was doing interviews at the festivals, but when the last interview finished around eight o'clock and the headline act hit the stage, I'd make up for lost time. Soon I'd be wandering about, not quite sure where I was, and I wasn't the only one. LJ would gather us all up when the headline act finished and make sure we got back to the hotel.

Lisa, our programme assistant, was there from day one. She's really into the new rock: Linkin Park, Blink 182 and so on. She was brilliant at keeping me up to date, she was still there when Rock Radio turned into RealXS then XFM. Later there was an opportunity in sales, so she moved over to that side of the business and she's doing well.

In the early days Father Ted was a bit like marmite. Some listeners loved him, some couldn't stand him – but as the years passed he got funnier and funnier on air, took lots of risks and was more often than not in the office for a bollocking.

It helped that Angela was into rock, and that she was a terrier, a fabulous salesperson, who not only made the sale, but liked to look after the client and make sure any campaign produced results.

Another one needing a special mention is Ciaran, the station manager. He was definitely one of the boys, well up for a laugh, and always open to suggestions from the team to make things better.

Finally, I've got to give a mention to Stephanie McCrackin, she worked steadily behind the scenes, doing all the unglamorous stuff. An irreplaceable member of the team.

28. WHAT'S NEXT

The people who matter ~ plans for the future

I'd like to close my book by mentioning a few people.

Billy Sloan made his name by slagging anything that was popular, especially established rock bands. I get on fine with Billy; even though he's been a lifelong teetotaller, he used to come into my shop as a teenager, so I have a soft spot for the guy. He was into punk, so he'd buy the Clash, the Stranglers, all that stuff, at one single a week. I remember him coming in one day to tell me he was going down south to see this up-and-coming band called The Sex Pistols. Their first single was just out. I was amazed by his enthusiasm when he came back the following week to tell me that this band was the future of rock'n'roll. They'd only played for twenty minutes, but according to Billy, they were brilliant.

I'm still friendly with most of my fellow DJs from the Radio Clyde days, but Gary Marshall is special. He's a DJ's DJ. Although he was firmly pop-orientated, he really knew what he was doing. He gave me all sorts of great tips, especially when it came to keeping a programme flowing.

Gary did a double-header on Clyde with Ross King for a while. Ross has done very well – he's GMTV's Hollywood correspondent – but in the early days they called themselves The Sunshine Boys and played off each other. Ross was always hungry looking for a step up. At an after-show party he'd always be chatting away to the movers and shakers, whereas Gary would just have a blether with anyone. I'm not slagging anyone off – they were just two different kinds of people. Both were cool, but they had different drives and ambitions.

Gary ended up on Westsound Radio in Ayr for a while, and so did I at one point, one night a week. I'd do Friday from six until nine in the evening, then drive up to Clyde for the Friday Night Rock Show. Gary and I would often have a blether as we changed over. He was always keen to show me a few wee tips. Just small things that you didn't particularly need on the Friday Night Rock Show, but for a daytime slot, they were invaluable. All his advice came to the fore when I got the call from Rock Radio to do a daytime show. It was nerve-racking, I was going right out of my comfort zone, but at least I had those tips from Gary to keep me on track. I'll always be grateful to him for that.

Another great pal of mine in the business is Paul Carlin, known to all and sundry as 'Carnage'. I remember the night he got the name. He was working as one of the producers on Rock Radio, and we used to have RAJAR Nights, when the audience figures would come out. Regardless of the ratings, the bosses would take us out for a piss-up. On this particular night they took us to a casino on the Clydeside. So it was a meal and unlimited drink – whatever you wanted: a double brandy, a pint of heavy, whatever. The lightweights started to leave around ten o'clock, and by midnight there were four of us left.

I'd just managed to get a double JD and coke before the bar tab ran out. Paul, however, had missed the round. So he picked up a pint tumbler with about an inch left in it, and went round the tables gathering up all the slops. Vodka, guinness, brandy, champagne… he got about three quarters of a pint, then he started drinking it. He managed to get about half of it down him until he stopped and let out an immense rift.

Eventually I got a taxi home in one direction and he got a one in the other. That night he was the original bouncy man; but the next day, with a massive hangover, he looked like death warmed up. After that, we called him Carnage.

Ricky Warwick is another great friend of mine. I first met him in 1988 when he gave me a cassette of his unsigned band The Almighty. I still have it. Throughout their career, I remained close with them, and I was sad when they split up in 1996. Ricky continued to write songs and tour solo, and I was always happy to have him in the studio, and to have him playing the Rock Radio Birthday Bash in 2007 (along with Stumpy, The Almighty's drummer). Two years later I was delighted to hear that Ricky was the new singer in Thin Lizzy, a role that he fitted perfectly. After touring extensively, they recorded a new album – but out of respect for the late Phil Lynott, they changd their name to Black Star Riders.

Without Paul Murdoch I'd never have got round to writing this book. His encouragement, help and input was invaluable.

Martin Kielty, who's been a stalwart of the Glasgow rock scene for many years, was a great help getting the book to the finishing line.

I also want to thank Jean, my partner. I got married in 1980 and had two wonderful, talented children; but the marriage broke up after thirty-two years. That's just the way it is these days. I wasn't expecting it; it just happened. However, I'm eternally grateful to have met Jean. I only hope she feels the same way, as there are a few examples of my behaviour that may leave her less than impressed… For example, the first call I got after signing on again as an extra, was for BBC drama Shetland, starring Dougie Henshall. I was offered three days' work in Paisley. Jean was initially delighted that her man was going to be on the telly, and spent the next two days telling her cronies all about it. You can imagine her disappointment, however, when I came home from the first day's filming to tell her I was playing a patient in an old folks' home, in a wheelchair,. She said, 'I can't tell my pals that!' It was even more disappointing six months later when we watched the show. After my three days filming, all you saw was my wheelchair being pushed down the corridor… and when it turned right, you got an excellent view of my right foot! Such are the rewards as an extra.

I met Jean when I was going though the divorce and we got on great. She didn't know anything about rock music but I suppose it's true what they say: opposites attract. Because of the divorce I had to sell my dream house, my big pad in the country, but Jean generously offered me to be her bidie-in, and we've been happily together now for over four years. On air, I affectionately call Jean 'her indoors'.

As most men do, I have favourite items of clothing, even though they should probably have been binned long ago. In my case, it was a pair of old boxer shorts. Grey, slightly tattered, and with a few wee holes – but so comfy. Within the first week of moving in, however, Jean announced, 'They should be in the bin, Tom.'

I said, 'No, no… they're my favourites. I've had them for years!'

Then, one night, as I was putting some rubbish into the outside bin I noticed this pair of boxers in the bin. I thought, 'This is an outrage!' I took them back into the house, waved them under her nose and said, 'What's this?'

Jean was all sweet and innocent. 'I don't know…'

I said, 'It must have been the next door neighbour. These grey boxers of mine must have blown into their back lawn from our washing line, they've picked them up with a pair of tweezers and put them in our bin.'

At that, Jean admitted the crime. 'Alright, I confess, it was me!' She added, 'I'm not going to wash these boxers ever again! They're done. They're a disgrace. I'll buy you another pair.'
I have to report: it's happened again since, with a couple of my old t-shirts. Ah well… there are more important things in life.

I'd been seeing Jean for a few weeks when I was working on the third Two Rivers Rock Festival in Paisley. I was compere for the day and I asked her to come along. She was enjoying herself until, late in the afternoon, I took her to a pub for a drink and a sandwich. A lady, who will of course remain nameless, came running up to me, arms outstretched, declaring her undying love. She asked if I'd give her an autograph, and lifted up her t-shirt to display her well-presented new brassiere. She handed me a black felt tip pen and told me to get on with it. Glancing sheepishly at Jean, I obliged.

She then apologised to Jean, blamed the drink and asked Jean if I was her man. Jean admitted to the crime. So the lady shouted over to her man, 'Johnny, get your arse over here! Drop your kegs so Jean can autograph them!'

One of the things we had in common from the start was travelling. Jean loves to travel and so do I. A few months after we met, we booked a cruise to the Canaries, and we found a Southampton hotel that offered a taxi to the port the next morning, so we could leave the car for a week. The great day arrived – we set off from Glasgow early and arrived at the hotel at five o'clock in the evening. On checking in, the receptionist asked what time we wanted transport to the port, and what ship we were on. When we said it was the Britannia, she said, 'Are you sure?'

She called for her manager, who finally blurted out, 'Britannia sailed today, Saturday, at four o'clock.'

We said, 'No, she sails tomorrow, Sunday, at four o'clock. Look at our documents…' Oops – we'd made an arse of it. We'd got the sailing day wrong, and as we were arriving at our hotel, our fellow passengers were settling in and exploring the boat. Our ship had sailed.

Jean was inconsolable; but a calm head plus a credit card saved the day. Next morning we got the bus to Gatwick, caught a flight to Maderia, the first port of call, checked into a hotel for a couple of nights, and then waited for the ship. I'm still paying for it! Next time, we'll check our dates a bit more carefully.

At the time of writing, we're waiting for Ofcom, the body in charge of broadcasting, to decide who'll get the 96.3FM licence for Glasgow. It has an increased signal strength from the Rock Radio days, making it more likely that it can turn a profit as a standalone business. Four companies have applied, including one called Rock Radio Glasgow. It's supported by a number of local businessmen who feel there's a need for an alternative to stations playing broadly similar music. The Rock Radio Glasgow application has also received overwhelming support from local people who want a station that plays the music that they want to hear.

My hope is that the bid will be successful, that I'll get a job on the station, and that my amazing adventure will continue a bit longer.

If it doesn't work out, I have no job and not much chance of getting one at my age. So I'll take up golf again, continue going to Falkirk matches and make full use of my Glasgow Warriors rugby season ticket. I'll take her indoors on the occasional holiday and allow her to take me shopping twice a year. I'll spend even more time with my lovely grandchildren. And I'll look back over the past sixty-odd years with a smile.

AFTERWORD

I've had two nicknames over the past few years and we swithered over which one to use for the title of the book. Firstly there was 'The Beard of Doom'. Kieron Elliot, first presenter of the breakfast show on 96.3 Rock Radio, started calling me that during the handovers between our shows. It stuck, and for the past few years people have frequently come up to me at gigs and said, 'Hello, Beard Of Doom, how are you?'

The second nickname, which we went for as the title, is 'The Godfather of Rock'. It goes back to the Radio Clyde days. I actually have no memory however of how it started, or who came up with it. If it was you, please get in touch and let me know.

Digging out the photos for the book proved to be a mammoth task. I just have too many, so it was difficult selecting which ones to use. So I've set up a website – www.tomrussellrocks.com – where many of the other photos are available to view.

There are so many stories I've remembered while putting the finishing touches to the book, but we had to draw the line somewhere. Apologies if you're disappointed that your particular story hasn't made it – I need to keep some up my sleeve…

If you fancy following me on twitter: TomRussell666

On Facebook: Tom Russell Beard Of Doom

My website is: tomrussellrocks.com

MARTIN KIELTY is the author of five novels and eleven rock history books including Apollo Memories, SAHB Story: The Tale Of The Sensational Alex Harvey Band and Chris Glen: The Bass Business.

He's a regular contributor to Classic Rock and Metal Hammer magazines plus a range of newspapers, periodicals and websites. He also writes for television and theatre, and appears on STV Glasgow. He's a former manager of The Sensational Alex Harvey Band and The Rezillos, an active drummer, and a former presenter on 96.3 Rock Radio. www.martinkielty.com

TUESDAY TAKEOVER PLAYLISTS

BLACK STONE CHERRY

Alterbridge - Isolation
Stone Temple Pilots - Down
Slipknot - Psychosocial
Black Syone Cherry - White Trash Millionaire
Sevendust - Waffle
Led Zeppelin - Ramble On
Rolling Stones - Gimme Shelter
Black Stone Cherry - Killing Floor
Soundgarden - Rusty Cage
Rod Stewart - Hot Legs
Lynyrd Skynyrd - Gimme Back My Bullets
Bad Company - Rock N Roll Fantasy
Free - Wishing Well
Black Stone Cherry - In My Blood
Silver chair - Israelis Son

MOTLEY CRUE (NIKKI SIXX)

E.L.O. - Can't Get It Out Of My Head
David Bowie - Rebel Rebel
Nine Inch Nails - The Hand That Feeds
Lynyrd Skynyrd - Gimme Back My Bullets
Cheap Trick - On Top Of The World
Van Halen - Running With The Devil
Hole - Samantha
New York Dolls - Showdown
Motorhead - Killers
Montrose - Space Station *5
T-Rex - The Slider
Kiss - Deuce

Judas Priest - Grinder
Cypress Hill - Rise Up
Slade - Gudbuy T'Jane
Moby - Come On Baby
Queen - Ogre Battle
UFO - Doctor Doctor

ROB ZOMBIE

Frank Zappa - Hungry Freaks, Daddy
Faces - Miss Judys Farm
Rob Zombie - Pussy Liquor
Butthole Surfers - Tonque
Allman Brothers - Whipping Post
Billy Preston - Space Race
Alice Cooper - Muscle Of Love
The Cure - Caterpillar
Harry Nilson - Jump Into The Fire
Rob Zombie - What
Mott The Hoople - Alice
Rolling Stones - Rocks Off
Slade - Get Down and Get With It
Sonic Youth - Starpower
Sweet - Sweet FA
Lou Reed - Hanging Around
Manfred Mann - Blinded By The Light
Iggy Pop - Nightclubbing
Badfinger - No Matter What
Rob Zombie - Lords Of Salem

ZAKK WYLDE

Black Label Society - Crazy Horses
Led Zeppelin - Black Dog
Rolling Stones - Street Fighting Man
Elton John - Tiny Dancer
Black Sabbath - Into The Void
Alice In Chains - Dam That River
Soundgarden - Outshined
Neil Young - Unknown Legend
Jimi Hendrix - Little Wing
Eagles - Hotel California
Allman Brothers - Midnight Rider
Lynyrd Skynyrd - I Know A Little
AC/DC - Highway To Hell
Bad Company - Shooting Star
Black Label Society - Spoke In The Wheel
Ozzy Osbourne - Miracle Man
Damage Plan - Save Me
Judas Priest - Riding On The Wind
ZZ Top - Beer Drinkers and Hell Raisers
Black Label Society - Darkest Days

ALTERBRIDGE (MYLES KENNEDY)

Black Sabbath - Mob Rules
The Who - Baba O'Riley
AC/DC - Touch Too Much
Alterbridge - Isolation
David Bowie - Suffragette City
Queen - We Will Rock You
Motorhead - We Are The Road Crew
Rush - Subdivisions
White Stripes - Icky Thump

UFO - Love To Love
Led Zeppelin - Going To California
Guns N Roses - Welcome To The Jungle
Pink Floyd - Comfortably Numb
AC/DC - Let There Be Rock
Police - Synchronicity 2
Alterbridge - Wonderful Life
Led Zeppelin - The Rain Song
Whitesnake - Still Of The Night
Ozzy Osbourne - You Can't Kill Rock & Roll
Elton John - Levon
Slash - Back From Cali
Led Zeppelin - No Quarter
Alterbridge - Blackbird

MR BIG (BILLY SHEEHAN)

David Lee Roth - Yankee Rose
Mr Big - Addicted To That Rush
Byrds - Eight Miles High
Yardbirds - Lost Woman
Mr Big - To Be With You
Judas Priest - Breaking The Law
Iron Maiden - Run To The Hills
David Lee Roth - Shy Boy
Beatles - If I Fell
Mr Big - Green Tinted 60's Mind
Bryan Adams - Summer Of 69
AC/DC - Night Prowler
Rush - Spirit Of Radio
Mr Big - Colorado Bullfrog
Yes - Roundabout
Pink Floyd - Money
Mr Big - Alive and Kicking

PAUL WELLER

Kinks - I'm Not Everybody Else
Primal Scream - Kill All Hippies
Tame Impala - Desire Be Desire Go
Paul Weller - Moonshine
David Bowie - Moonage Daydream
The Strokes - Someday
Iggy Pop - Search and Destroy
Pink Floyd - Lucifer Sam
Paul Weller - Wake Up The Nation
Caravan - A Place Of My Own
Velvet Underground - Waiting For The Man
Black Keys - The Only One
The Coral - Jacqueline
Paul Weller - Up The Dosage
Little Richard - Slippin' and Slidin'
Plan B - Stay Too Long
Stereophonics - Dakota
Dr Feelgood - She Does It Right
Wild Beasts - All The Kings Men
Libertines - I No Longer Hear The Music
Paul Weller - Two Fat Ladies

GLENN HUGHES

Terry Reid - Dean
Free - I'll Be Creepin'
Traffic - Empty Pages
Buffalo Springfield - For What It's Worth

Neil Young - A Man Needs A Maid
Sly & The Family Stone - If You Want Me To Stay
Stevie Wonder - Visions
Prince - Diamonds and Pearls
Free - Fire and Water
CSNY - Carry On
Humble Pie - Hot and Nasty
David Bowie - Station To Station
Glenn Hughes - I Don't Want To Live That Way
Rolling Stones - Gimme Shelter
Tommy Bolin - Lotus
Black Crowes - Soul Singing
Jimi Hendrix - Freedom
Led Zeppelin - When The Levee Breaks
Rainbow - Catch The Rainbow
Beatles - A Day In The Life

MANIC STREET PREACHERS

Free - My Brother Jake
Aerosmith - Back In The Saddle
Sex Pistols - Did You No Wrong
Alice In Chains - Them Bones
Dinosaur Jr - Start Choppin'
Billy Squire - Lonely Is The Night
Faces - Debris
The Clash - Safe European Home
Beatles - Paperback Writer
Dead Kennedys - California Uber Alles
Jesus & Mary Chain - April Skies
E.L.O. - Last Train To London
Black Sabbath - Neon Nights
Hanoi Rocks - Boulevard Of Broken Dreams
Guns N Roses - It's So Easy

Husker Du - Sorry Somehow
Echo & The Bunnymen - My Kingdom
Teenage Fanclub - Star Sign
Stevie Wonder - Higher Ground
The Skids - A Woman In Winter
Smashing Pumpkins - Cherub Rock
Simple Minds - Life In A Day
Rolling Stones - Happy

TOTO (STEVE LUKATHER)

Beatles - I Saw Her Standing There
Jimi Hendrix - Purple Haze
Steely Dan - Kid Charlemagne
Rolling Stones - Honky Tonk Woman
Lukather - Ever Changing Times
Pink Floyd - Comfortably Numb
Genesis - Firth Of Fifth
Cream - Crossroads
Joe Walsh - Rocky Mountain Way
Yes - Roundabout
Van Halen - Eruption
The Who - Won't Get Fooled Again
Rage Against The Machine - Bulls On Parade
Bob Scaggs - Breakdown Dead Ahead
Michael Jackson - Beat It
Randy Newman - I Love LA
Lukather - Hero With 1000 Eyes
Cheap Trick - Voices
Jeff Beck - Where Were You
Toto - Hold The Line

STATUS QUO

Andrew Gold - Lonely boy
Johnny & The Hurricanes - Red River Rock
Eagles - The Last Resort
Status Quo - All I Really Wanna Do
E.L.O. - Can't Get It Out Of My Head
Led Zeppelin - Dyer Maker
Snow Patrol - Chasing Cars
Beatles - Across The Universe
Pink Floyd - Comfortably Numb
AC/DC - Whole Lotta Rosie
Everly Brothers - Temptation
Status Quo - Marguerita Time
David Bowie - The Man Who Sold The World
Bob Seger - Old Time Rock & Roll
Killers - Read My Mind
The Move - Fire Brigade
Manfred Mann - Davy's On The Road Again
Jimi Hendrix - Hey Joe
Little Richard - Lucille
Beatles - I Am The Walrus
Status Quo - In The Army Now

WOLFMOTHER

Neil Young - Don't Let It Bring You Down
Beatles - Don't Bring Me Down
Bob Dylan - Man In Me
AC/DC - Jailbreak
Donovan - Jennifer Juniper
Jimi Hendrix - Burning Of The Midnight Lamp
Steve Miller - Fly Like An Eagle
Kate Bush - Wuthering Heights

Stevie Nicks - Leather and Lace
Doobie Brothers - Long Train Running
Willie Nelson - To All The Girls I've Loved Before
Kiss - Shandy
Bonnie Tyler - Total Eclipse Of The Heart
Supertramp - Dreamer
Led Zeppelin - The Grunge

GENESIS

Jimi Hendrix - Hey Joe
Don Henley - The End Of The Innocence
Paul Carrack - How Long
Beatles - Paperback Writer
Seal - Crazy
Steely Dan - Ricky Don't Lose That Number
E.L.O. - Mr Blue Sky
Steve Winwood - Back In The Highlife
Led Zeppelin - Kashmir
Simon & Garfunkel - America
Beatles - Twist and Shout
Kinks - You Really Got Me
Jimi Hendrix - Purple Haze
Extreme - Rest In Peace
Gerry Rafferty - Baker Street
Stevie Wonder - Superstition
Genesis - I Know What I Like

MEGADETH (DAVE MUSTAINE)

Guns N Roses - Used To Love Her
Megadeth - Liar
Danzig - Mother
Lamb Of God - Beating At Deaths Door
Alice In Chains - Game
Motley Crue - Too Fast For Love
Skid Row - I Remember You
Opeth - To Bid You Farewell
Faith No More - Take This
Black Sabbath - Evil Woman
Type O Negative - Anaesthesia
Nevermore - Dreaming Neon Black
Metallica - Unforgiven 2
Strapping Young Lad - Love
Iced Earth - I'd Die For You
Thin Lizzy - Still In Love With You
Red Hot Chilli Peppers - Breaking The Girl
Anthrax - Crush
AC/DC - The Jack
Testament - Leave Me Forever
Pantera - This Love

DON AIREY

Jimi Hendrix - Purple Haze
Beatles - She's So Heavy
Cream - NSU (live)
Nice - America
Deep Purple - Rat Bat Blue
Mahavishnu Orchestra - Birds Of Fire
Mountain - Never In My Life
Ram Jam - Black Betty

Led Zeppelin - All Of My Love
Rainbow - All Night Long
Whitesnake - Still Of The Night
Alice In Chains - Rooster
Pantera - Walk
EMF - Unbelievable
Jeff Beck - Rice Pudding
Ozzy Osbourne - Mr Crowley
Yes - Close To The Edge
Joe Bonamassa - Ballad Of John Henry
Fleetwood Mac - Oh Well
Derek & Dominoes - Layla
The Move - Brontosaurus
Focus - Sylvia
Beatles - Dig A Pony
Korn - Blind

STEREOPHONICS

Temple Of The Dog - Say Hello To Heaven
Pearl Jam - Alive
AC/DC - Down Payment Blues
Nirvana - In Bloom
Blind Melon - No Rain
Four Horsemen - Rocking Is My Business
Lemonheads - Rudderless
Red Hot Chilli Peppers - Scar Tissue
Stereophonics - Innocent
Black Crowes - Remedy
Thin Lizzy - The Boys Are Back In Town
Black Sabbath - War Pigs
The Prodigy - Firestarter
Led Zeppelin - Ramble On
Faces - Stay With Me

Free - Mr Big
Stereophonics - She's Alright
Aerosmith - Love In An Elevator
Lynyrd Skynyrd - Saturday Night Special
Rolling Stones - Gimme Shelter
John Lee Hooker - Dimples
Soundgarden - Superunknown

ALICE IN CHAINS

AC/DC - It's A Long Way To The Top
Jimi Hendrix - Manic Depression
Alice In Chains - Acid Bubble
Queen - Fat Bottomed Girls
Beatles - I'm Only Sleeping
William Shatner - Lucy In The Sky
Iron Maiden - Still Life
Billy Joel - Big Shot
Iggy & The Stooges - Search and Destroy
Led Zeppelin - Immigrant Song
Van Halen - Ain't Talking About Love
UFO - Mother Mary (live)
Focus - Hocus Pocus
Black Sabbath - Hand Of Doom
Aerosmith - Seasons Of Wither
Alice In Chains - Last Of My Kind
Black Flag - Damaged 2
Pink Floyd - Comfortably Numb
Ozzy Osbourne - You Can't Stop Rock & Roll
Alice In Chains - Black Gives Way To Blue

RICKY WARWICK

Ramones - I Wanna Be Sedated
Motorhead - Ace Of Spades
Thin Lizzy - Do Anything You Wanna do
Johnny Cash - Ring Of Fire
The Cult - Wild Flower
Megadeth - Peace Sells
Iron Maiden - Running Free
Ricky Warwick - Hanks Blues
Stiff Little Fingers - Alternative Ulster
Def Leppard - Dogs Of War
Therapy - Screamager
Cheap Trick - Surrender
Rolling Stones - Tumbling Dice
Steve Earle - Copperhead Road
AC/DC - Shot Down In Flames
Sex Pistols - God Save The Queen
The Almighty - Jonestown Mind
Big Country - Fields Of Fire
SAHB - Vambo
Guns N Roses - Welcome To The Jungle
New Model Army - No Rest
Metallica - Battery
GBH - Give Me Fire
Lynyrd Skynyrd - Simple Man
Supersuckers - Born With A Tail
Ricky Warwick - Tattoos and Alibis
The Clash - London Calling
Bruce Springsteen - Radio Nowhere
Gaslight Anthem - Great Expectations

TEN YEARS AFTER

Buddy Rich - Jumpin' At The Woodside
Roy Orbison - Only The Lonely
Everly Brothers - Gone GoneGone
Hollies - Stay
Steve Miller - Children Of The Future
Eagles - Take It Easy
Pink - Dear Mr President
Jimmy Smith - Theme From Carpetbaggers
Byrds - Mr Tambourine Man
Sam Cooke - Shake
Ten Years After - Slip Slide Away
Temptations - Ball Of Confusion
Bruce Springsteen - Blinded By The Light
Smokey Robinson & The Miracles - My Girl
Propellerhead's - Velvet Pants
Amy Winehouse - Back To Black
Led Zeppelin - How Many More Times
Beatles - Twist and Shout
Rolling Stones - Honky Tonk Woman
Foo Fighters - Cheer Up Boys
Ten Years After - I'm Going Home

JOURNEY

Beatles - A Day In The Life
Beatles - Hey Jude
Rolling Stones - Satisfaction
The Who - I Can See For Miles
The Who - Won't Get Fooled Again
Cream - Sunshine Of Your Love
Santana - Everybody's Everything

Journey - Separate Ways
Police - Roxanne
Journey - Stone In Love
Jimi Hendrix - All Along The Watchtower
Jimi Hendrix - Little Wing
Free - All Right Now
Jeff Beck - Shapes Of Things
Journey - Faithfully
Pink Floyd - Comfortably Numb
Sly & The Family Stone - Dance To The Music

MARILLION

Van Halen - Running With The Devil
Family - My Friend The Sun
Jimi Hendrix - Voodoo Child
Ben Folds Five - Underground
Jellyfish - The King Is Half Undressed
Marillion - The Uninvited Guest
Mott The Hoople - Whiz Kid
BB King - How Blue Can You Get
Todd Rundgren - Bread
King Crimson - Frame By Frame
Porcupine Tree - The Sound Of Muzak
Peter Gabriel - Here Comes The Flood
Toad The Wet Sprocket - Walk On The Ocean
Steely Dan - Kid Charlemagne
Marillion - Hard As Love
Camel - Lady Fantasy
Grizzly Bear - Southern Point
Crowded House - Into Temptation
Blur - Coffee and TV
Transatlantic - Out Of The Night
The Wishing Tree - Fly

Radiohead - Wolf From The Door
Pink Floyd - Comfortably Numb
UFO - Love to Love
Hawkwind - Silver Machine
Wolfmother - Vagabond
Rolling Stones - Angie

FIVE FINGER DEATH PUNCH

Faith No More - From Out Of Nowhere
Soulfly - Eye For An Eye
Accept - Balls To The Wall
Disturbed - Inside The Fire
Killswitch Engage - Arms Of Sorrow
Metallica - Master Of Puppets
Testament - The New Order
Exodus - The Toxic Waltz
Slayer - Silent Scream
Korn - Did My Time
Five Finger Death Punch - Dying Breed
Opeth - Ghost Of Perdition
Alice In Chains - Check My Brain
Anthrax - State Of Euphoria
Motorhead - Killed By Death
Machine Head - Davidian
Airbourne - Girls In Black
Lamb Of God - Walk With Me In Hell
Fear Factory - Obsolete
Marilyn Manson - Irresponsible Hate Anthem
Slipknot - Left Behind
Five Finger Death Punch - Canto 34
Judas Priest - Dissident Agressor
AC/DC - Rif Raff

MEAT LOAF

Nirvana - Smells Like Teen Spirit
Nickelback - Something In Your Mouth
Green Day - American Idiot
Rolling Stones - Undercover Of The Night
Led Zeppelin - Stairway To Heaven
Bon Jovi - Living On A Prayer
Stevie Ray Vaughn - The House Is A Rockin'
Aerosmith - Rag Doll
Peter Gabriel - Sledgehammer
Pink Floyd - Money
Eagles - Life In The Fast Lane
Bob Seger - Old Time Rock N Roll
Police - Message In A Bottle
The Who - My Generation
Meat Loaf - Love Is Not Real
Queen - Crazy Little Thing Called Love
Kings Of Leon - Use Somebody
Jimi Hendrix - Foxy Lady
Meat Loaf - Los Angeloser

NAZARETH

Little Richard - Lucille
Rolling Stones - Brown Sugar
The Band - The Weight
Elvis Presley - Heartbreak Hotel
Allman Brothers - Black Hearted Woman
Black Sabbath - Paranoid
Led Zeppelin - Rock N Roll
Otis Redding - Try A Little Tenderness
Free - Fire and Water
Marvin Gaye - Can I Get A Witness

Bob Dylan - Tangled Up In Blue
Kings Of Leon - Sex On Fire
Warren Zevon - Boom Boom Mancini
Little Feat - Rock n Roll Doctor
The Move - Brontosaurus
Robert Palmer - Simply Irresistible
Tom Petty - Listen To Her Heart
Chuck Berry - Promised Land
Deep Purple - Highway Star
Frankie Miller - Be Good To Yourself

BULLET FOR MY VALENTINE

AC/DC - You Shook Me All Night Long
Alice In Chains - Them Bones
As I Lay Dying - Within Destruction
Avenged Sevenfold - Almost Easy
Blacktide - Shockwave
Bullet For My Valentine - Tears Don't Fall
Deftones - My Own Summer
Faith No More - Last Cup Of Sorrow
Iron Maiden - The Trooper
Judas Priest - Turbo Lover
Killswitch Engage - My Last Serenade
Lamb Of God - Redneck
Metallica - Unforgiven
Pantera - Hostile
Slipknot - Disaster Pieces

JETHRO TULL (IAN ANDERSON)

Frank Zappa - Dirty Love
Steelye Span - Thomas The Rhymer
Spin Doctors - Jimmy Olsens Blues
Captain Beefheart - Big Eyed Beans From Venus
Evanescence - Bring Me To Life
The Nice - America
Blackmores Night - Rainbow Blues
Foreigner - I Wanna Know What Love Is
Jethro Tull - Watching Me, Watching You
Fleetwood Mac - Oh Well
Fleetwood Mac - Man Of the World
Captain Beefheart - When it blows its stacks
Frank Zappa - Dynamo Hum
Spin Doctors - What Time Is It
The Nice - Diamond Hard Blue Apples Of The Moon
Jethro Tull - Too Many Too
MC5 - Kick Out The Jams
Led Zeppelin - Kashmir

RATT

Cream - Crossroads
Captain Beefheart - Buggy Boogie Woogie
Buffalo Springfield - Bluebird
Deep Purple - Smoke On The Water
Alice Cooper - Schools Out
Ratt - Last Call
Jimi Hendrix - All along The Watchtower
Led Zeppelin - Going To California
Lynyrd Skynyrd - Gimme 3 Steps

THUNDER

Beatles - Happiness Is A Warm Gun
Jimi Hendrix - Manic Depression
Led Zeppelin - Ten Years Gone
Thunder - Backstreet Symphony
The Who - The Punk & The Godfather
Steely Dan - Do It Again
Edgar Winter - Frankenstein
Van Halen - Running With The Devil
Family - Burlesque
Derek & Dominoes - Bell Bottom Blues
Thunder - A Better Man
Montrose - Space Station No 5
Robin Trower - Day Of The Eagle
Rolling Stones - Tumbling Dice
Tom Petty - Breakdown
Nirvana - Come As You Are
Free - Ride On Pony
Neil Young - Southern Man
Thunder - I Love You More Than Rock n Roll
Deep Purple - What's Going On Here
AC/DC - Whole Lotta Rosie

BACHMAN TURNER OVERDRIVE (RANDY BACHMAN)

Free - All Right Now
Spencer Davies Group - Gimme Some Loving
Rolling Stones - Brown Sugar
The Who - Baba O'Riley
Chris Rea - Fool If You Think It's Over
Chuck Berry - Memphis Tennessee
Shadows - Dance on
Procul Harum - A Whiter Shade Of Pale

Tornadoes - Telstar
Bachman Turner - Rolling Along
The Animals - House Of The Rising Sun
Beach Boys - Good Vibrations
Jimi Hendrix - All Along The Watchtower
Joe Walsh - Rocky Mountain Way
Beatles - And I Love Her

EXTREME

Led Zeppelin - The Crunge
Van Halen - Outta Love Again
Queen - Dragon Attack
Pat Travers - Snorting Whiskey
David Bowie - Fame
Dr Dre - California Love
Journey - Lady Luck
Aerosmith - Dream On
Beastie Boys - Sabotage
Genesis - Down And Out
Nikka Costa - Can't Never Did Nothing
Heart - Magic Man
System Of A Down - Vicinity Of Obscenity
Rage Against The Machine - Down Rodeo

30 SECONDS TO MARS

Guns N Roses - Welcome To The Jungle
Lynyrd Skynyrd - Tuesdays Gone
Van Halen - Running With The Devil
Journey - Don't Stop Believing
U2 - Where The Streets Have No Name
Nine Inch Nails - Terrible Lie
30 Seconds To Mars - This Is War

Pink Floyd - Comfortably Numb
Nirvana - Heart Shaped Box
Fleetwood Mac - Don't Stop
Michael Jackson - Billie Jean
Depeche Mode - Personal Jesus
30 Seconds To Mars - Closer To The Edge
Led Zeppelin - Stairway To Heaven
Bob Dylan - Subterranean Homesick Blues
Boston - More Than A Feeling
The Cure - Prayers For Rain
Soundgarden - Black Hole Sun
Temple Of The Dog - Hungry
30 Seconds To Mars - Kings & Queens

DEF LEPPARD (JOE ELLIOT)

SAHB - Vambo
UFO - Natural Thing
Ricky Warwick - Johnny Or Elvis
The Who - 5.15
Cybernaughts - Time
Wolfmother - Woman
Todd Rundgren - Overture Mountain Top And Sunrise
10cc - Second Sitting Last Supper
Down 'n' Outz - Shouting And Pointing
Rush - A Farewell To Kings
Neil Young - Needle And The Damage Done
Wings - No Words
Kiss - Flaming Youth
Mott The Hoople - Whizz Kid
SAHB - Boston Tea Party

SLASH

Slash - Back From Cali
Aerosmith - Sweet Emotion
Queen - Tie Your Mother Down
Led Zeppelin - Black Dog
Black Sabbath - Sabbath Bloody Sabbath
AC/DC / Those About To Rock
Slash - Doctor Alibi
Metallica - Master Of Puppets
Megadeth - Peace Sells
Led Zeppelin - Whole Lotta Love
Ted Nugent - Stranglehold
Cheap Trick - Gonna Raise Hell
Deep Purple - Space Trucking
Slash - By The Sword
Aerosmith - Back In The Saddle Again
Alterbridge - Rise Today
Rolling Stones - Gimme Shelter
Thin Lizzy - Thunder & Lightning
Queen - Fat Bottomed Girls
Slash - Starlight

SLAYER

Slipknot - Get This
Nine Inch Nails - March Of The Pigs
Pantera - Becoming
Jucifer - Pontius Of Palia
Children Of Bodom - If You Want Peace
Adolescents - I Hate Children
Black Label Society - Genocide Junkies
AC/DC - Walk All Over You
Judas Priest - Stained Class

Suicidal Tendencies - You Can't Bring Me Down
Iron Maiden - Iron Maiden
Black Sabbath - The Wizard
Led Zeppelin - Immigrant Song
Machine Head - Davidian
Arch Enemy - My Apocalypse
Slayer - Hate Worldwide
Burst - Visionary
Deep Purple - Highway Star

SLIPKNOT (COREY TAYLOR)

Foo Fighters - Long Road to Ruin
Green Day - Holiday
Metallica - Whiplash
AC/DC - Walk All Over You
Motley Crue - Too Young To Fall In Love
Y&T - summertime Girls
REM - End Of The World
Bush - Greedy Fly
Cars - You've Got Tonight
The Hives - Walk Idiot Walk
Thin Lizzy - Jailbreak
Alice In Chains - We Die Young
Motorhead - Iron Fist
Ratt - Round And Round
The Jam - In The City
Dead Kennedy's - Holiday In Cambodia
Europe - Rock The Night
Tool - 46 And 2
Killers - Somebody Told Me
Nirvana - Aneurysm

MAX CAVALERA

Dillinger Escape Plan - Farewell Mona Lisa
Converge - Axe To Fall
Prong - Power Of The Damager
Fear Factory - Power Shifter
Cavalera Conspiracy - Inflicted
Morbid Angel - Dominate
Entombed - Left Hand Path
Celtic Frost - Procreation Of The Wicked
Municipal Waste - The Wrong Answer
Warbringer - Total War
Agnostic Front - Addiction
Chromags - We Gotta Know
Biohazard - Tales From The Parkside
Black Sabbath - A Hole In The Sky
Slayer - World Painted Blood
Motorhead - Ace Of Spades
Probot - Red War
Cavalera Conspiracy - Sanctuary

STEVE HACKETT

Rolling Stones - I Wanna Be Your Man
Rolling Stones - Route 66
The Who - My Generation
Joni Mitchell - Morning Morgantown
Beatles - Eleanor Rigby
CSNY - Everybody I Love You
Cream - Tales Of Brave Ulysses
Yardbirds - The Nazz Are Blue
Steve Hackett - Sleepers
Bonnie Tyler - Lost In France
Traffic - No Face, No Name, No Number

Joni Mitchell - Coyote
Bob Dylan - Rainy Day Woman
Mahavishnu Orchestra - Vision Is A Naked Sword
Rolling Stones - Paint It Black
Beatles - I Am The Walrus
Richard Harris - MacArthur Park
Jimi Hendrix - All Along The Watchtower
John Mayalls Bluesbreakers - Key To Love
Steve Hackett - Nomads
Beatles - I'm Only Sleeping
Spencer Davies Group - Stevies Blues
Rolling Stones - Ruby Tuesday
Steve Hackett - Tubehead

ALTERBRIDGE (MARK TREMONTI)

Celtic Frost - The Throne To Emperor
Kings X - Dogman
Meshuggah - Bleed
Testament - Trial By Fire
Bad Brains - At The Movies
Metallica - Orion
Eric Johnson - Cliffs Of Dover
Death Angel - Voracious Souls
Alterbridge - Isolation
Bad Company - Bad Company
Stevie Ray Vaughan - Lenny
Arc Angels - See What Tomorrow Brings
Black Flag - My War
Alterbridge - Blackbird
Jeff Buckley - Hallelujah
Pantera - Walk
Metallica - Am I Evil
Slayer - Alter Of Sacrifice

Alterbridge - Ties That Bind

SKUNK ANANSIE

Sepultura - Roots
Korn - Right Now
Horehound - Dead Weather
Noisettes - Scratch Your Name
Doves - Kingdom Of Rust
Alterbridge - In Loving Memory
Stone Temple Pilots - Dead And Bloated
Biffy Clyro - Some Kind Of Wizzard
Pendulum - Granite
Skunk Anansie - My Ugly Boy
Virgin Marys - Bang Bang Bang
Jimi Hendrix - If Six Were Nine
Slipknot - Duality
Bette Davis - Anti Love Song
Weezer - Pork And Beans
Skindred - Roots Rock Riot
Kings X - Dogman
The XX - VCR
Creed - Overcome
Bullet For My Valentine - Hearts Burst Into Fire
Pearl Jam - Rearview Mirror
Skunk Anansie - Charlie Big Potato
Band Of Skulls - Diamonds And Pearls
Nirvana - In Bloom
Marilyn Manson - Beautiful People

PAPA ROACH

Red Hot Chilli Peppers - Under The Bridge
Faith No More - Naked In Front Of The Computer
Wutang Clan - Cream
Thin Lizzy - Thunder And Lightning
Queen - The Show Must Go On
Led Zeppelin - When The Levee Breaks
Deftones - Engine Number Nine
Social Distortion - Down On The World Again
Pixies - Gouge Away
At The Drive In - One Arm Scissor
The Refused - New Noise
AC/DC - Thunderstruck
Nirvana - Smells Like Teen Spirit
Johnny Cash - Man In Black
Nine Inch Nails - Head Like A Hole
The Prodigy - Smack My Bitch Up
Pantera - Walk
Korn - Blind
Foo Fighters - My Hero
Elvis Costello - Watching The Detectives
Aerosmith - Walk This Way
Guns N Roses - Welcome To The Jungle
Poison - Look What The Cat Dragged In
Jay Z - 99 Problems
Tricky - Tricky Kid

THE WILDHEARTS (GINGER)

King Blues - Head Butt
Sinead O'Connor - Daddy I'm Fine
Trail Of The Dead - Wasted State Of Mind
Foxy Shazam - Oh Lord
Von Hertzen Brothers - Miracle
Band Of Horses - Is There A Ghost
Against Me - Born On The FM Waves
Queen - It's Late
Y&T - Squeeze
Tubes - She's A Beauty
Grandaddy - Now It's On
Alkaline Trio - Continental
Distillers - City Of Angels
Whale - Hobo Humpin' Slobo Babe
Fishbone - Bonin' In The Boneyard
Devin Townsend - Bend It Like Bender
Jason & The Scorchers - White Lies
Sparks - Wacky Women
Wildhearts - Vernix
Good Rats - Rat City In Blue
Biffy Clyro - Glitter And Trauma
Graham Coxon - Jamie Thomas
Yeah Yeah Yeahs - Zero